D0906209

MONEY FOR NOTHING

Money for Nothing

POLITICIANS, RENT EXTRACTION,
AND POLITICAL EXTORTION

Fred S. McChesney

Harvard University Press

Cambridge, Massachusetts, and London, England • 1997

Library of Congress Cataloging-in-Publication Data

McChesney, Fred S., 1948–
  Money for nothing : politicians, rent extraction, and political
extortion / Fred S. McChesney.
    p.   cm.
  Includes bibliographical references and index.
  ISBN 0-674-58330-2 (alk. paper)
  1. Bribery—Economic aspects. 2. Extortion—Economic aspects.
3. Lobbying—Economic aspects. 4. Pressure groups—Economic
aspects. 5. Political corruption—Economic aspects. I. Title.
HV6301.M33 1997
364.1'323—dc21   96-47873
                                     CIP

To Elaine

With gratitude, admiration, and love

Contents

Figures

Tables

Preface

The foundation of this book is an article on rent extraction published in 1987. That model of rent extraction—extortion by politicians, of the sort to be defined shortly—has subsequently won increasing acceptance among at least one group of social scientists. Its acceptance has undoubtedly been helped by empirical demonstrations of its validity. Still, the phenomenon of rent extraction is not acknowledged universally; it is perhaps not even familiar generally. In this book I hope for improvements along both lines.

This book follows the intellectual tradition of the Virginia school of political economy and public choice. The point of departure in that tradition is the use of standard economic principles, both substantive and methodological, to analyze political behavior. The crux of the economic approach, in turn, is that politicians—like everyone else—are guided chiefly by the goal of advancing their personal interests. It is not serving the public interest but furthering their own welfare (measured in votes, money, power, or whatever) that motivates politicians and their bureaucratic agents.

Admittedly, this fundamental approach—analyzing and predicting political behavior in terms of how it advances politicians' own welfare—is one that the Virginia school of political economy shares with other adherents to the public-choice approach, in both political science and economics. But the Virginians' particular contribution, as described by one longtime observer, William C. Mitchell, in a 1988 article, is their "theory of the failure of political processes": "Essentially the theory is focused on the perverse incentives embedded in rules of collective choice that necessarily enable redistribution to dominate efficiency . . . Accordingly, inequity, inefficiency, and coercion are the most general results of democratic policy formation. For more than twenty-five years, Virginia economists have developed and related these themes to a variety of institutional and policy settings."

This book aspires to contribute to that Virginia-school analysis of governmental "inequity, inefficiency, and coercion," particularly the last of those. It adds a new set of "institutional and policy settings." In those settings, government is modeled as, and then is shown to perform as, an obstacle to rather than facilitator of economic well-being. The book explains how political extortion via "rent extraction" figures in politicians' maximization of their own welfare personally, to the detriment of society generally.

The theory of political benefit through rent extraction builds straightforwardly on Gordon Tullock's 1967 model of rent seeking, which along with his later work in the same vein continues to illuminate debates in far-flung areas of economics and law. Tullock's contribution has become an Archimedean lever in many different domains. Like many others, I owe him a large intellectual debt.

Others have helped me straighten out my thinking about rent extraction at several junctures over the years. Many colleagues have commented on earlier articles: Howard Abrams, Terry Anderson, Henry Butler, Louis De Alessi, Frank Easterbrook, Ernest Gellhorn, Thomas Hazlett, Dwight Lee, Jonathan Macey, William MacLeod, Roger Meiners, Mark Moran, Timothy Muris, Sam Peltzman, Paul Rubin, Mark Ramseyer, Steven Salop, David Schap, William Shughart, Alan Sykes, John Wenders, Bruce Yandle, and Gordon Tullock himself. Others have been generous with telephone calls and letters to reinforce certain points, to provide new examples and note further implications, and to point out errors: Donald Boudreaux, William Fischel, Thomas Hammond, Jack High, P. J. Hill, and Richard Wagner.

Special acknowledgment is due to several special people. As both critic and editor, Richard Epstein has been extremely generous with time and insights. I learned a lot about tax politics, and even a little tax law, from conversations and collaborations with Richard Doernberg. I acknowledge with special gratitude repeated criticism and assistance from David Haddock, Robert McCormick, and Robert Tollison. Many ideas developed here first germinated in discussions with Richard Higgins during our time together at the Federal Trade Commission. Another veteran of those days, William Shughart, read and criticized the entire manuscript and made innumerable improvements.

The fact that almost all those named above are personal friends, many of long standing, has made the enterprise much more enjoyable—for me, at least. Their willingness to impose costs on themselves to benefit me disproves the frequent claim that *homo economicus* is but a selfish, short-run maximizer.

I gratefully acknowledge the financial assistance of the Earhart Foundation. In addition, Enrico Colombatto and his International Centre for Economic Research (ICER) in Turin contributed a great deal, including the in-kind emoluments that are so important to finishing a book: time and space, peace and quiet. Alessandra Calosso at ICER and Catherine Phillips at Emory University provided valuable administrative assistance on their respective sides of the Atlantic. Radine Robinson at Emory and Mary Finn at Northwestern University greatly facilitated final production of the manuscript. At the Emory University School of Law, I benefited from the excellent research help of Michael Kaeding and Kelly O'Reilly. The understanding of Dean Howard O. Hunter and the generosity of the Robert T. Thompson family continue to afford me splendid research opportunities that would otherwise be lacking. I am especially grateful for their continued encouragement and support.

The mere proposal to set the politician to watch the capitalist has been disturbed by the rather disconcerting discovery that they are both the same man. We are past the point where being a capitalist is the only way of becoming a politician, and we are dangerously near the point where being a politician is much the quickest way of becoming a capitalist.

—G. K. CHESTERTON

Introduction

> The rights of the king who will rule you will be as follows. He will take your sons and assign them to his chariots and horses, and they will run before his chariot . . . He will set them to do his plowing and his harvesting, and to make his implements of war, and equipment of his chariots. He will use your daughters as ointment-makers, as cooks, and as bakers. He will take the best of your fields, vineyards, and olive groves, and give the revenue to his eunuchs and his slaves. He will take your male and female servants, as well as your best oxen and your asses, and use them to do his work. He will tithe your flocks and you yourselves will become his slaves.
>
> —1 SAMUEL 8: 11–17

Surveys reveal a majority of Americans believing that government is run for special interests, not the public interest. This awareness represents a triumph for the so-called economic theory of regulation. The economic analysis of regulation focuses on the ability of government to create artificially high returns (profits) for "special-interest groups" at the expense of taxpayers and consumers. The essential insight of the economic model is that legislation and regulation are sold to the highest bidder in political markets, just as other goods and services are sold in more familiar commercial markets.

This is not to deny that governments also create wealth, by enforcing contracts and property rights, providing public goods, and so forth. But wealth-reducing redistribution to favored individuals and groups is the conspicuous hallmark of modern government, at all levels (for example, Scully 1995). For the favors, private interests (often acting through their political action committees, or PACs) pay politicians in several ways, including campaign contributions, in-kind benefits, and other forms of recompense. The sales are often overt—monetary contributions are supposed to be a matter of public record—and "PAC excesses" have become standard fare for editorial hand-wringing in the press. From the standard populist perspective adopted by the media, the payments too frequently indicate that fat-cat lobbyists have corrupted a basically upright but weak legislator. Some of that criticism is deserved, but it falls too heavily on the

1

buyers. Politicians who sell the legislation deserve opprobrium also. It takes two to tango.

Moreover, much of the criticism betrays a misunderstanding of why private interests are paying, and what they are paying for. The standard model of politicians and their contributors—those infamous "special interests"—treats contributions as being made for political favors. So viewed, many episodes of private payment are simply inexplicable, as students of the relations between politicians and private groups have increasingly noted.

Why, for example, would Nelson Rockefeller, on behalf of the Rockefeller family, with its important financial and management interests in industries like banking, insurance, and transportation, thank Congress for laws that seemed to *restrain* the Rockefellers' ability to make political contributions (Aranson and Hinich 1979)? Why do industries like toiletries and cosmetics, which are unregulated and want to stay that way, "pump hundreds of thousands of dollars to federal candidates" directly, besides spending millions of dollars in states where regulation is threatened (Kaplan 1990)? Similarly, if money is being made available to politicians for favors, why would American banks importune regulators like the Federal Election Commission for regulations making it illegal to lend to politicians?[1] Why are many lobbyists employed to persuade politicians *not* to act, with payments being made to induce nonactivity?

> The nation's largest banking company [Citicorp] employs eight registered lobbyists in its Washington office. In addition, six law firms represent Citicorp's interests on Capitol Hill. No one should judge this strike force ineffective by how little banking legislation gets through: The lobbyists spend most of their time blocking and blunting changes that could hurt Citicorp's extensive credit-card operations, student-loan business or ever-broadening financial-service offerings.[2]

The answer suggested here is that payments to politicians often are made, not for particular political favors, but to avoid particular political disfavor, that is, as part of a system of political extortion, or "rent extraction."

The basic notion of rent extraction is simple and derives from the biblical quotation above. Because the state, quite legally, can (and does) take money and other forms of wealth from its citizens, politicians can extort from private parties payments *not* to expropriate private wealth. The term "wealth extraction" would perhaps be closer to the essence of the political extortion process.

In that sense, rent extraction—receiving payments not to take or destroy private wealth—is "money for nothing," in the words of the song. Money is paid in exchange for politicians' doing nothing, when they could do something. Rent extraction represents a conscious, welfare-maximizing strategy for politicians personally. The practice resembles the "mud farming" practiced by the disreputable characters in Faulkner's *The Reivers.* Mud farming was a simple extortion (extraction) scam. By night, farmers plowed up and then watered down stretches of the dirt roads that ran alongside their houses. By day, when cars sank into the nocturnally created mud, drivers had a choice: abandon their entire investment (the car) or hire the mud farmer and his mules to haul them out. Rather than lose the entire asset, of course, drivers chose to hand over a part of its value for help.[3]

The essence of mud farming—rent extraction—is thus the mounting of a credible threat of loss, then selling back to those otherwise victimized reprieve from that loss. The most obvious sort of rent (wealth) extraction is observed, with increasing frequency, when legislators threaten to impose taxes (in 1 Samuel, to "tithe your fields"). Threatened taxes then elicit payments for tax forbearance from private parties whose wealth would otherwise be taken by the tax man. Because rounds of tax changes have become such visible spectacles of rent extraction, and perhaps the most lucrative source of private wealth paid over to politicians, this book frequently uses the tax policy process to illustrate the extraction model's workings. Yet the rent-extraction model applies not just to taxation but to regulation generally; consequently, many nontax episodes of political extortion are also presented.

The presentation alternates between the more and the less technical. I seek to convince two groups of the existence and importance of rent extraction in the overall fabric of political activity: social scientists who require a technical, deductive method (model, implications, tests); and general readers satisfied with a more heuristic, inductive approach. The essence of rent extraction is modeled in Part I. Part II then demonstrates, both anecdotally and more technically, how rent extraction actually is practiced, including the problems of enforcing the political contract when politicians agree merely to extract some wealth rather than take it all. Part III then extends the model to investigate issues related to rent extraction, such as use of earmarked taxes and incentives to organize to lobby government. The final chapter discusses a number of unanswered questions concerning political extortion.

I

THE MODEL

1

Background: The Economic Theory of Regulation

> In general, the art of government consists in taking as much money as possible from one party of the citizens to give to the other.
> —VOLTAIRE

Until some thirty years ago, only certain forms of government regulation—public utility regulation, for example—were of much interest to economists. The modern welfare and regulatory state, developing since the late nineteenth century (Anderson and Hill 1980) and flowering in the 1930s, had elicited little attention among most economists as late as 1960. Moreover, what little notice economists did pay came in the form of normative (welfare) models, not positive analysis. These normative models were typically armchair discussions of the perceived need for regulation in the presence of "market failure," and of the design of optimal regulation. There was little positive analysis of the actual working of regulation or (even more important) of how or whether its performance was superior to market outcomes. The mere fact that markets were imperfect was regarded both as establishing the normative case for regulation and as obviating the need for further study of how regulation actually worked.[1]

This longtime normative approach among economists produced several results. First, since all markets—like all human institutions, or indeed like all humans—are imperfect, regulation of any market could be justified. And since the "need" for any regulation could be justified in welfare-economic terms, whatever regulation that did result was treated as imposed from outside the market-economic system by government actors (politicians and bureaucrats) who were motivated by that same desire of maximizing social welfare. Regulation was "exogenous": it happened because the normative welfare models showed it should happen.

Imposed exogenously, regulation typically was treated as something that government did *to* regulated firms. Like children, markets might be better off for correction of their failures, but they could hardly be expected to like the medicine they were made to swallow. So, at least implicitly,

7

regulation was something regulated firms would prefer to avoid if they could. Rate regulation supposedly constrained public utilities, for example, to lower levels of profit than could be earned otherwise.

In the 1950s and 1960s, however, suspicions increasingly arose that the standard economic model was missing the essence of regulation.[2] Suspicion set in because observed regulation so often diverged from economists' models of optimal regulation. Some regulation seemed merely ineffectual (for example, Stigler and Friedland 1962). Other regulation was acknowledged to be economically wrongheaded, but the errors were excused. Any error was supposedly innocent, due either to ignorance or to good-faith mistake (for example, Coase 1959; Friedman and Schwartz 1963).

But neither of those descriptions accorded well with economists' fundamental presumption that people act (singly or through institutions) so as rationally to maximize their own welfare. It hardly seemed purposeful, maximizing activity for politicians and bureaucrats to incur positive costs of their own to regulate and impose costs on the regulated in return for zero effect or in furtherance of demonstrated error. Increasingly, too, it was noted that firms often seemed to want—even seek—regulation, as opposed to being victimized by it (see Posner 1974). Clearly, for example, regulated carriers were far from averse to regulation by the Interstate Commerce Commission.

Ineluctably, both the theoretical and empirical inconsistencies raised the larger question whether economists' basic model of regulation was correct in the first place. But in social science, it takes a model to beat a model. The prevailing welfare model of regulation, while clearly shaky, had no competitors. As of 1970, no systematic alternative model of regulation was yet forthcoming. Intellectual progress in understanding regulation required a change in perspective. Any new approach would have to explain the observed regulatory regimes—socially costly on net but often popular with their supposed victims. It would have to do so in terms of economists' basic assumption of purposeful, rational action by the politicians and bureaucrats responsible for regulation and by the firms that sought it.

The breakthrough was not long in coming, once the deficiencies of the existing models were perceived and the right questions were asked. If some economic agents wanted (demanded) regulation and government provided (supplied) it, was something akin to exchange going on? If so, what were the determinants of supply and demand? Asking those basic economic questions led George Stigler (1971) to produce his celebrated article, which focused counterintuitively on the ability of regulation to *benefit* its supposed victims.

The Stigler Model

In a nutshell, the Stiglerian interpretation of regulation was the traditional economic model of cartelization. But the Stigler model is one in which government imposes and enforces the anticompetitive restrictions, rather than private firms' doing so. If expected political rents net of the costs of organizing and procuring favorable regulation are positive, then producers will demand regulation. If payments sufficient to compensate politicians for the costs of creating regulation are forthcoming, they will supply it.

Many of Stigler's substantive points about regulation were not new.[3] The innovation lay in his conceptualization of regulation in terms of a familiar economic model, that of exchange. What, he asked, were the *benefits* that the state could provide to an industry, and what were the *costs* of obtaining those benefits? The benefits in particular were clear:

> The state—the machinery and power of the state—is a potential resource or threat to every industry in the society. With its power to prohibit or compel, to take or give money, the state can and does selectively help or hurt a vast number of industries . . . The central tasks of the theory of economic regulation are to explain who will receive the benefits or burdens of regulation . . . Regulation may be actively sought by an industry, or it may be thrust upon it. A central thesis of this paper is that, as a rule, regulation is acquired by the industry and is designed and operated primarily for its benefit. There are regulations whose net effects upon the regulated industry are undeniably onerous; a simple example is the differentially heavy taxation of the industry's product (whiskey, playing cards). These onerous regulations, however, are exceptional . . . (Stigler 1971, p. 3)

Dubbed the "economic theory of regulation," Stigler's new construct radically altered economists' perceptions (and their research agendas). Thereafter, economists shifted from asking normatively how the world ("society," "mankind") could be made better off by some optimal regulation, and from merely noting that regulation did not seem to work the way it was supposed to. Economists instead came to recognize that, as a strictly positive matter, government regulation had the power to create benefits that were unavailable other than through politics, or were more cheaply available through politics.

These benefits are, for better or worse, called *rents*. The notion of rent is a slippery one, largely because economists themselves have never agreed upon any one conventional use for the term (Alchian 1987). As used here, however, "rent" will refer to returns to the owner of an asset in excess of the level of returns necessary for him to continue using the asset in its current employment. Thus, a rent is any return above what the owner would earn in the asset's next-best alternative use.

In the basic exposition of the economic theory of regulation typically used, the example of benefits conferred by the state is that of government-created monopoly. In Figure 1.1, let D represent the demand curve for a product—that is, the price (P) that consumers would be willing to pay for given quantities (Q) of a good or service. With all firms facing identical marginal and average costs of production (C), and with costs understood to include a competitive rate of return to all factors of production (including entrepreneurial skill), competition among firms will cause total output of Q_c to be sold at price P_c. Any one firm's attempt to sell at a price above

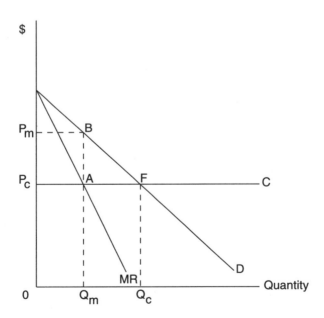

Figure 1.1 The Stigler model of economic regulation

P_c, say P_m, will cause competing firms to undercut that firm's price, since acceptable rates of return can be earned at the lower price, P_c.

Suppose, however, that all firms agree not to compete on price, and instead to charge the higher price, P_m. The higher price means that less of the good will be sold, but the reduced quantity sold (Q_m) can command a higher price. The difference in price times the units sold, rectangular area P_cP_mBA, is *rent* to producers, since that portion of the price (returns) is not necessary to induce production of the units produced. The firms would have been willing to produce Q_m even at the lower price P_c, where returns amount to only $0P_cAQ_m$. Or, to put the point a slightly different way, even if the rents represented by the rectangular area were somehow to disappear, producers would still produce the Q_m they produce with the rents. The higher price is superfluous, serving no useful economic function.

This description of rent creation by private agreement is no more than the standard depiction of monopoly or cartel, achievable (in principle at least) by contractual devices like price fixing. Private agreements are notoriously unreliable as a long-run source of rents, however. Would-be contracting parties with different costs will find it difficult to agree before the fact on the terms (prices, quantities to be produced and by whom) of any price-fixing cartel. Agreement on the distribution of gains after the fact will likewise be difficult. Parties may contract now but cheat later on the agreement, once their competitors raise their prices. These and other problems had already come to be well understood in the 1960s (for example, McGee 1960). Particularly troublesome for any private agreement is the freedom of other firms to enter the industry and take sales away from the contracting parties by undercutting the agreed-upon cartel price.

It is here that traditional monopoly theory meets the economic theory of regulation. With its ability to legalize price fixing, to police cartelizing agreements with taxpayer funds, and especially to restrict entry into markets, regulation can often perform rent-creating functions more efficaciously than private parties themselves can. By legally requiring government-issued "certificates of convenience and necessity" to enter industries like airlines, trucking or hospitals, the state can regulate entry (including specific conditions of entry) in ways unavailable to private parties. It is the state's ability to apply the force of law to any monopolizing arrangement that frequently makes regulation a superior mechanism for creating rents.[4]

The rents created are seemingly just transfers from consumers to producers via higher prices. The fact that producers' benefits are transfers is not to say, however, that rent creation has no economic implications overall.[5] There is a loss of consumer welfare, the BAF triangle in Figure 1.1 represented by the reduction in production from Q_c to Q_m.[6] Goods go unproduced even though consumers would be willing to pay the costs of their production. Even were the rents from government monopolization or cartelization mere transfers, society would be poorer for the lost exchanges of goods for which demanders were willing to pay the price of supply. This is a "deadweight" (pure) loss, since there is no countervailing benefit transferred to producers. But producers are presumably indifferent to this deadweight loss, since they themselves are better off for the transfer they do receive.

Other costs are of concern to producers, however. Government-sponsored monopoly does not just happen; it must be created—there are no free lunches in rent creation. Since the rents are a return to producers over and above that available in other, competitive markets, producers will—indeed, must—expend resources to attain them. To obtain politically created rents, private interests will have to provide something valued by politicians themselves. Producers must incur these costs themselves. In Stigler, as in most of the succeeding literature, the quid pro quo to politicians for politically created monopoly consists primarily of votes. But cruder forms of costly consideration also play an important role.

> Regulatory decisions can also elicit campaign contributions, contributions of time to get-out-the-vote, occasional bribes, or well-paid jobs in the political afterlife. Because the more well-financed and well-staffed campaigns tend to be the more successful and because a self-interested politician also values wealth, he pays attention to these resource (money) consequences. Accordingly, groups that may themselves be too small to offer many votes directly in support of a regulatory policy can nevertheless affect that policy by delivering other valuable resources. (Peltzman 1989, p. 7)

For simplicity, all these "valuable resources" used in pushing politically for rent creation will be referred to as "lobbying" costs.

In the model of cartelization by private agreement (for example, price fixing), the costs of government-created rents are measured societally by the time and money that could have gone to more productive ends that instead are invested in forming and enforcing cartels (deciding on optimal prices and outputs, enforcing output restrictions). With government creation of rents, the costs also include those of lobbying government for cartel creation and enforcement. If the rents represented by rectangular area P_cP_mBA in Figure 1.1 total $1,000, producers rationally will spend up to $999.99 to acquire them.[7]

These expenditures, incurred in the process typically dubbed "rent seeking," also are losses to society, in addition to the deadweight loss mentioned above (Tullock 1967). They represent resources diverted from production of new wealth to the transfer of existing wealth from purchasers to sellers. And because resources must be used in lobbying for rents, many (perhaps most) of the returns available from government cartelization actually represent further economic loss, not mere transfers from consumers.

Reduced to its essentials, then, the economic theory of regulation is the study of government creation of rents through the mechanism of law (including bureaucratic administration of law). Regulations seeming ineffectual or mistaken when measured by the standards of welfare maximization frequently cease to seem so when they are viewed as rent-creating devices for groups or industries favored politically. A regulation may appear mistaken in welfare-economic terms, but that does not mean its consequences were unintended. Rather, the regulation may just be a rent-creating device for its beneficiaries, who hardly care about its overall welfare-economic implications as long as they gain personally. But the transfers (rents) earned come at the cost of deadweight losses suffered by transferees, plus the economic costs of lobbying (rent seeking). Demanders of regulatory rents will lobby for their creation up to the point where the returns equal the costs of obtaining them.

Extending the Theory of Political Rents

The model of monopolization-by-government used here to illustrate the economic theory of regulation reproduces the points made graphically by Gordon Tullock (1967) and descriptively by Stigler (1971). Many interesting aspects of this first model have not been covered here. But for purposes of the rent-extraction model on which this book concentrates, two additional points should be made.

Rent Creation Is a Many-Splendored Thing

Not long after Stigler launched his new model, observers began to note that although the model certainly advanced the understanding of some forms of regulation, it did not seem applicable to many other types. Much regulation apparently did not benefit producers at the expense of consumers. Just a few industries had the kind of benefits modeled in Figure 1.1, the legal ability to set prices and/or restrict entry. As Richard Posner observed, for example, "The 'consumerist' measures of the last years . . . are not an obvious product of interest group pressures, and the proponents of the economic theory of regulation have thus far largely ignored such measures."[8]

In response to the criticisms, the original economic theory of regulation has advanced considerably. Because political action can redistribute wealth from any person or group to any other, it is now seen that regulation may entail many forms of lobbying and rent creation, other than those creating rents for producers at consumers' expense (Aranson 1990; Olson 1995). It is not necessary for present purposes to cover all the different forms of government regulation studied subsequently, since good summaries are available elsewhere (Posner 1974; Tollison 1982; Aranson 1990). However, one particular form of regulation does bear further scrutiny.

This second form of rent creation entails the creation of inframarginal (or Ricardian) rents via regulation. In that model, an entire industry of producers does not seek regulation to benefit itself at the expense of purchasers. Instead, some relatively homogeneous subgroup of producers lobbies for and obtains regulation that benefits itself at the expense of another subgroup of producers. For example, large capital-intensive firms in an industry may benefit themselves by securing government intervention in the labor market, such as by imposing a minimum wage, that disadvantages their smaller, more labor-intensive rivals.[9]

It will later prove useful to summarize diagrammatically this raising-rivals'-costs (or "cost predation") model. Figure 1.2 depicts an industry in which producers have differing amounts of some firm-specific, fixed-cost asset (including entrepreneurial ability). The industry supply curve in the absence of regulation (S_0) thus is upward sloping. Returns to specific assets come out of producers' surplus, 0AD. These returns are rents, as that term was defined earlier: returns to the asset's owner above the returns necessary to induce the owner to keep the asset in its current use and producing at a given level.[10] The returns are unnecessary to continue production using specific assets, because, by definition, the assets are already in existence and can be employed only in their particular use. Since the relevant costs of investment have already been incurred and the assets have no value in another use (including as scrap), a net return of even $.01 will suffice to induce their employment. The owner will use the asset as long as marginal cost only (for example, depreciation) is covered.

In the raising-rivals'-cost model, regulatory measures are identified that increase costs for all firms, but proportionately more for marginal firms, when the industry supply curve is shifted to S_1. A regulation increasing the cost of labor, for example, will affect firms with relatively large capital investments less than those using proportionately more labor than capital in production. Higher overall costs due to regulation mean higher prices to consumers, and so a lower quantity produced. Reduced quantities mean that rents earned on some existing production will be lost because of regulation. But for capital-intensive producers, costs may rise less than prices do, creating new rents exceeding the old rents lost. To inframarginal, capital-intensive producers, regulation is advantageous—that is, they would pay politicians to effect it—as long as there is an increase in rents on net.

In Figure 1.2, area I is greater than area II (CDEF > AC0). The gains from higher prices exceed the losses due to fewer sales at higher cost. Firms with the high capital investments, and therefore lower marginal (labor) costs, in particular gain. The capitalized value of the increased rent flow defines the maximum payment producers would make to politicians in return for regulation.

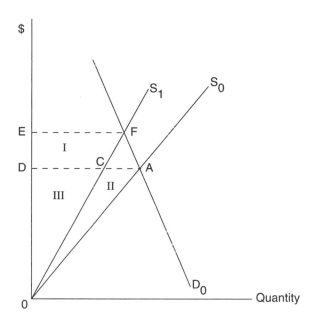

Figure 1.2 The raising-rivals'-costs model of regulation

This cost-predation model has been found to describe accurately many forms of labor, environmental, broadcast, and other regulation, and the politics behind their enactment.[11] The cost-predation strategy differs from Stiglerian cartelization in that only some firms in the industry gain while others lose. Industry cooperation to obtain rents for all firms is replaced by rivalry among industry subgroups to benefit some firms at others' expense. This cost-predation model will be considered again in Chapter 2.

Gainers versus Losers in a Multiparty Context

The focus on winning versus losing firms raises a second point concerning the basic economic theory of regulation. In the political lobbying over raising rivals' costs (above, by a minimum-wage increase), it should not be expected that potential losing firms will just sit on the political sidelines. As Sam Peltzman (1976) has explained, potential losers in the game will also be players in the politics surrounding rent creation. A dollar of rent obtained by one individual or firm is a dollar lost by another.[12] If A finds it worthwhile to spend her resources lobbying Congress for transfers from B, it often will be worth B's while to lobby Congress against the transfers sought by A.

Predictably, politicians will not be willing to give A everything she wants and B nothing. The ultimate form of regulation chosen will entail some benefit to one side and some loss to the other. Returning to Figure 1.1, assume now that consumers join together to lobby against price increases that reduce their consumer surplus. The monopoly created politically to benefit producers will not entail the maximum-benefit price increase to P_m, but only to some intermediate point between P_m and P_c.

In effect, there is a market for regulation as for any other economic good. But that market is not one where a sole demander (producers) purchases from the supplier (government), as originally modeled by Stigler. Rather, it is an auction market, where various groups of potential winners and losers vie for the amounts and kinds of rent creation that government can supply. In this more sophisticated Stigler-Peltzman model, regulation is sold by auction to the highest bidder, like any number of other things (houses, paintings). But typically, no one person ends up owning all of the particular type of asset being auctioned.

The notion of regulation as a multiparty auction for rents has implications, too, for groups' incentives to organize. In the economic theory of regulation, organization of special-interest groups is unambiguously good. Larger organizations can draw on the resources of more people, increasing total bid size and so the likelihood of obtaining the desired regulation. Smaller groups can, by controlling free riding, more effectively organize their lobbying (Stigler 1974). Groups that are not organized, such as consumers in the original Stigler model, will see more of their surplus transferred to organized producer groups.

Gaps in the Rent-Creation Model of Regulation

The economic theory of regulation thus has evolved into a more complex description of the various ways government regulatory power can be turned to private ends. Important limitations of the standard economic theory of regulation remain, however. Three shortcomings are particularly noteworthy.

First, despite the growing realization that "government" is not an abstract entity but a group of politicians and their bureaucratic agents, the role of the politician has not been integrated satisfactorily into the model. By the ordinary assumptions of economics, the politician must be treated as a rational individual, seeking to maximize his own personal welfare. This statement is simply a tautology, however, saying just that the politician does what he does because he wants to do it. The truly useful exercise is identifying the ways in which politicians can improve their own lots—identifying the "arguments in their utility functions," to use the standard jargon—and then locating the constraints on them as they attempt to maximize utility.

In this sense, the economic theory of regulation has been deficient. The basic model, including its raising-rivals'-cost variant, focuses on private purchase of political rents. As in a standard market model of exchange, including auctions, politician-brokers respond to private demands for rents with a supply of regulation, but they do not actively enter the market for rents with their own demands.[13] As Tullock (1993, p. 26) summarizes, "politicians are modelled as providing a brokering function in the political model for wealth transfers." Their own utility functions and the constraints on their utility maximization are not part of the standard rent-creation story. This assumption is perhaps in keeping with the consumer-sovereignty model of private markets, but the applicability of that model to political markets is questionable. Clearly, a politician himself actively seeks votes, campaign contributions, and other forms of recompense, contracting to receive a supply of goods or services from private parties in response to his own demands. Only rarely, however, have social scientists considered whether "the politician demands funds" on his own initiative, and what the consequences of those independent demands are.[14]

Modeled just as a faceless broker among competing private demands, the politician has not been well integrated into the economic theory of regulation. He has remained a "mystery actor" (Tollison 1982, p. 592), a passive auctioneer among competing private rent-seekers (for example, McCormick and Tollison 1981). His role has been "subsumed" (McCormick 1984, p. 14), with little explicit consideration given to the ways in which the politician himself benefits from creating rents for private parties. This role of the politician is at fundamental variance with a principal tenet of economic models, that the actors therein are rational maximizers of their own welfare and interested in that of others only insofar as it advances their own.

This first gap in the standard theory in turn forces recognition of a second failing. Since little thought has been given to the ways that politicians themselves benefit from their elected positions, so has little attention has been paid to ways other than rent creation that a politician can obtain benefits from private individuals. Observers note that creation of rents does not seem to explain many of the regulatory statutes that legislators have enacted. Yet the principal theorists of the economic model cling to procrustean notions of rent creation to describe regulation, even when some groups clearly are made worse off, and even when those losses outweigh the gains to other groups.

Consider Peltzman's summary (1989) of his earlier (1976) model, in which consumers in effect bargain politicians down from price P_m in Figure 1.1 to some lower, intermediate price. Consumers are still made worse off, since the truly competitive price, P_c, is no longer available, thanks to political intervention in the market. Moreover, consumer losses will always be greater than producer gains, since consumers suffer both the monetary transfer to producers and the nonmonetary deadweight loss from higher prices. Inexplicably, though, Peltzman describes the outcome he originally expounded, in which "consumers can offer some votes or money for a small departure from the cartel equilibrium" (1989, p. 6), as involving a *sharing of created rents:*

> The notion that no single economic interest captures a regulatory body plays a prominent role in the 1976 article by Peltzman. He derives an equilibrium in which the utility-maximizing politician allocates benefits across groups optimally . . . As a result, politicians

normally hire the services of all groups. A similar statement applies within groups. Given the usual constraints on discrimination, *regulators will allocate benefits across consumer and producer groups* so that total political utility is maximized.[15]

This passage is curious. Note that both groups are bidders for the politicians' favor. Yet consumers lose in the process, and net losses result overall: consumer losses are greater than producer gains. Nonetheless, Peltzman describes the sequences as "allocating benefits across [both] consumer and producer groups," even though the former is a loser, not a beneficiary, from the process.

But the politician presumably has gained in the process, since he has gone ahead and lifted price above the prevailing competitive price P_c. Herein lies a seeming anomaly, and a third gap in the Stigler-Peltzman theory of economic regulation. The ability of politicians to gain, not by creating rents for some but by causing losses to others, has never been considered. How does a politician gain from imposing net losses? If fuller consideration were given to the ways in which politicians can benefit themselves, and if the economic model examined not just the gains to some groups from regulation but also the losses to others, might a fuller understanding of the regulatory state emerge?

That is the subject of the rest this book. The notion of rent extraction addresses the three deficiencies in the conventional economic theory of regulation described above. In particular, it challenges the basic economic perception of regulation as rent creation. The reason that the conventional rent-creation model cannot explain many forms of regulation, it is proposed here, is precisely because other sources of gains to politicians and bureaucrats themselves have not been considered systematically. One of these is rent extraction.

The rent-extraction model focuses specifically on politicians. It views them not as mere brokers redistributing wealth in response to competing private demands, but as independent actors making their own demands to which private actors respond. The conceptual reversal of roles in turn forces consideration of the ways other than rent creation that politicians can gain from private parties. The basic rent-extraction model to be developed now shows how politicians reap returns first by threatening and then by forbearing from the expropriation of private rents already in existence.

2

Rent Extraction: The Theory of Political Extortion

Governments show thus how successfully men can be imposed on . . .

    —HENRY DAVID THOREAU

Now I ask you: why does a man want to be a General? And I answer you: because he can drive anywhere in Russia—with postillions and adjutants rushing on ahead to get him his next team of horses. They won't give them to anybody else.

    —NIKOLAI GOGOL

Extraction of Politically Created Rents

As was shown in Chapter 1, the basic economic model of regulation—even in its more complex, post-Stiglerian form—remains one of rent creation. Rent creation is the standard perspective undoubtedly because, even after the embellishments to the model described, the economic model of regulation remains one of *exchange* (Peltzman 1989, p. 7). Politicians and their beneficiaries conclude a bargain that, like the typical contract, makes them both better off. Newly created rents are exchanged for votes and money; the multiparty auction allocates rents across groups. To the understandable confusion of lawyers, economists frequently use the word "bribe" to describe the "consideration" (the lawyers' term) paid over—quite legally—to politicians in return for regulatory favors.

It is not surprising that, perhaps instinctively, economists would turn to models of contract (exchange) to model regulation. Economics is often described as the study of the allocation of scarce resources among competing ends (Robbins 1930, p. 16). The principal mechanism by which scarce goods and services are allocated in market-based economies is exchange. Thus, economists have been interested in exchange since the development of economic science as a distinct discipline. Adam Smith began *The Wealth of Nations* (1776) with a description of people's "propensity to truck, barter and exchange one thing for another."

20

But analysis of regulation via a contract-based model entails three conceptual problems. First, the essence of contract is Pareto superiority: contracting parties are better off, and no one is worse off. That is obviously not true in the regulatory setting, where the benefits to producers (to some extent shared with politicians) come at the expense of consumers.[1] This point has led to a generalization of Stigler's initial model by Peltzman, as already discussed, and by others (for example, Becker 1983). But there remains the problem of how to fit these losses into an overall notion of regulatory exchange or contract.

Second, consider that the "contract" between regulator-supplier and regulated beneficiary is not an ordinary legal contract. Payment is made in order to make the private party better off, and in the process the politician gains as well. But were the politician to take the money and then refuse to create the rents, the aggrieved private party would have no legal recourse. The law effectively does not prohibit an agreement involving money in exchange for political favors (although, as explained in Chapter 3, it does regulate it). But the law does not enforce it, either.

The rent-creation contract is not illegal, but extralegal. The parties to the regulatory contract therefore must find their own, self-help ways to ensure that the promised performance is rendered on both sides. In this sense, rent creation is no different from any number of private exchanges made every day, in which individuals rely on one another's good faith and the desirability of continued relations, not the courts, for enforcement of the agreement.

Describing regulation as essentially a contract between politicians and regulated beneficiaries entails a third conceptual question: might other sorts of relationships also exist between the two groups? In the real world, voluntary contracts do not make up the complete set of human interactions. This fact has long been appreciated by game theorists, who study and model both cooperative (for example, Axelrod 1984) and noncooperative (for example, Schelling 1963) human behavior. People are thrown together involuntarily—on one side at least, if not both—in settings involving torts, even crimes, such as theft.

Obviously, these interactions do not leave both sides better off. But to the criminal (thief), the fact that his victims suffer while he gains is of scant importance. His only concern is whether he gains more through the involuntary exchange (theft) than he could by any voluntary exchange.[2]

In short, bribery (contract) is not the only form of interaction observed in the world. "In the general case, the individual will observe two ways to persuade: by a threat and by a bribe."[3] In the course of the ordinary day, an individual will typically combine bribes to some people (for example, his spouse) with threats to others (for example, his children) in order to induce the behavior that is desired or expected. Other people do the same with him: his boss probably relies on a combination of carrots and sticks.

Why would politicians not use the same dual strategy in their dealings with people? Certainly, private beneficiaries may pay bribes (legal or illegal) to politicians for regulatory largesse. But instead of or in addition to accepting bribes, might not politicians also take, or extort, from private parties?[4]

A politician has alternative ways to interact with private parties. He may seek votes or money from producers and offer rents from consumers in exchange, as in the orthodox economic theory of regulation-as-bribery.[5] But a politician may also make his demands on private parties, not by promising benefits, but by threatening to impose costs—a form of political extortion or blackmail. If the expected cost of the act threatened exceeds the value of what private parties must give up to avoid legislative action, they rationally will surrender the tribute demanded of them. With constant marginal utility of wealth, a private citizen will be just as willing to pay legislators to have rents of $1 million created as she will to avoid imposition of $1 million in losses. With declining marginal utility of income, the citizen will pay more to avoid the losses than she will to obtain the gains.

Once the politician is seen as an independent actor in the regulatory process, his objective function cannot be treated as single-valued. He will maximize total returns to himself by equating at the margin the returns from votes, contributions, bribes, power, and other sources of personal

"Calvin and Hobbes," © Watterson. Dist. by Universal Press Syndicate. Reprinted with permission. All rights reserved.

gain or utility. All these, in turn, are positive functions not only of private benefits he confers but also of private costs he agrees not to impose.

The political strategy of cost forbearance can assume several forms. Perhaps most obvious is the threat to deregulate an industry previously cartelized. Expected political rents created by earlier regulation are quickly capitalized into firm share prices. If politicians later breach their contract and vote unexpectedly to deregulate, shareholders suffer a wealth loss. Rather than suffer the costs of deregulation, shareholders will pay politicians a sum, up to the amount of wealth loss threatened, to have them refrain from deregulating. And in fact one routinely observes payments to politicians to protect previously enacted cartel measures. Dairy interests pay handsomely for continuation of congressional milk-price supports; physician and dentist political action committees (PACs) contribute large sums for continuation of self-regulation (Sabato 1984, pp. 133–137).

Subsequent payments to avoid postcontractual opportunism by politicians are to be distinguished from contractual payments to enhance rent longevity *ex ante*. Both politicians and rent recipients gain when the durability of regulation can be increased, that is, when legislators are held to longer contracts. But new arrivals on both sides succeed to the interests of the original contracting parties. A legislator not party to the original bargain has less incentive to abide by the political rent-creation deal struck by his predecessors unless he too is compensated. Guaranteed rent durability is thus impossible. Among owners of firms, subsequent purchasers of shares with expected rents capitalized into their prices are vulnerable to extraction of previously created rents on the part of opportunistic politicians. Payments to political newcomers to secure performance of previously negotiated contracts earn no rents. Rather, they protect against windfall losses that new legislators could impose otherwise.

Political Extraction of Private Rents

The durability problem for politically created rents has been discussed at length elsewhere[6] and is not the focus of this volume. But recognition of the rent-extraction opportunities that capitalized cartel rents represent to politicians suggests that similar strategies may offer gains to politicians when other sorts of rents exist. In particular, it leads one to focus on the capital value of *privately* created rents and politicians' predictable responses to their existence, including how that value might be extorted, or extracted. It remains to formalize the extraction process more rigorously within the standard economic model of regulation, showing how, from the standpoint of the maximizing politician, extraction of existing rents may be a more valuable strategy than creation of new rents.

The Model

Consider again the model of rent creation by cost predation (raising rivals' costs). Figure 2.1 is similar to Figure 1.2, used in the preceding chapter to describe cost predation. As before, in an industry whose firms have differing amounts of a firm-specific, fixed-cost resource, the supply curve without regulation (S_0) is upward-sloping. The returns to that specialized capital, producers' surplus 0AD, are rents. They are purely *private* rents, however, not governmentally created ones. They represent returns to inborn special talents (say, athletic ability) or some other asset whose supply is not readily augmented (a prime selling location), plus investments made earlier in those assets that now yield a flow of returns over time. Most important, they represent economically "good rents," ones resulting from mutually beneficial exchange. Allowing asset owners to realize the rents is a necessary condition for inducing optimal levels of investment in assets.[7]

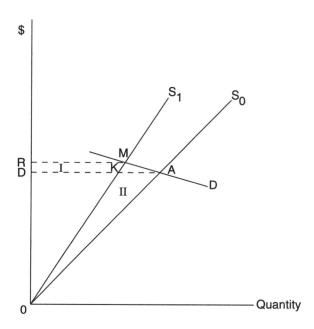

Figure 2.1 Net losses from raising rivals' costs

The original Figure 1.2 showed how net inframarginal (or so-called Ricardian) rents could be created for that industry by imposing costs so as to shift S_0 to S_1. But now, for the new industry in Figure 2.1, demand (D) is more elastic than was demand for the industry in Figure 1.2. Suppose that in this second industry with more elastic demand the same political measures are suggested to shift S_0 to S_1. What will the political outcome be?

With the same cost-increasing measures being proposed, precisely the opposite result will obtain. The area of rents created for at least some firms is smaller than the rents lost: overall area I (DKMR) < area II (0AK). Industrywide, the loss of existing rents ("good rents") at current production levels is greater than the new (politically created) rents available from raising rivals' costs, because the higher price causes production levels (quantity demanded) to decline. The politically created rents are smaller than the rents from private capital already in existence. In contrast to the first rent-creation case (Figure 1.2), politicians proposing to regulate in the second industry (Figure 2.1) would find that firms in the industry potentially affected would pay *not* to be regulated. That is, politicians could be rewarded by threatening to impose costs so as to shift S_0 to S_1, then allowing themselves to be bought off in return for not actually imposing those costs.

In other words, the politician would be paid, not for political rent creation, but for withholding action that would destroy existing private rents. Private parties' willingness to pay for cost-raising measures to create rents is a function of the price elasticity of demand, as the comparison between Figures 1.2 and 2.1 shows. However, recognition of the opportunities for political profit from threatening action and then being bought off raises the question whether such a strategy is available to politicians more generally. The answer is yes. In fact demand elasticity is largely unimportant whenever an industry is characterized by large stocks of capital earning rents and producers' surplus.

To see why, consider again Figure 1.2. Increasing costs for all firms—but more for marginal firms—creates inframarginal (Ricardian) rents by shifting the supply curve to S_1: area I is larger than area II (CDEF > AC0). To inframarginal, capital-intensive producers, regulation is advantageous. Hence, the beneficiaries will pay politicians to effect it.[8] The capitalized value of the net increased rent flow defines the maximum payment producers would make to politicians in return for regulation. As the difference between areas I and II grows, the politicians' "take" from the process increases.

But rent creation by a governmentally mandated shift from S_0 to S_1 is not the only option open to politicians. Existing *private* rents rewarding specific capital assets (areas II + III) are already greater than the rents that can be created by regulation (area I): 0AD > CDEF. As demonstrated below, regulatory measures could be identified that would expropriate the producers' surplus 0AD by legally mandating either lower prices or higher costs. Once such regulation is threatened, the price that producers would pay politicians in return for governmental inaction would exceed any payment for rent-creating regulation. (Henceforth, the payments made to avoid full expropriation of this privately created producers' surplus 0AD will be referred to as payments of extraction.)

Faced, then, with a choice between the two strategies, a regulator would not in the situation portrayed maximize the benefits to himself by creating new rents. Rather, he would threaten to expropriate existing private rents and then forbear from doing so, extracting a smaller part of the rents as payment for not taking all of them. (The conditions under which rent extraction is politically preferable to—that is, more valuable than—rent creation are explored later in this chapter.) As with threatened deregulation of government cartels, payments must be made to protect rents. But unlike the cartel case, in which rents were created by government itself, a legislator threatening to expropriate private rents is paid to let firms earn returns on capital they have created for themselves.

Methods of Extracting Private Rents

Having located private capital stocks whose returns will come out of producers' surplus, how can legislators extract a share of that surplus? Two general strategies represent threats to private producers' returns on their capital: reductions in price and increases in cost. Acting collectively, politicians can use either strategy to induce private payments not to extract rents.[9]

Legislative Threats to Reduce Prices
One way to threaten producers' privately created surplus is to lower prices legislatively below levels that would otherwise prevail in the market. Any measure that reduces price necessarily reduces the level of producer surplus that can be earned. One straightforward way to threaten that surplus is to threaten price controls, a threat that predictably would elicit offers of

payment from affected producers in exchange for politicians' withdrawing the proposed controls.

A variant on extracting rents by threatening (and then forbearing from) imposing price controls is threatening to withdraw a privilege that the state has arrogated to itself (such as occupational license, a corporate charter, a building permit). These privileges are themselves typically not the source of rents, since they ordinarily are easily obtained and do not foreclose entry in any effective way. Licenses, corporate charters, and building permits, for example, are supposedly available to all applicants upon the satisfaction of prespecified conditions. But threatening to revoke charters or permits is equivalent to threatening to reduce to zero the price the firm can legally charge. As Richard Epstein (1993) has explained, selective denial of these privileges unless certain wealth is surrendered provides a fertile source of rent extraction from victims so denied. Epstein argues forcefully that these practices should be voidable as "unconstitutional conditions."

Threats of price controls or license revocation are obvious ways to menace producers' rents so as to garner payments to remove the threat; both practices are examined in greater detail in Chapter 3. But more indirect ways to lower prices legislatively are also available. Consider firms' fixed-cost investments in brand-name capital or reputation, which are especially important in securing repeat patronage over time. All firms may produce otherwise equivalent products, but some will have incurred greater costs in past periods (for example, by advertising) to make their names, logos, trademarks, and quality familiar to consumers. Advertising creates a capital stock, returns from which accrue over time. Once created, the capital is specific to the firm and enables the firm in a later period to incur lower costs to guide purchasers to its products and to guarantee the quality of the goods or services that it sells. Rival firms without brand-name capital must incur higher costs in that same later period to make their names and product quality as well known and trustworthy to buyers.[10]

This situation is illustrated in Figure 2.2 for two representative firms. Industry supply and demand establish the equilibrium price, 0D. Firm X has been in business and has advertised for years; firm Y has just started in business. Both firms provide identical products of equivalent quality at the same marginal cost ($MC_X = MC_Y$). But customers cannot evaluate product quality prior to purchase; hence there is buyer uncertainty. Both firms guarantee quality, but in different ways. Firm X relies on its investment in brand-name capital in prior periods, its customers paying a premium for the credible guarantee of quality that the reputation capital provides. To offer an equivalent guarantee, firm Y must incur other fixed costs in the current period, such as having an independent laboratory test its product quality and publicize the fact that it is just as good as X's. The higher current expenses make Y's average costs higher than X's: $AC_Y > AC_X$. The premium (AB) that X's customers pay for the reputational guarantee earns rents (ABCD).

But X's rents can be reduced or destroyed by government intervention. Politicians can pass legislation to have administrative agencies guarantee quality or truthful information by imposing minimum quality standards or mandatory information-disclosure regulations. Government agents then would police the market for quality and truth, substituting both for the brand-name capital invested earlier by firm X and for the current testing that firm Y would have commissioned to guarantee quality. To the extent that it substitutes for private reputational capital, government regulation destroys the premium value of X's private capital while relieving the firm without reputation, Y, of any current costs to warrant its own quality.

The threatened government intervention would lower price, eradicating the producers' surplus compensating firms for their earlier investments. Rather than have politicians depreciate their capital stock, firm X would pay up to ABCD per period for nonintervention in the market. Even if regulation "only" substitutes for activities currently provided privately, it reduces the expected returns to prior private investments and so, over time, the amount firms are willing to invest. In the new equilibrium firm Y would earn no rents from the regulation and so would offer politicians nothing for it. The only gains to politicians in this case come from threatening to extract X's privately created rents.

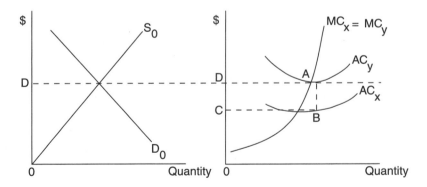

Figure 2.2 Rent extraction by threatened price reductions

Legislative Threats to Raise Costs

Just as proposals to institute price-lowering regulation imperil private rents, so do regulations that threaten to increase costs. The strategy of extracting rents by raising costs is just as straightforward as that of imposing price controls. Consider the situation portrayed in Figure 2.3, in which legislators threaten an excise tax or other per-unit cost of 0C. Rather than suffer the net loss in producers' surplus that would result, area I minus area II (0AEC − BDFE), firms earning rents will offer to compensate legislators to refrain from imposing the costs.

The extraction option is not mere blackboard economics. In fact politicians practice rent extraction routinely. "Milker bills" is one term used by politicians to describe legislative proposals intended only to "milk" private producers for payments not to pass the rent-extracting legislation.

> Early on in my association with the California legislature, I came across the concept of "milker bills"—proposed legislation which had nothing to do with milk to drink and much to do with money, the "mother's milk of politics" . . . Representative Sam, in need of campaign contributions, has a bill introduced which excites some constituency to urge

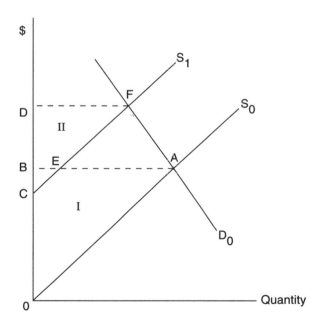

Figure 2.3 Rent extraction by threatened cost increases

Sam to work hard for its defeat (easily achieved), pouring funds into his campaign coffers and "forever" endearing Sam to his constituency for his effectiveness . . . (Stubblebine 1985, pp. 1–2)

"Cash cows" is another name for legislation threatened in order to milk contributions and then not passed. "Rarely do these cash-generating pieces of legislation ever pass. But . . . they sprout again every Congress, replenishing the coffers of lawmakers" (Abramson 1990). With proposed product-liability legislation, Washington politicians for years "have been feeding off the contributions from political action committees and the fat retainers that product-liability legislation has generated," so "product liability legislation will remain in legislative limbo—a cash cow with plenty of milk left." Money flows from PACs on both sides of the issue. According to Ralph Nader, "The bill is a PAC annuity for members of Congress. It's like rubbing the golden lamp" (ibid.).

"Juice bills" is another moniker attached to bills submitted only "for the cash that can be squeezed out of them," as noted in one account of the California legislature.

One prime example: repeal of unitary taxation, which would save foreign companies operating in California as much as $500 million in state corporate taxes. Strongly backed by Japanese and British interests, the bill has been debated in each of the past three sessions but has yet to come to a vote. Insiders complain that legislators are dawdling because they have become hooked on the thousands of dollars of lobbyist lucre it generates. Another example: between 1979 and 1982, California's oil industry spent $2.5 million to prevent the imposition of a severance tax, which is a levy on oil shipped out of the state. (Doerner 1986)

Newsweek reports that pieces of menacing legislation are also known as "fetcher" bills: "bills introduced solely to draw—fetch—lavish treatment from lobbyists. Usage: 'Let's toss in a fetcher on prohibiting the sale of Japanese-made Christmas-tree lights.'"[11]

Newsweek refers to "fetcher" as a term from the Midwest; the practice of "fetching" seems particularly active in Illinois. One study of the Illinois legislature (quoted in Aranson 1981, p. 253) referred to legislators who "introduce some bills that are deliberately designed to shake down groups which oppose them and which pay to have them withdrawn. These bills are called 'fetchers,' and once their sponsors develop a lucrative field, they guard it jealously." Even in Washington, Illinois legislators profit from "fetchers."

> Rep. Jim Leach quietly introduced a bill a few days ago aimed at reducing speculation in financial futures. Barely 24 hours later, the Iowa Republican learned that Chicago commodity traders were gunning to kill his proposal. Rep. Leach said one Illinois lawmaker told him the bill was shaping up as a classic "fetcher bill," a term used in that state's Legislature to describe a measure likely to "fetch" campaign contributions for its opponents. Sure enough, one of the first to defend the traders was Democratic Rep. Cardiss Collins of Illinois, recipient of $24,500 from futures-industry political action committees. She called on colleagues in the Illinois delegation to beat back the Leach bill and watch out for similar legislation. (Jackson and Ingersoll 1987)

In the economic theory of regulation, rent creation is to rent extraction as, more generally, bribery is to extortion. With the former (rent creation/bribery), the beneficiaries of political action compensate the politician for increasing their welfare. With the latter (rent extraction/extortion), persons whose welfare would otherwise be diminished by political action compensate the politician for not effectuating that diminution. The ultimate implications for the payors themselves are completely different, of course, although the politician is enriched either way.

The outside observer may often find it difficult at the time to distinguish the motivation for payments to politicians. "Bribery and extortion substantially overlap and have for centuries . . . the same envelope filled with cash can be both a payment extorted under a threat of unfairly negative treatment and a bribe obtained under a promise of unfairly positive treat-

"Calvin and Hobbes," © Watterson. Dist. by Universal Press Syndicate.
Reprinted with permission. All rights reserved.

ment."[12] In theory, as Avner Greif, Paul Milgrom, and Barry Weingast (1994, p. 754) note, one would look at quantity responses to the payment. Effective cartelization (rent creation) would lead to the new cartel's reduction of quantities produced; removal of the threat of expropriation should cause the previously threatened firm or individual to produce more. But in practice, measuring the quantity response will not be easy.[13]

Those approached by politicians have less difficulty distinguishing the reasons for the approach. To "milked" or "squeezed" victims, and to those whose favors are "fetched," the process in which they are forced to participate is frequently seen just as extortion to avoid future losses, not as a chance to join in any auction for new rents.[14] One PAC director is quoted as saying that invitations to purchase tickets to congressional receptions "are nothing but blackmail" (Sabato 1984, p. 86). Likewise, "The 1972 reelection effort for President Nixon included practices bordering on extortion, in which corporations and their executives were, in essence, 'shaken down' for cash donations" (ibid., p. 5). Brooks Jackson's remarkable insider study of the Democratic Congressional Campaign Committee (1988, p. 5) finds that the committee "pressures business lobbyists for campaign money in ways that sometimes amount to intimidation."[15] The threats are made quite openly. One newspaper reported, for example, that "House Republican leaders are sending a vaguely threatening message to business political action committees: Give us more, or we may do something rash."[16]

The Costs of Rent Extraction

In the early days of economists' study of the social cost of monopoly (including government-created monopolies and cartels), the actual economic costs of monopoly appeared to be slight. The rents created thereby seemed mere transfers from one group (consumers) to another (producers), with little net social loss. The deadweight welfare loss associated with the transfer, while real, was repeatedly estimated empirically to be rather small. It was only when Gordon Tullock (1967) explained how competition for the transfer payments (rent seeking) converted transfers into real resource losses that the true social costs of monopoly were appreciated.

Superficially, the losses from rent extraction might also seem like mere transfers from asset owners to politicians. But for reasons similar to those in the rent-creation debate, the economic implications of regulation that is threatened but ultimately not imposed when politicians are bought off are nonetheless important. The producers' surplus compensating firm-specific capital is inframarginal, but this fact does not mean that its potential expropriation by politicians has no allocative consequences. Even if politicians eventually allow themselves to be bought off, their minatory presence reduces the expected value of entrepreneurial ability and specific-capital investments. True social losses would result in several ways.

First, the possibility that government may reduce returns to their capital unless paid off naturally reduces firms' incentives to invest in the first place. The portent of rent extraction also induces inefficient shifts to investment in socially less valuable but politically more mobile or salvageable (that is, less firm-specific) forms of capital as insurance against expropriation. Most obviously, these shifts include investments made in the "underground economy" (Alm 1985), where they cannot be reached by government. The underground economy has grown so large in response to government attempts to tax, regulate, or ban activities like gambling, prostitution, or drugs—activities that routinely furnish rent-extraction opportunities to government agents—that "money-laundering" is now said to constitute the third-largest business in the world (Robinson 1994).

Regardless of whether the extraction strategy causes investments not to be made at all, or to be made in less valuable but also less vulnerable areas, the economic impact is the same. The allocative efficiency losses from politicians' ability to extract the returns from private capital in the industry threatened are measured by the difference between the wealth-maximizing investments that would be made, but for the extortion threats, and those that are made. The consequences are like those of common extortion[17] or of ordinary theft. "One way of minimizing loss by theft is to have little or nothing to steal. In a world in which theft was legal we could expect this fact to lead to a reduction in productive activities."[18] If you own nothing, you have nothing to lose.

In effect, an important similarity between capital expropriations in less-developed countries and "mere" regulation in developed nations has been overlooked. In both settings, the very presence of a threatening government will reduce private investment, all else equal (Eaton and Gersovitz 1984). The resulting welfare losses would be measured by the value of specific capital and other investments that firms would have made, but for the fear (uncertainty) over subsequent expropriation and the cost of purchasing protection from politicians. These similarities are detailed further in Chapter 3.

The first cost of the rent-extraction phenomenon is thus the disincentive to create new capital whose returns will subsequently be vulnerable to expropriation, and so exposed to the possibility of later extraction. However, creation of new wealth flows also depends on the size of existing capital stocks that will be enlisted for production. The value of existing capital is also diminished by the possibility that it will be extracted. "[I]f private property depends on the payment of bribes, then the bribe to be extorted can be the full value of the property and, hence, the property has no value" (Tullock 1974b, p. 67). In a hypothetical world in which no new capital was going to be created anyway, an increased ability of politicians to extract rents would diminish the value of existing capital.

Third, one must include in the total social cost of rent extraction the transaction (including bargaining) costs incurred in the extraction process—just as private blackmail and extortion are undesirable for similar reasons.[19] To the extent that there is a socially positive opportunity cost to politicians' time, losses follow from negotiating over the division of the surpluses generated by private investment. Obviously, private capital owners' time entails that same cost. And the process consumes other sorts of real resources as well (for meals, lawyers, and other in-kind expenditures), just as rent creation does (Mixon, Laband, and Ekelund 1994). Add to those losses the very real (capital and labor) costs of operating the legislative process (studies, hearings, meetings, debates) necessary to making expropriation threats credible when milker, squeezer, and fetcher bills are proposed.

Finally, the reckoning of transaction costs must also include the deadweight costs of hiding resources so as to avoid their being subject to extraction in the first place, and the effects of that concealment on bargaining costs. As J. Patrick Gunning has noted (1972, p. 22), different incentives to hide resources distinguish bribes (here, rent creation) from extortion (rent extraction). With bribery, the payor will pursue a mixed strategy of convincing the other side (politicians) that he has some resources, enough to pay the other's reservation price, but no more. But with possible extortion, the strategy is the simpler one of hiding the existence (or value) of the resource altogether. Hiding money to avoid threats of taxation, for example, is a large part of the international money-laundering enterprise.

Extracting Private Rents versus Creating Political Rents

Extraction of private rents and creation of political rents need not be mutually exclusive strategies for politicians. Maximum gains for legislators may involve a combination of the two. In Figure 1.2, for example, politicians could create rents in area I (CDEF) by imposing regulation while threatening to expropriate the remaining producers' surplus in area III (0DC). Increasing minimum wages could benefit capital-intensive firms at the expense of their labor-intensive rivals; at the same time, a lump-sum tax could extract the value (that is, the discounted present value of the stream of quasi-rents over time) to be earned by that capital. The maximum private payment forthcoming from the combined tactic, areas I plus III (0EF), would exceed that from merely threatening rent expropriation with regulation (0AD).

But a combined strategy of rent creation and rent extraction is not necessarily optimal to politicians. Political rent creation (of either the Stiglerian or raising-rivals'-costs sort) requires restriction of output. That restriction in turn diminishes the current stock of expropriable producers' surplus, since it reduces the number of units sold on which rents can be earned. *Ceteris paribus,* greater rent creation therefore means more forgone rent extraction. Particularly because the political processes of creating or extracting rents are not costless to legislators, the gains may justify using only one or the other strategy in a particular market. (The relevant costs include the sheer transaction costs of creating and extracting rents, the subject of Chapter 7.) Thus, among economists who have recognized that governments transfer wealth not just among subgroups of citizens but also directly to themselves, one finds examples of some industries enjoying cartelization (rent creation) while others suffer threats of extortion (rent extraction). Greif, Milgrom, and Weingast (1994), for example, discuss the cartelization of some sellers (members of craft guilds) simultaneous with expropriation from others (merchant sellers) by medieval European city-states.

The relative gains from the two strategies, and thus the optimal political mix of created (political) and extracted (private) rents, are a function of industry supply and demand conditions. The more inelastic industry demand, the greater the relative attraction of political rent creation, all else equal. Similarly, if industry supply is perfectly elastic, there is no producers' surplus and so no opportunity for rent extraction. On the other hand, as industry demand becomes perfectly elastic, extraction of private rents becomes the only plausible political strategy. Similarly, a large stock of specific (nonsalvageable) capital increases the relative attraction to politicians of private rent extraction.

Of course, producers themselves would rather buy new rents than pay to protect their own existing rents. But as between the two possibilities, it is politicians who own (subject to any constitutional limitations) the effective property rights to decide whether rents will be created or extracted. In some markets, rent-creation opportunities for politicians may be minor compared with those for extracting returns to private capital. For example, ease of new entry or closeness of substitutes may make rent-creating cartelization futile. At the same time, the presence of large specific-capital stocks would make the same industry vulnerable to rent extraction.

Gathering information about supply and demand elasticities, entry costs, and the size and mobility of capital stocks is costly to politicians.[20] The specter of rent extraction naturally will induce private owners of expropriable capital to try to hide the size (value) of their capital stocks, a tactic that increases the costs to politicians of discovering how much producers would pay to avoid expropriation.[21] But political threats to act have the effect of instituting an auction market among private parties.

> [L]egislatures work on the presence or absence of opposition. Legislation for which the claim can be made that some group will benefit, if only modestly, and which induces no opposition is almost certain to pass. Thus, introduction of a milker bill which does not generate the expected opposition to its passage, as evidenced by resources devoted to lobbying for its defeat, indeed will pass. By contrast, milker bills which generate the anticipated opposition will fail. Contrasting these outcomes usually makes an effective case for generating the lobbying resources. (Stubblebine 1985, p. 18)

An auction not only drives competitive bids for legislative favors higher but also reveals which firms stand to gain and which to lose, plus the magnitude of the respective effects.

The auction thus provides valuable information whether regulatory action or inaction will be more lucrative to politicians themselves; it helps to identify the likely payors and to set the amounts of compensation to be paid. Particularly since legislators may not know the size of the rents potentially expropriable, they may prefer to make good their threat in order to elicit bids revealing the true size of the private capital stock. Actual enactment of legislation raises to unity the probability of rent-destroying measures, subject to firms' buying legislative repeal. Legislation that would destroy rents can be enacted with a delayed effective date to allow firms to mobilize and bid to remove or alter the statute. This has been the pattern observed, for example, in response to the Energy Policy and Conservation Act of 1975, which forces auto firms to build different mixes of large and small cars from what consumers demand, and therefore lowers profits (Henderson 1985). Since 1975 auto firms have repeatedly lobbied the

Department of Transportation to delay or alter standards on auto emissions, and have had to fight off a series of congressional attempts to increase the strength of the original legislation.[22]

Because the maximum gains to legislators depend on some knowledge of elasticities and the size of private rents, there may also be gains from specialization in identifying industries with expropriable producers' surplus and in determining how best to extract it. If so, legislators predictably would delegate cost-imposing functions to specialized bureaucratic agencies. By threatening or actually imposing costs, these outside agents create a demand for politicians to mitigate the costs.

Use of specialized agencies to impose costs has a second advantage to politicians. Although they may act at the behest of elected officials, bureaucrats will be perceived by at least some rationally ignorant voters as independent. Information about the regulatory process is costly to obtain, and so it may appear that misguided agencies rather than politicians themselves are responsible for the costs threatened. Designation of institutions like the Federal Trade Commission (FTC) and the Securities and Exchange Commission as "independent agencies" may further the perception in some voters' eyes that politicians are less responsible for agency activities. Further, the appearance may not be purely illusory. Congressional monitoring of agencies is costly. Some of what agencies do, therefore, will not be known to a legislator until constituents bring it to her attention.

The rent-extraction model thus sheds light on the recurring controversy whether bureaucratic agencies "run amok," free of congressional constraints, or whether they function as closely controlled creatures (agents) of Congress, a controversy illustrated by conflicting views of the FTC.[23] Politicians' ability to extract rents means that neither view may capture fully the essence of Congress-agency relations. In a given situation, a politician may have less incentive to monitor specialized agencies *ex ante*, while they consider and adopt cost-imposing measures more cheaply and carefully than Congress itself could. There would be more incentive for legislative surveillance of agency actions *ex post*, in order to locate opportunities for alleviating those costs (for a fee, of course). An agency like the FTC might be allowed to file legal actions against particular firms, such a tactic then eliciting requests for politicians' intervention to remove the costs imposed by bureaucrats' investigations and prosecutions—precisely the pattern that has been identified for antitrust cases brought by the FTC (Faith, Leavens, and Tollison 1982).

The Strategy of Rent Extraction

The political strategy of milking extractive payments from private-investment values can succeed only to the extent that threats to expropriate returns to capital are credible. Credibility may not be easily achieved. With any given firm or industry, producers and politicians are seemingly locked in a game of "chicken," creating some incentive on producers' part to call politicians' bluff and refuse to pay.

As a numerical example, suppose that a politician can credibly imperil $30,000 of a person's wealth by some legislation (for example, a tax). But the politician in fact would prefer not to tax, if an attractive payment from the tax victim can be negotiated. Any money actually taken by the tax would go to the government treasury, and so has only trivial value, say $2,000, to him personally. Alternatively, the politician would be willing not to legislate if a payment greater than $2,000 (say $10,000) was paid to him personally.

The politician thus has two choices: extract the $10,000 personal payment, or expropriate the whole $30,000. The private person's choices are whether or not to ante up the $10,000. These four possibilities result in the accompanying payoff matrix (with quadrant letters A through D in brackets). In each quadrant the individual's losses are shown first, with the politician's gains in parentheses.

		Individual	
		No payment	Payment
Politician	No expropriation	$0 ($0) [A]	$10,000 ($10,000) [B]
	Expropriation	$30,000 ($2,000) [C]	$40,000 ($12,000) [D]

The matrix illustrates the key elements of the extraction strategy. In [C], the politician threatens a loss of $30,000 (the tax), but the potential gain to him is only $2,000. That sum is less than the gain to him in [B], where the individual threatened pays the politician $10,000 not to be harmed. Knowing that the actual gain to the politician from expropriating (taxing) is relatively small, the individual might be tempted to call the politician's bluff and offer nothing, hoping that the threatened tax actually will not be imposed (quadrant [A]). In that case the politician's only gain would come from actually expropriating (taxing), leaving both parties worse off collectively in [C] than they would be in [B].

Political Credibility

This matrix illustrates the politician's dilemma. Well-informed individuals facing him will realize that he would prefer to be paid off rather than legislate. So he must convince them that although he would prefer not to expropriate, he will do so, however reluctantly. That is, the threat to expropriate—which is not the politician's preferred strategy—must be credible.[24]

But the politician has several advantages. First, the politician still gains something if he taxes, albeit not as much as he would if he were bought off. Second, the more the putative victim would lose from legislation, the less plausible the strategy of calling the politician's bluff becomes. For example, David Laband (1986, p. 409) found that stoplight windshield-washers' threats of extortion at city intersections are more credible (and therefore made more often) against women. Women fear more for their physical safety in such confrontations, meaning the potential loss to them is greater than that for men, and so they are more likely to pay.

Moreover, a politician's demonstrated willingness actually to expropriate private rents in one situation provides an instructive lesson to other firms or industries that will increase their incentive to pay in their turn. "[P]oliticians may sometimes have to enact legislation extracting private rents from owners who do not pay up, just as the *Cosa Nostra* occasionally burns down the buildings of those who fail to pay its protection levies" (Tullock 1993, p. 74). That is, rent extraction from the perspective of the politician is a repeat game. To make credible expected later threats to destroy others' capital, politicians may sometimes have to enact legislation extracting private rents from owners who do not pay. In the private extortion setting, windshield-washing at stoplights, Laband (1986) observes that a common tactic to induce payments from those not wanting the services "offered" is to cover the windshield with soapy water and then walk away, returning only if payment is forthcoming—which it often is. Likewise, politicians can always legislate now and sell repeal later, much as the Civil War law on the draft ordered conscription but allowed draftees to buy their way out.[25]

The credibility—and thus the political attraction—of expropriation threats is also a function of the strength of constitutional rules that protect private property and contract rights from governmental taking.[26] Legislative threats to expropriate returns to private capital will elicit fewer payments to politicians, the more likely it is that capital owners can later have any expropriative legislation voided constitutionally in the courts. However, the level of constitutional scrutiny of legislative expropriations involving private contract and property rights has diminished throughout the late nineteenth and twentieth centuries (Anderson and Hill 1980; Epstein 1985). The scope for credible legislative threats against private capital has expanded apace. In effect, as courts have retreated from affording constitutional protection against legislative takings, potential private victims are forced to employ more self-help remedies by buying off politicians rather than submit to even more dire expropriative regulation.

Political Opportunism

Politicians thus have at their disposal several ways to make their threats credible, avoiding quadrant [A] and creating an incentive for would-be victims to try to buy off the threat. In addition to credibility, however, the politician has a second potential problem to overcome in eliciting private payments to avoid expropriation. That is the worry of opportunistic behavior by politicians.

To return to the payoff matrix presented above, the politician prefers quadrant [D] to either [B] or [C] separately, since in [D] the politician secures not only the $10,000 payment from the individual but also (by expropriating via taxation the $30,000) a second benefit of $2,000 for himself. The individual, then, does not get what he paid for. But people are not stupid. Knowing that the politician may take his money and then expropriate anyway, the individual may refuse to make the payment. The fear of potential opportunism by the politician—the victim's fear of ending up in [D]—thus risks leaving the parties in [C], which neither of them prefers to [B].

This sort of opportunism, or "double-crossing," is a common problem in any extortion context, including that of rent extraction.

> A person making a threat faces a double problem. On one hand, his
> threat must be credible. The intended victim must believe there to be
> a significant chance that the threat will be carried out if and only if he
> does not accede to it; otherwise, he may have insufficient reason to
> bow to the will of the threatener. On the other hand, the victim must
> believe that if he *does* reward the threatener, he, the victim, will gain

thereby and not merely set himself up for further threats . . . Difficulties in making threats combined with possibilities of miscalculation lead to the risk that demands will be rejected and threats actually executed. (Shavell 1993, p. 1878)

As with credibility, though, there are factors that would tend to land the parties in [B] rather than [C]. In particular, rent extraction is a repeat game from the perspective of the politician. A reputation for keeping one's word—avoiding the opportunism that causes the parties to end up in [D]—thus is valuable to a politician. The issue is somewhat complex, however, and further discussion is deferred to Chapter 5.

Conclusion

The rent-extraction model elaborated in this chapter is essentially a model of extortion by politicians. They are paid not to legislate—money for nothing. The model extends the economic theory of regulation to include the gains available to politician-maximizers from alleviating costs threatened or actually imposed on private actors by legislators themselves and by specialized bureaucratic agencies. Status as a legislator confers a property right not only to create political rents but also to impose costs that would destroy private rents. In order to protect these returns, private owners have an incentive to strike bargains with legislators, as long as the side payments to politicians are lower than the losses expected from the law threatened.

Their ability to impose costs enables politicians to demand payments not to do so. As with rent creation, the process of rent extraction in the short run might seem to involve only transfers—from capital owners to politicians, rather than from consumers to producers. But the long-run implications are the more important ones. The transfers required to protect returns to private investments create disincentives to invest in valuable specific capital in the first place. Even when politicians eventually eschew intervention, the mere threat and the payments required to remove it must distort private investment decisions.

The model of rent extraction set out here in no way undermines the orthodox model of rent-creating regulation; rather, it supplements the rent-creation model by recognizing alternative sources of political gains.[27] Indeed, Stigler's original article foreshadowed a complementary rent-extraction model: "The state—the machinery and power of the state—is a potential resource or threat to every industry in the society. With its power to prohibit or compel, to take or give money, the state can and does selectively help or hurt a vast number of industries . . . Regulation may be actively sought by an industry, or it may be thrust upon it."[28] Conditions that make political rent creation relatively unattractive to politicians make private rent extraction more attractive. The relative attraction of rent extraction has also increased as constitutional protection of private rights has diminished.

True, credibility issues, problems of political opportunism, and perhaps other imperfections in private-capital protection may create disincentives for capital owners to buy off legislators—just as opportunism and political-rent protection may discourage payments for rent creation. Yet rent creation is an ongoing, frequently observed phenomenon of modern politics. The complementary question thus is posed: do private actors in fact pay significant sums to induce government *not* to act?

That is the question addressed in Part II, where much evidence of actual rent extraction is presented. Despite the political impediments to contract, then, the demonstrated willingness of capital owners to purchase protection indicates that appreciable capital stocks are credibly imperiled by regulations that are never actually enacted.

If so, one cost of government regulation has been missed. Heretofore, the economic model has identified several different costs of government regulation: deadweight consumer loss, resources expended as private parties seek rents, and costs of compliance with regulation (Tullock 1967; Posner 1975; Rogerson 1982; Fisher 1985). To these should be added the costs of protecting private capital, even when politicians ultimately are persuaded not to regulate. As Part II demonstrates, there is no such thing as a free market.

II

DEMONSTRATIONS

3

Observing Extortion:
The Practice of Rent Extraction

Do what we can, summer will have its flies. If we walk in the
woods, we must feed mosquitoes.

—RALPH WALDO EMERSON

The previous chapter elaborated a basic economic model of political
extortion. The model is one of rent extraction, not rent creation as in the
standard (Stigler-Peltzman) economic theory of regulation. Individuals do
not bribe a legislator to improve their lots in life. Rather, payments are just
extorted—individuals are made to pay, rather than suffer welfare (wealth)
losses. A few examples of rent extraction—"juice," "fetcher," and "milker"
bills—were provided in passing. But the emphasis was on the theory of
rent extraction and on contrasting it to more familiar notions of rent-creating government regulation.

One aspect of the rent extraction model noted in Chapter 2 was the
importance of politicians' threats of expropriation being credible. Obviously, unless the specter of expropriation is credible, no private extraction
payments will be forthcoming. This chapter provides anecdotal evidence
to demonstrate that rent extraction is indeed a frequently used tactic in
politicians' overall portfolio of ways to benefit from their offices. Particular
attention will be paid to the most obvious episode occurring in this
country's recent political history, the 1986 Tax Reform Act. As will be
seen, private parties do find expropriation threats credible, as evidenced by
their payments to avoid the actions threatened.

Forms of Private Tribute Paid to Politicians

Politicians' process of using the portent of unfavorable legislation to milk
and squeeze private groups for contributions hardly corresponds to the
legislative process as taught in eighth-grade civics classes. In the civics-class
version, bills typically originate in one chamber (either the House or the
Senate), proceed through formal hearings and committee and staff work,

and then are reported to the full chamber, which votes and sends the bill to the other chamber. Once each chamber agrees on its own version of the bill, any differences are resolved in conference. The compromise bill must then be approved by both chambers and sent to the president for his signature.

This civics-class outline of legislation ignores a key part of the process—lobbying by special interests or their lobbyist agents. The relationship between special interests, acting through lobbyists, and legislators is central to understanding much of the legislative process. In 1985, for instance, as the Tax Reform Act was taking shape, nearly 8,000 lobbyists paid $49 million to persuade Congress, an amount that averages more than $91,000 per congressman and senator. The lobbyists' payments exceeded by over 50 percent the $32.7 million that U.S. taxpayers paid as salaries to their 535 senators and representatives.[1] High as these figures may seem, those from just nine years later are even greater. In 1994 the number of registered congressional lobbyists had grown by some 50 percent, to almost 12,000.

The payments to politicians take many forms, including campaign contributions, speech and personal appearance fees, and in-kind benefits.[2] Sometimes even nonelected officials are included in the largesse dispensed. In the following typology of payment methods, the focus is on recent taxation episodes (including the momentous 1986 Act), since these have been so frequent and are so obviously used to extract private wealth. But the methods detailed here to avoid invidious tax treatment are the same as those used to avoid other forms of rent extraction.

Campaign Contributions

The most obvious form of compensating legislators is to give money to them personally or to their campaigns. In 1985 political action committees (PACs) gave members of the House Ways and Means Committee and the Senate Finance Committee more than twice as much in campaign contributions as they did in 1983, a comparable non-election-year period but one in which no major tax legislation had been threatened. According to a Common Cause study based on reports filed with the Federal Election Commission, the fifty-six members of Congress' two principal tax-writing committees raised $6.7 million from PACs in 1985, compared with $2.7 million in 1983, when major tax changes were not on the congressional agenda. Campaign contributions to committee members totaled $19.8 million—nearly double the $9.9 million raised in 1983. Another study (see

Doernberg and McChesney 1987a, p. 937) found that the average PAC contribution to Ways and Means Committee members was 31 percent higher than the average received by all House members. Ways and Means and Finance Committee members, accounting for only 10.5 percent of the Congress, collected 23.5 percent of the $15 million given by PACs to all members of Congress during the first six months of 1985.

As the data suggest, a period during which tax reform is formulated can be particularly profitable for members of the tax-writing committees. Not surprisingly, the most influential members of those committees garner the most contributions.[3] Not all Ways and Means or Finance Committee members accepted PAC money or honoraria. One who did not, Andrew Jacobs, commented that "[t]he only reason it isn't considered bribery is that Congress gets to define bribery" (Maraniss 1983).

The value of campaign contributions to politicians is often misunderstood or underestimated. Regardless of whether a legislator faces serious opposition in an upcoming election, political appetites for contributions remain voracious. As former Senator Russell Long once told a lobbyist, "a U.S. Senator is primarily interested in two things—one, to be elected, and the other, to be reelected" (Fessler 1986, p. 798). Even if the opposition faced by an incumbent this time is unimpressive, there is no such thing as too much money; one never knows who the next opponent will be. In 1993 Bob Carr, the new chairman of the House Appropriations subcommittee that controls "billions of dollars in transportation funds," collected $332,000 in campaign contributions during the first six months of his chairmanship. This was "almost four times his receipts for the same period in prior election cycles. Mr. Carr is unapologetic about his headlong pursuit of campaign funds. 'I've run against millionaires four times in the last 12 years,' he says. 'I have to start early. I have to assume the worst and hope for the best'" (Rogers 1993b).

This approach to political contributions is hardly that of a politician who sits passively by, waiting for rent seekers to approach him to begin a rent-creation auction. The attitude reflects rather an active need to raise money and a search for likely sources. The need to stockpile money has grown as the cost of maintaining one's office has ballooned. "Long dubbed the mother's milk of politics, money now seems more like cocaine. While the average American family earns $35,000 a year, the average senator must raise $35,000 every 20 days throughout his or her term to meet the $4 million minimum cost of a competitive campaign."[4] Recent senatorial races, like the 1994 Feinstein-Huffington race in California, indicate that a $4 million price may soon look like a bargain in many political contests. Political fundraising is now taught in graduate school and has spawned an entire industry of consultant-specialists, at least some of whom are paid with "a cut of the proceeds" (Kuntz 1995, p. A4).

Perhaps the value of campaign contributions is underestimated also because federal law apparently limits both the amounts that can be given and the ways politicians can use the money. But observers agree that the apparent limits on both donation amounts and uses of money are generally illusory. Even under the stricter campaign statutes and regulations enacted during the 1970s, the laws are so easily overcome that one might almost suspect they were not really enacted to constrain their enactors.

For example, PAC contributions have been limited to $5,000 per candidate per election for a congressional candidate, but the limit is easily circumvented. As an example, ALIGNPAC, a PAC formed by insurance sellers, avoided the limit in 1985–86 in order to ward off rent-extracting tax legislation. ALIGNPAC's donors were life-insurance salesmen seeking to preserve favorable tax provisions on the cash value of their products (Jackson 1988, p. 131). The insurance PAC circumvented the limit by having its members make checks payable directly to Senator Packwood in an amount up to $1,000. The PAC leaders periodically "bundled" the contributions and delivered them to Packwood's campaign headquarters. In this way, Senator Packwood received more than $168,000 in 1985 from a group ostensibly limited to a $5,000 contribution. This practice of "bundling," whereby a PAC skirts donation limits by having members donate directly to candidates, thus avoiding bumping up against any legal limit of its own, has long been controversial—and lucrative for politicians.[5]

Multiple PACs with the same purpose can also avoid the $5,000 limitation. As a result, there were about one hundred insurance-industry PACs by the mid-1980s. Finally, although there are limits on PAC contributions to candidates, federal election law does not limit independent expenditures by a PAC made without consultation with, or the cooperation of, any candidate or campaign (Sabato 1984, pp. 96–107). For example, the Realtors' PAC spent almost $200,000 during 1981–82 to help candidates who supported pro-realtor legislation (ibid., p. 97). Often such "soft money" contributions, as they are known, will be made to a political party or organization (for example, the Democratic Congressional Campaign Committee) but are obviously destined for the use of politicians, not the organization itself, which is merely a conduit.

The biggest misunderstanding about political contributions, though, probably does not concern supposed donation amounts. There seems to be more popular confusion about supposed limits on the uses to which politicians and candidates can put the funds. PAC contributions in principle must be used for campaign rather than personal expenses. The distinction, however, is so fuzzy and its enforcement so infrequent as to make it meaningless. "In the 15 years that the personal-use prohibition has been on the books, the FEC [Federal Election Commission] has never punished anyone for violating it, and the broad power over how campaign money is used has remained one of lawmakers' most prized perks" (Wartzman 1994a). As a result, little practical distinction exists between the spending of funds donated for true campaign objectives as opposed to those for personal use.

Politicians are always and everywhere campaigning, or at least claiming to be. "A 1992 report by the citizens' lobby Common Cause showed that . . . former Republican Rep. Robert Davis had his campaign pay nearly $225,000 between 1978 and 1990 for 'travel, lodging, meals—virtually everything he did in Michigan,' his home state" (Wartzman 1994a). Politicians have successfully justified as campaign rather than personal expenditures things like country club dues, Kentucky Derby tickets, buying and leasing of cars, travel and entertainment expenses, football tickets, liquor, insurance for works of art, bronze figurines for investment, golf clubs and golf-related expenses, trips abroad, and tax-sheltered investments (Jackson 1985d; Freda 1993; Wartzman 1994a). Even when a political race seems not to require much campaign spending, expenditures are still made out of campaign funds for seemingly personal purposes: "In 1990, U.S. Sen. Sam Nunn purchased a car as part of the $1.2 million he spent on his re-election, which was uncontested, according to a Congressional Quarterly analysis of campaign spending" (Sherman 1993). And as discussed further below, politicians use campaign money to defend against lawsuits with allegations ranging from drunken driving to sexual harassment to financial transgressions (Thomas 1993).

The Federal Election Commission in 1993 was considering new regulations to list items that would automatically be considered as personal and thus illegal. On the proposed list of things henceforth to be deemed "personal use" were funeral, cremation, and burial expenses for deceased politicians; the FEC said at the time that it was "aware that campaign funds have been used" to cover such costs (Wartzman 1994a). The new regulations would also prevent politicians from paying themselves salaries out of campaign funds. But all these limitations have yet to be enacted.

If further examples are needed that supposed campaign funds really amount to personal emoluments, consider what can happen when a politician tries to pass off expenses as government-related (and therefore fully reimbursable from the government), but the expenses are subsequently determined not to be job-related. In that case, the politician will be ordered to return the money to the Treasury or whatever agency paid him. But then, politicians may just take the money from their personal campaign funds to reimburse the Treasury for what has formally been declared a personal expense.[6]

Additionally, many current legislators have been able to create de facto retirement funds by keeping unspent campaign contributions for their personal use after leaving Congress. Senators and representatives thus could use money supposedly contributed to finance campaigns to create their own form of "individual retirement account." Although the law has now changed to outlaw these de facto IRAs, Congress exempted all members in office as of January 8, 1980, from the statute. Many legislators retired with campaign war chests thereby converted into personal funds. That law has now been tightened, but the change seems to make little difference in view of the continuing ease with which campaign funds can be used for personal spending anyway.

Speaking and Appearance Honoraria

Campaign contributions are not the only way to get money to politicians personally. Private parties can pay legislators cash "honoraria" for personal appearances and speaking engagements. Depending on the limits legislated for speaking fees, which change frequently, many senators have earned more from speeches than from their official government salaries. And, not surprisingly, the big gainers from honoraria have been those with the greatest ability to impose costs on private individuals and firms: members of tax-writing committees.

In 1984 tax-panel members received more than $1 million in honoraria, or approximately 20 percent of the total $5.2 million paid to all members of Congress. In 1985 senators earned more than $2.4 million in honoraria. Of that amount, the twenty members of the Finance Committee earned more than $660,000, or more than 28 percent of the total. The single largest recipient was Finance Committee member Robert Dole, who received $127,993. Of the thirteen senators receiving honoraria totaling

$40,000 or more, six were Finance Committee members. For the House of Representatives, twenty of the thirty-nine members who earned $25,000 or more in honoraria served on the Ways and Means Committee. The recipient of the greatest amount in the House, $137,500, was Dan Rostenkowski, at that time chairman of the Ways and Means Committee.[7]

There are disclosure requirements and limits on how much legislators can collect annually in outside fees, but these limits are easily circumvented. Moreover, on reaching the maximum allowed, a politician can make a well-publicized donation of the fees to charity. Disclosure requirements and fee limits also do not apply to politicians' spouses, who thus pick up fees of their own from lobbying organizations. Finally, speaking honoraria have typically been available to congressional staff as well. As one report (Yang 1989) summarized, "some important staffers take thousands of dollars each year from companies and groups that have much to win or lose in legislation."

In-Kind Benefits

Campaign contributions and honoraria are but two of the methods used to bestow favors on those in a position to impose costs on private interests. Many donors combine their pecuniary contributions with lavish in-kind benefits, as the movie industry has done. Then-Senator (now Governor) Pete Wilson of California received $50,000 from film industry PACs in 1985 and the first part of 1986; movie executives donated thousands of dollars to Representative Rostenkowski's PAC. But in addition to the financial largesse has come much free entertainment for legislators from the Washington office of the Motion Picture Association (MPA). When the MPA was seeking an investment-tax break, a "senior Democratic member of the Ways and Means Committee, California Representative Fortney ('Pete') Stark, treated about 50 of his friends to a private screening of an Alan Arkin film in the Motion Picture Association's 70-seat theater," with food and drinks provided by the MPA. One executive of the MPA noted that entertainment and help in fund-raisers is something the MPA does "[f]or the people who have been good to us . . . We try to reward people" (Jackson 1986). Politicians seeking reelection find that businesses and lobbyists also make their facilities available for nothing or at greatly reduced prices; Brooks Jackson (1988, p. 18) reports that a cigarette manufacturer worried about higher excise taxes provided its private airplane to ferry politicians from Washington to California on fundraising trips.

Economists, political scientists, and others interested in the political process may underestimate the relative importance of in-kind payments to politicians in the total costs of legislatively mandated transfers. Nonpecuniary costs are not as easy to track but may well be greater than the monetary transfers to politicians. As one study noted, "Overt cash bribes attract attention and invite regulation . . . it is commonly understood that lobbying effort may be indirect, as when trips, fancy meals or golf rounds are provided legislators, and their family and associates" (Mixon, Laband, and Ekelund 1994, p. 172). In fact the same statistical study finds that with other factors held equal, the number of restaurants and of golf courses is greater in state capitals, where the amount of in-kind transfers to politicians would predictably be greater.

In-kind donations are also important in swaying nonelected, but nonetheless key, participants in the legislative process. Most important are congressional staff personnel, whose role in the legislative process is increasing. Not even counting the explosion in the size of congressional committee staffs, the personal staffs of Washington legislators have grown remarkably. House members' staffs almost tripled from 1960 to 1992; Senate personal staffs have more than tripled (Califano 1994). In many respects, staff members function as substitutes for the legislator himself, conducting business on behalf of constituents and reportedly even writing statements for the *Congressional Record,* statements that are nominally delivered by the legislator, who in fact may never have seen them (Abramson and Rogers 1991). With the growth in the number of congressional committees and subcommittees—not to mention the amounts of time politicians increasingly spend in raising more and more money—the work of drafting and changing bills destined for voting on the floor increasingly falls to the committee staffs.

For example, staffers do the actual drafting of tax legislation and often have the ear of members of the tax-writing committees, making it valuable for private interests to attract their attention. Congressional staff members are not prohibited from accepting in-kind contributions as part of speaking engagements, seminars, or fact-finding trips. Thus, during consideration of the 1986 Tax Reform Act by the Ways and Means Committee, the Equitable Life Assurance Society flew a dozen congressional aides along with spouses or guests to New York City; put them up at the Plaza Hotel; and entertained them at the U.S. Open tennis tournament, restaurants, and a Broadway show. During the debate over Clinton-administration attempts to overhaul the health-care system (which, as described below, included imposition of controversial price controls), doctors, insurers, pharmaceutical companies, and the American Medical Association entertained key congressional staff members "lavishly."[8]

Legal Contributions versus Illegal Payments

Both the rent-creation and rent-extraction models of regulatory activity are based on payments to politicians in return for services (that is, on a notion of extralegal contracts). The contracts are not legally enforceable, but at the same time do elicit bargained-for performance on both sides. The constant blur of money changing hands in Washington, state capitals, and anywhere else politicians are in control is certainly consistent with these models. The contracts may be extralegal, but manifestly the contracting process works.

Occasionally in this maelstrom of campaign contributions (often used for purely personal purposes), personal honoraria, and in-kind benefits, legal authorities manage to locate behavior that violates the laws against bribery and extortion.[9] But not often, for at least three reasons. For the most part, the similarity between illegal bribery/extortion payments and ordinary, quite legal political contributions makes rent extraction easy to practice without fear of legal consequences. As the leading legal expert on bribery and extortion, James Lindgren (1993, p. 1707), says, "It's notoriously difficult to separate bribery (or extortion) from gifts, tips, campaign contributions, and log-rolling."

Moreover, the only other person who knows about the proffered payment is usually the politician—who would be just as liable or guilty for taking money illegally as the payor would be. Politicians naturally recognize the illegality of many offers. As Representative "Pete" Stark of California (quoted in Jackson 1988, p. 48) said, "I've got guys coming into my office who are felonies waiting to happen. I've got dipshits talking about tax amendments, and in the same breath talking about raising money. You could put them in jail for that." But accounts of politicians' actually reporting the offerors to legal authorities are apparently nonexistent.

Finally, legal action against extortion would require agents of one group of politicians (the executive branch) to prosecute another group (the legislative branch), in a prosecution to be adjudicated by a third group (the judiciary) typically appointed by the first (the executive). The difficulties in this respect are obvious, and typically the exposed extortioner is allowed simply to retire without any legal action (or even a demand that the money be repaid). In England the owner of Harrod's department store revealed in October 1994 that he had been the victim of parliamentary extortion from 1987 to 1989, when he was seeking government permission to purchase the store. In addition to in-kind contributions demanded by members of Parliament (for example, store merchandise) he paid from 8,000 to 10,000 pounds sterling monthly to lobbyists working with MPs. One MP (also a minister) admitted the political extortion and simply resigned. There were no reports of any repayments or of any sanctions against him (Barbash 1994).

It is interesting, too, that in the exceptional cases in which legal action is actually brought against politicians, they are free to use campaign funds to defend against the accusations. In addition, accused politicians are permitted to raise funds separately for their defenses. They do so regularly, and with great success. Minnesota Senator David Durenberger, for example, escaped multiple charges of corruption with a sentence of just probation plus a $1,000 fine. But it cost him almost $1 million in legal fees to do so.

> To pay them, Senator Durenberger first tapped his campaign fund for $115,000 and then did what 15 other members of Congress—and one sitting president and his wife—have done in recent years: He set up a legal defense fund.
>
> Those 17 funds have raised nearly $7 million in donations, making money no object for public officials seeking counsel for job-related legal problems—congressional ethics probes, felony trials on public corruption charges, investigations by special counsel . . . (Berkman 1995)

As the same account notes, "The lightly regulated funds give targeted officials the wherewithal to wage pricey legal battles, while offering special interests a new way to win friends and influence people."

The payments detailed here are not necessarily all made to avoid extortion. As was noted in Chapter 2, politicians practice both rent creation and rent extraction; private individuals and firms transfer money for both reasons. But the ability of politicians to raise money by creating and selling rents has long been understood. (Indeed, as Peter Aranson points out [1981, p. 252], the popular revulsion against paying politicians presupposes that payments are made for special favors, since the calls for reform constantly focus on limiting what individuals can give—not the total of what politicians can take.) The focus here is on the underrecognized phenomenon of politicians' threats to take and of money then being paid to avoid extraction of existing wealth. What remains to be seen, then, is the various ways that politicians can and do practice rent extraction.

Extracting Rents by Threats

Chapter 2 noted that threatened political action of two sorts predictably will induce firms to pay in order to obtain inaction. Legislation that either lowers prices or increases costs will reduce the returns to firms' invested capital, and so will furnish useful political threats. Concerning the former, threats to shut down a firm altogether are a particularly draconian form of price reduction—a threatened price reduction to zero. With respect to the latter, threats of taxation are especially potent. Rather than suffer a capital loss from either source, lower prices or higher costs, firms and individuals will pay politicians either not to enact the threatened measures or, if regulation has already been passed, to repeal it.

Threats to Lower Prices

Threats to decrease prices legislatively below market-determined levels, followed by removal of the threat once contributions are made by the firms affected, are a common rent-extraction strategy. Since the fifty states regulate a good many industries more pervasively than does the federal government, the locus of price-lowering threats (followed by payoffs to cancel the threat) has often been the states. So, for example, one reads constantly about state attempts to lower interest rates (the price of borrowing) being proposed for consumer and mortgage credit but ultimately being withdrawn or killed in committee when the industry pays up.[10] In other words, these bills are quintessential "fetchers."

The same tactics are used at the federal level. The history of the Federal Trade Commission's "Used Car Rule" provides a good example of the gain to politicians from threatening to lower price by substituting government guarantees of quality for those already provided by high-reputation sellers (a process described in theoretical terms in Chapter 2). In 1975 Congress statutorily ordered the FTC to initiate a rulemaking to regulate used-car dealers' warranties.[11] The FTC promulgated a rule imposing warranty and auto-defect disclosure requirements; in the meantime, Congress had legislated for itself a veto over FTC actions. Thus was created an opportunity for legislators to extract concessions from car dealers to void the FTC warranty and disclosure measures—provisions that Congress itself had demanded. And in fact, upon promulgation of the rule in 1982, used-car dealers and their trade association, the National Auto Dealers Association (NADA), descended on Congress, spending large sums for relief from the proposed rule. One study found that "[o]f the 251 legislators who supported the veto resolution and ran again in 1982, 89 percent received contributions from NADA, which averaged over $2,300. This total included 66 legislators who had not been backed by NADA at all in 1980, before the veto resolution vote. Just 22 percent of the 125 congressmen who voted against NADA received 1982 money, and they averaged only about $1,000 apiece" (Sabato 1984, p. 134). With these concessions exacted, Congress vetoed the very rule it had ordered.[12]

But this was not the end of the story. The Supreme Court later invalidated the legislative veto, which meant that Congress' veto of the FTC used-car rule was likewise invalid. The invalidation perhaps suggested that the car dealers had been duped in paying for legislative repeal. But the actions of the Federal Trade Commission provide a telling example of how supposedly "independent" agencies in fact complement congressional regulatory strategies. The agency reacted to the Supreme Court's decisions in such a way as to preserve the legislative contract struck with the dealers. The FTC recalled its proposed rule and essentially gutted it.

Conditions in the used-car industry conform closely to those proposed in Chapter 2 as conducive to a political strategy of rent extraction. As George Stigler himself noted (1971, pp. 9–10), cartelization of the used-car industry would be difficult. Start-up costs are low; there are no artificial entry barriers (for example, licensing requirements); and units of the product have different qualities, making enforcement of cartel pricing difficult. By comparison, the industry is susceptible to a strategy of rent extraction. Quality uncertainty (the risk of getting George Akerlof's "lemon") is a problem, leading sellers to invest heavily in reputational capital.[13] By requiring and policing seller disclosure of warranty and defect information, government would have substituted for sellers' investments in quality-assuring reputation. Rather than suffer the capital losses that regulation would entail, firms predictably would—and did—compensate legislators not to intervene.

The value of price-control threats has been well illustrated more recently. Indeed, perhaps no single episode in recent American politics has generated as much money for legislators as the health-care plan proposed by President Clinton in 1993 but ultimately killed by Congress in 1994. Although the term "price controls" was not used in the Clinton plan, there is no doubt that economically the plan amounted to widespread controls.[14] It would have set fees charged by doctors and hospitals, limited annual spending on health care, restrained insurance premiums, and limited prices on drugs.[15]

The human and other capital possessed by doctors, hospitals, and pharmaceutical firms (especially those with large investments in research and development) is extraordinary, totaling in the billions of dollars. Not surprisingly, then, the reaction of those whose prices would have been controlled was swift, with lucrative results for politicians.[16] Under the headline "Medical Industry Showers Congress with Lobby Money," the *New York Times* reported:

> As Congress prepares to debate drastic changes in the nation's health care system, its members are receiving vast campaign contributions from the medical industry, an amount apparently unprecedented for a non-election year.
>
> While it remains unclear who would benefit and who would suffer under whatever health plan is ultimately adopted, it is apparent that the early winners are members of Congress. (Lewis 1993)

Contributions reportedly were 27 to 30 percent greater than in the prior nonelection year (1991). The bonanza for some legislators was phenomenal. Representative Jim Cooper, who worked for an alternative to the Clinton plan less destructive to the industry, had received between $500,000 and $1 million by April 1994, at which time the debate was still very much alive and so more contributions were on the horizon. "Representative Jim Cooper offers a simple explanation for his putting forward a health-care proposal: 'This is a pocketbook issue. It really matters to every family.' It has also become a pocketbook issue for Mr. Cooper, and whatever the fate of his health plan, he is already a winner" (Berke 1994).

Particularly alarmed, given their substantial stocks of immobile capital invested in ongoing research and new product development, were the major pharmaceutical companies. Early on, they were singled out by President Clinton as price-gougers and thus deserving of price controls. But who was gouging whom? Clinton administration speeches about its health-care proposals caused the value of pharmaceuticals' stocks to drop by huge amounts ($40 billion, by one account.)[17] Pharmaceutical firms' reactions to the rent expropriation that would follow from price controls was lavish. Individual companies' direct giving to politicians ran into the millions, with donations and advertising campaigns by industry groups costing millions more. "The situation is a case study of how one industry has been working to thwart an important part of the Clinton health plan, the effort to hold down drug costs [that is, prices]" (Lewis 1994).

The sums passing from the medical industry to politicians were not going to purchase special favors or create rents. Rather, they were payments to fend off political threats to extract private rents by lowering prices legislatively. As one official, describing payments made to stave off price controls in similar state statutes, summarized, these were contributions made in "lobbying for the status quo" (Fialka 1993). The Clintons' health-care hopes were dashed, but in the process the industry losses and the transfers to politicians were impressive, a point revisited in the next chapter.

Another current but ongoing price-control episode promises to yield substantial rent-extractive opportunities for politicians soon. In 1992 Congress authorized the Federal Communications Commission (FCC) to set prices for cable television. In doing so, the agency cut industry revenues by some 10 percent. Then, in 1994, the FCC voted to require a further 7 percent reduction. Not surprisingly, "cable operators have lobbied fiercely" against the rate cuts, but the cuts have remained in place (Carnevale and Robichaux 1994). One can only wait to see whether the rent losers from price controls and the politicians will find a price at which relaxation of the price controls is mutually advantageous.

The price-control examples just reported in medicine and in cable television at least would not deprive firms of all their capital. Often, however, more extreme regulation is threatened that effectively would expropriate a firm's entire market value by forcing it out of business. Such regulation is the ultimate in price controls, since it prevents the firm from producing and charging anything at all. These threats, when credible, naturally elicit offers of payment from the firms targeted.

Consider the breach-of-contract lawsuit brought in 1983 by Gerald Wallace, brother of Governor George Wallace, against the principal (Milton McGregor) of a dog-racing track in Alabama. Race tracks typically require a license from the state government to operate; such was the situation in Alabama. According to the complaint, Gerald Wallace was hired by the track and was to receive 5 percent of the firm's stock for his "services," but never got it. In a deposition made public in 1989, lawyers quizzed Gerald Wallace about what his "services" to McGregor were to be. Admittedly, they didn't include lobbying in the legislature, helping to draft the dog-track bill, or helping pass the local referendum on the track. The opposing lawyer finally asked, "What could you do for him [McGregor], Gerald?" The answer: "Well, Mr. McGregor knew that I could tell my brother to kill the bill and it would have been killed." In his lawsuit, Wallace thus complained that he had performed this service—*not* approaching his brother, the governor—but did not receive his stock (Nossiter 1989).

As the Wallace episode illustrates, the need for special legislation, occupational licenses, zoning or building permits, and the like just to do business all furnish a wonderful opportunity for extraction of private rents. Like race tracks, banks are controlled by state regulators. Banks that wish to expand typically need state permission; politicians either grant those permissions or can help get them. Thus, stories of money-for-expansion-permission in banking are commonplace (Seabrook 1994b). No one is paying for political favors, unless the mere right to do business is considered a special favor. The Citicorp lobbyists mentioned in the Introduction, for example, are involved in "fending off limits on banks' mutual fund sales, and fighting efforts to curb banks' use of financial derivatives," as well as lobbying for "an expansion of banks' ability to compete more directly with the securities firms, insurance companies and mutual funds" (Bacon 1993).

Other examples, just as revealing, could be presented to illustrate the point that politicians are very successful at extracting payments from firms just to grant access to markets. Recently, local telephone companies (the "Baby Bells") have been paying a small fortune to try to win congressional approval for access to long-distance telephone markets, which was closed to them by judicial order.

> To win friends on Capitol Hill, the Bells' political action committees have handed out $9.7 million in the past decade—overshadowing every other part of the industry, according to analysis by Common Cause. The Bells have hired scores of former federal officials, including two likely candidates for the 1996 Republican presidential nomination . . . The telephone association—which gets more than half of its $8 million in dues from the seven Bells—hosts lawmakers at conferences in such warm-weather sites as Key West and Orlando, Fla. . . . Each year, the Bells hand out tens of millions of dollars to chambers of commerce, rotary clubs and the like. In turn, the phone companies often find support for their legislative agency in the form of resolutions, letters, and phone calls to Capitol Hill. (Wartzman and Harwood 1994)

Likewise, tobacco companies have been forced to flood politicians' accounts with millions of dollars annually in fighting simply for the continued ability to sell their product.[18]

In that sense, the plight of the telephone and tobacco companies is the same as that of the other firms discussed earlier. The industry may be used cars, medicine, or cable television. In each industry, payments were made—just as Gerald Wallace supposedly was to get stock—as compensation just for the privilege of doing business. No supracompetitive rents were sought, other than those possibly available from doing normal business. The extractive payments are made for the right merely to sell one's wares at the market price.

In that sense, too, recognition of politicians' rent-extraction strategy recalls the problems discussed by Richard Epstein in his important *Bargaining with the State* (1993). Because Epstein has covered the problem so well in his book, little more needs to be said here, other than to note that "bargaining with the state" often just entails a slightly modified sort of rent extraction. The item bargained over might be an occupational license, a zoning permit, a corporate charter, or a building permit. These things cannot typically be the source of any rents, since they are supposedly available to all firms at equal cost and do not foreclose entry in any important way. Licenses, corporate charters, and building or zoning permits, for example, are supposed to be available to all applicants upon the satisfaction of prespecified conditions. But as Epstein explains, selective withdrawal or denial of these privileges unless certain additional wealth is surrendered provides a fertile source of rent extraction from victims so threatened.[19]

Consider the 1987 case of *Nollan v. California Coastal Commission* (483 U.S. 825), involving beachfront property owners who sought commission approval to replace their old beach houses with new ones. The government granted the Nollans permission to use their own property as they wished only after extorting an agreement from them (and many others in similar situations) to grant an easement giving access to the public—across their property—to adjacent public beaches. The only difference between the Nollans' predicament and Gerald Wallace's threat to the dog track was that Wallace was extorting for his own monetary benefit, whereas the California Coastal Commission was extorting for the in-kind benefit of others.

The case is also a reminder of the role of constitutional rules in obviating politicians' extortion opportunities. In the *Nollan* case, for example, the Supreme Court struck down the commission's attempt at wealth extraction as an unconstitutional condition. But the jurisprudence in this area generally furnishes little guarantee that similar instances of extortion will likewise be found constitutionally defective. In a subsequent case that seemed legally indistinguishable from *Nollan,* lower courts refused to apply the *Nollan* holding. Thus, in *Dolan v. City of Tigard* (512 U.S. 374 [1994]), Mrs. Dolan was able to avoid governmental extortion only by arguing all the way to the Supreme Court. An elderly widow, she wanted to expand the size of her store, but the city government of Tigard, Oregon, granted the necessary permit only on condition that she set aside part of her land in furtherance of public purposes and construct a pedestrian-bicycle path on another part. The land surrendered amounted to 10 percent of what Mrs. Dolan owned. When she challenged the obvious extortion, she lost at all levels of the Oregon courts, despite the Supreme Court's *Nollan* decision. Only her perseverance and the Supreme Court's willingness to hear her case (and ultimately to reverse the Oregon courts) resulted in the legally mandated result—and even then only by the barest five-to-four majority. But in how many instances of such extortion will the Supreme Court be willing or able to correct politically popular extraction of private wealth?[20]

Threats to Increase Costs

Chapter 2 also demonstrated that private rents can be extracted by threatening cost increases. There are many examples of payments to politicians to purchase government forbearance from imposing costs. Examples of recent threats include proposals to require financial institutions to start costly reporting and tax withholding on depositors' interest and dividend income—a measure that Congress passed and then repealed—and proposals to impose "unisex" premiums and benefit payments on insurance firms. Both episodes are difficult to explain using the standard economic model of regulation, as they consumed considerable political time and ended with no regulation at all being imposed.

But even if the regulation was never actually imposed, each measure would be attractive politically as a device that might ultimately elicit payments to legislators not to impose the threatened costs—which in fact each one did. The banking industry contributed millions of dollars to politicians in 1982 to obtain repeal of the statutory provision requiring banks to withhold taxes on interest and dividends. There are no precise figures on contributions to politicians to stop legislation banning insurance companies' gender-based rates and benefits, but their magnitude may be inferred from the American Council of Life Insurance's media budget of nearly $2 million in 1983 and 1984 to defeat the legislation (Sabato 1984, p. 125).

The most obvious cost that politicians can impose on firms and individuals is, of course, taxation. Payments for preferential tax treatment (that is, forbearance from expropriation) were mentioned earlier in the chapter, and the subject is addressed again from a different perspective in Chapters 5 and 6. But a few examples here will usefully illustrate the value of threatening excise-tax and income-tax legislation just to raise cash from private interests.

Excise taxes. Excise taxes diminish firms' wealth, as Figure 2.3 showed. Therefore, firms predictably would be willing to pay politicians not to impose them. In fact private interests do just that. Without even proposing an increase in the federal excise tax on beer, legislators for forty years extracted substantial revenue from brewers for not taxing their product. It was reported in the mid-1980s that "there hasn't been an increase in the 65-cent-a-case federal tax on beer since the Korean War, and nobody is seriously proposing one right now" (Jackson 1985b). But all the while, brewers were paying year after year not to be taxed. Although the tax ultimately was raised in 1991, a coalition of brewers and wholesalers had organized many years beforehand for the purpose of convincing key members of Congress not to tax. The coalition regularly invited members of the tax-writing committees to its meetings, paying honoraria of $2,000 per appearance, and thus purchased apathy toward new beer tax legislation for a generation. Although new beer taxes hadn't "generated much interest in Congress," the president of the brewery trade association said at the time, they "want[ed] to be prepared" all during the period of tax quiescence (ibid.).

As new industries become successful, they are increasingly likely to attract the attention of the tax man. As the politician locates new caches of private wealth, the political temptation to extract some of that wealth is quite predictable. One industry that has fared very well in the past twenty years is gambling, as states have liberalized their traditional legal constraints against it. But with success has come a rattling of the tax-saber, both in the states and in Washington, where in 1994 the White House announced it was taking under consideration a 4 percent federal excise tax on gambling receipts. "After recovering from their initial shock, casino operators, horse- and dog-track owners and Indian tribes with gambling facilities have wasted no time in lobbying the administration and Congress in the hopes of keeping the tax from ever being formally proposed" (Wartzman and Yoshihashi 1994b). That lobbying, of course, includes giving hundreds of thousands of dollars to politicians themselves, rather than suffer the much greater losses that would go into the Treasury in excise taxes (Wartzman and Yoshihashi

1994a). So far the industry has managed to fend off major taxation—but at the cost of considerable wealth extraction.

Threats to tax something like gambling are especially credible because the activity itself is considered to be "wrong" by a sizable number of voters. Taxing it therefore seems to offer electoral advantages to politicians, who by taxation could curry favor with those viewing the activity as unacceptable.[21] The fact that taxation offers electoral advantages also means that the interests threatened will have to pay even more to buy off the tax man, all other things being equal. So-called sin taxes are routinely threatened on traditional "sins" like gambling, tobacco, and alcohol, but are often not levied when sufficient payment is made to politicians. More recently, however, there have been calls for taxation of new "sins" like buying food high in saturated fat.[22] The calls can only be music to the rent-extracting politician's ears.

Income taxation. To illustrate further the workings of rent extraction through taxation threats, consider the ubiquitous private purchases of tax relief every time Congress opens the income-tax window—as it does routinely these days. For example, in connection with the Tax Reform Act of 1986, the drafting of which began the year before, it was reported that

> members of the tax-writing committees nearly tripled their take from political action committees during the first six months of this year, to $2.6 million, compared to the like period in the past two-year election cycle . . . the money is pouring in from . . . insurance companies that want to preserve tax-free appreciation of life insurance policy earnings, from horse breeders who want to keep rapid depreciation of thoroughbreds, from drug companies seeking to keep a tax haven in Puerto Rico, and from military contractors seeking to retain favorable tax treatment of earnings from multiyear contracts. (Jackson 1985c)

The money is not flowing for "special favors" via creation of new politically generated wealth, but to safeguard existing privately created wealth.

Even as politicians pronounce themselves increasingly concerned about budget deficits, the process of so-called tax carve-outs has become more noticeable. "Carve-outs" refer to situations in which politicians legislate tax changes that are revenue-increasing overall but that also include carefully pinpointed tax breaks sold back to favored individuals and industries. Beneficiaries of carve-outs sold as part of the Clinton 1993 tax increases included Hollywood filmmakers, described as "flush with Democratic campaign money." They also included Electronic Data Systems, which, having doubled its campaign contributions during 1992, accelerated that pace in 1993 as part of "an aggressive EDS lobbying campaign aimed at protecting its ability to quickly write off computer software assets obtained by acquiring smaller companies." In addition to hundreds of thousands of dollars in campaign contributions, the EDS effort to protect its revenues from the tax man included "tens of thousands of dollars in so-called soft money, 'party building' contributions that aren't subject to election-law limits" (Rogers 1993a).

No one would be so naive as to think that the contributions and tax relief are mere coincidences, causally unrelated. The cash pours in as long as taxation is on the legislative agenda, with money being matched by forbearance in taxing. According to Representative "Pete" Stark, a long-time member of the House Ways and Means Committee who ultimately retired early under an ethical cloud, "America needs a tax bill each year [to give] a little help to your friends" (Birnbaum 1985b). Further examples of payments from special-interest groups to retain favorable tax treatment during tax "reform" episodes are ubiquitous.[23]

To return to the momentous Tax Reform Act of 1986, for example, the Senate bill was loaded with special-interest breaks with nicknames like "the Marriott amendment," identifying the beneficiaries. The Marriott amendment carved out an exception to a proposed tax provison to limit certain business meal and entertainment deductions to 80 percent of actual expenses. A coalition of hotels and others heavily dependent on convention business convinced the Senate Finance Committee to exempt business meals provided as part of conventions. To qualify under this Marriott exception, however, Congress stipulated that the convention would have to include a speaker. Politicians thereby raised the demand for their own services as outside speakers. But politicians were also paid "up front" to enact the exception. As one former Treasury official put it at the time, "it helps if you've been a big supporter of [a] senator . . . I'm afraid that's democracy" (Murray 1986).

On the House side, likewise, provisions like the "Gallo amendment" were written into the Ways and Means Committee bill, to the enrichment of committee members. Ernest and Julio Gallo, California vintners with more than twenty grandchildren and a net worth estimated at $600 million at the time, faced a major wealth-reducing provision concerning generation-skipping transfer taxes. (Generation-skipping taxes are designed to ensure that wealth is taxed at each generational level by placing a special tax penalty on bequests, such as from a grandfather to a granddaughter, that skip a generation.) The Gallo brothers, through lobbyist channels, then were able to convince House Ways and Means Committee members to adopt a favorable amendment to allow the bequests that they wanted to make. The Gallo clan at the time had made at least $325,000 in campaign donations in previous elections and "were still giving heavily while lobbying for estate-tax relief" (Jackson 1988, p. 116). But obviously it was money well spent: they thereby avoided taxes on $104 million.

The record abounds with other examples of campaign donations followed closely by favorable legislation (Sabato 1984, p. 125; Malbin 1984). Thus, although the 1986 amendments to the basic income-tax provisions of the Internal Revenue Code were hailed as major tax reform,[24] they also became a bonanza for the reformers. Correspondents following Congress noted that "President Reagan's effort to overhaul the federal tax system has resulted in a financial windfall for the campaign coffers of most members of Congress' tax-writing committees" (Pressman 1985; see also Hanlon 1986).

Three essential points emerge. First, any tax "reform" promulgated by Congress—even reform that truly is welfare increasing—often is only as much reform as someone is willing to purchase. Second, the purchases are payments to avoid infliction of new economic pain or to obtain reform of painful provisions already in existence, in return for surrendering privately created wealth. Payment is made to keep what one has earned, not to generate economic rents. And finally, politicians can use threatened tax changes to generate income for themselves, even when no change ultimately ensues. Private wealth is "gold in them thar hills," and so there is money in proposing and then withdrawing new tax provisions that would take some of the gold.

It may be tempting to blame the entire process of procuring favorable tax provisions and avoiding harmful ones on the private beneficiaries who pay. This is the predictable populist perspective, reminiscent of a James Stewart movie but with a more cynical ending: cigar-smoking lobbyists in three-piece suits bamboozle an upright but weak legislator trying to do his best under the circumstances. But it is not the description provided by those inside the process, who have witnessed systematic rent extraction up close (for example, Sabato 1984; Birnbaum and Murray 1987; Jackson 1988). They describe a frequently reenacted sequence in which politicians seek out various interests to learn how much they would pay—how much can be extracted—to avoid politically imposed losses.

Given the benefits to politicians themselves, one should anticipate that they would actively seek contributions rather than wait for lobbyists to come to them. The now-annual legislative tax seasons have in fact become noteworthy for politicians themselves taking the initiatives to generate funds. In the landmark legislation of 1986, "legislators began tapping contributors for dollars almost immediately after the 1984 campaign came to an end," using threats of harmful legislation to extract funds from the special interest PACs (Pressman 1985, p. 1807). The arm-twisting is rarely subtle and often verges on the flagrant, as shown by the story (quoted before in Chapter 2) that appeared during the 1985–86 tax season: "House Republican leaders are sending a vaguely threatening message to business political-action committees: Give us more, or we may do something rash" (Jackson 1985a). As discussions of new taxes began in 1985, tax lobbyists said that they had not seen "such ravenous appetites for contributions in a non-election year before" (Jackson 1985c).

Some might object to the interpretation here that payments for tax relief manifest political extortion. They might claim that the fact that lobbyists play some role in the legislative process does not mean the game is one of rent extraction. Perhaps lobbyists are essentially information providers, arming busy legislators with the facts they need to make welfare-increasing decisions under unavoidable fiscal constraints. The PAC funds and other inducements that lobbyists provide could just be devices to direct legislators' attention to lobbyists' information, much like advertising in the private sector that ultimately inures to the information-providers' benefit and at the same time increases social welfare. That competing hypothesis, and another, are tested in the next chapter. Before turning to them, however, one other realm of flagrant rent extraction merits mention.

Rent Extraction Abroad

In perennially underdeveloped countries, it has long been acknowledged that an important reason for economic atrophy is the frequent grant of special favors, instead of reliance on markets, to determine who will provide goods and services. The favored recipients of governmental favors thereby expect to be able to charge supra-market prices and thus, depending on what it has cost them to get the special favors, earn supracompetitive returns. This process of rent creation abroad is ubiquitous and well understood in the economic-development and rent-seeking literature.[25]

However, governments abroad are just as adept at extorting existing private rents and wealth. The economic implications of that process have received relatively little attention. True, the importance of outright expropriation is generally acknowledged (for example, Eaton and Gersovitz 1984). Often for reasons of politics, foreign governments nationalize firms, seizing their physical assets and thereby cutting off the flow of future profits.

The ability to nationalize, however, also creates a credible threat from which politicians can be bought off. However popular politically, nationalization is a drastic economic step. By cutting off a firm's future profit flow, the government ends the possibility of extracting (say, by taxation) a portion of that flow for itself (for example, Wang 1994). Merely threatening wealth can be a profitable alternative to seizing firms and their assets, when asset owners are thereby made to pay to buy off the threat. At the margin, one would expect to see a revenue-maximizing government practice each of these various forms of revenue generation.[26]

Particularly when the "government" is synonymous with a single individual (a monarch or dictator) or small group (junta, royal family), it may be difficult to distinguish expropriation from extraction. When the peasants line up outside the castle with a portion of their produce and chickens for the king, are they being taxed or paying to avoid the imposition of a tax? Practically, the distinction is meaningless to both payors and the payee.[27] Yet some forms of wealth extraction practiced in underdeveloped countries are flagrantly unrelated to any formal, legislated system of taxation. As Andrei Shleifer and Robert Vishny write, distinctions between extortion and taxation are "blurred by the fact that the treasury is indistinguishable from the sovereign's pocket. Yet for most governments, the distinction is material and shows how corruption substitutes for taxation."[28]

In Zaire, for instance, "citizens are sometimes arrested simply to get the payoffs" (Davidson 1991). Similar payment-for-freedom incidents are reported elsewhere.[29] Extorting money from foreigners as a condition for doing business (Epstein's "unconstitutional conditions" at work abroad) is rife in underdeveloped countries.[30] Just as in more developed nations, requirements for licensure are surefire ways to engender rent extraction.[31] The examples, both historical and current, are almost endless. As Shleifer and Vishny report (1993, p. 608), for example,

> In India, taking a road between two towns indeed requires paying a bribe in every village through which the road passes. Taking goods inland in Zaire is more expensive because of corruption than bringing them from Europe by ship to a port. In 1400 there were 60 independently run tolls along the Rhine. Along the Seine there were so

many tolls that to ship a good twenty miles cost as much as its price. In contrast, rivers in England were free of such tolls, which in part explains the ability of England to develop specialized, commercial agriculture feeding London, the world's center of commerce.

But for personal enrichment by a politician, perhaps no one has ever run a more successfully ambidextrous operation—creating rents for a price with one hand while extracting existing private rents with the other—than Brazil's President Fernando Collor de Mello. The president operated "an extortion and influence-peddling system" on such a scale that it was later called "an assault on the state" (Brooke 1992, p. 42). The amounts of money collected personally through extraction were staggering. Investigators have established that at least $32 million was paid, and "believe they uncovered only about 10 percent to 30 percent of the total cash flow" (ibid., p. 31). Previously, as a local mayor, Collor sold tax relief worth $100 million to some sugar-cane interests for $20 million in payments to him; selling tax relief to other sugar-cane planters followed. Once he became president, it was exceptionally lucrative to Collor to establish a supposedly anti-inflation program that froze all bank deposits over $1,200 for eighteen months. "The program was a colossal failure, producing suicides, heart attacks, a 4 percent plunge in economic activity—and barely a dent in inflation."[32] Brazilians might have thought the policy well-intended but mistaken—until they learned that Collor was selling companies relief to unfreeze their capital for a 10 percent commission (ibid., p. 45).

As was noted in Chapter 2, rent extraction as practiced in more modern nations is really much like threats of outright capital expropriations in less-developed countries. It is rarely recognized that the two phenomena are essentially one and the same. The specter of loss may be from "modern" regulation or "Third World" nationalization, impersonal taxation or personal arrest, anti-inflation price controls or anti-inflation freezes on bank accounts. But however and wherever made, government threats to private rents work alike, and regardless of method have the economic consequences of legalized theft: reduced investment, shift of assets into less valuable but less expropriable forms, and expenditures for hiding wealth or otherwise keeping it away from the extractors. Citizens of "developed" nations find the expropriative antics of foreign despots exotic, sometimes even laughable. But the shakedowns practiced by their own politicians are different only in the complexity, camouflage, and rhetoric surrounding the expropriation threats and ultimate extraction schemes.

4

Validating the Model: Empirical Tests of Rent Extraction

> In order to erect a corporation, no other authority in ancient times was requisite in many parts of Europe, but that of the town corporate in which it was established. In England, indeed, a charter from the king was likewise necessary. But this prerogative of the crown seems to have been reserved rather for extorting money from the subject . . . Upon paying a fine to the king, the charter seems generally to have been readily granted.
>
> —ADAM SMITH

The power of the sovereign enables him to create new wealth, both by contracting with his subjects to do certain things (such as creating public goods) and by guaranteeing the enforceability of private contracts they make among themselves. But that same power enables him to transfer wealth, both among subgroups of citizens and directly to himself. David Haddock (1994) insightfully refers to this tradeoff as "the sovereign's dilemma."

The dilemma resides in the tradeoff between the sovereign's ability to assist his subjects' creation of private wealth and his ability to appropriate wealth to himself. As the state's power grows, its ability to create wealth grows, since that power can be used to enforce private contracts and other property rights more effectively. But enhanced power also raises a greater specter of governmentally forced transfers, either between contesting private parties or directly from either of them to the sovereign power itself. What are mere transfers in the short run are, of course, destructive of private wealth creation in the long run. "The simplest economic view of the state as an institution that enforces contracts and property rights and provides public goods poses a dilemma: A state with sufficient coercive power to do these things also has the power to withhold protection or confiscate private wealth, undermining the foundations of the market economy."[1] The relationship between a strong state and a wealthy state thus becomes more complicated as state power grows. Greater strength implies both better protection of wealth-enhancing activities (contract, private property) and greater threats to the wealth generated thereby.

The phenomenon of wealth expropriation by strong states has been evident for a long time, probably since the appearance of states themselves. Government edicts without a threat of violence are mere suggestions. But as Thomas Sowell (1980, p. 74) points out,

> The fact that actual violence does not usually occur in no way under-mines the crucial importance of violence in the outcome. Most armed robberies also do not lead to actual violence: common sense usually causes the victim to turn over his money without a fight and causes the robber to take the money and go . . . The government's threat-ened violence is not direct corporal punishment for violating laws and regulations. Rather it is a threat to take assets by force—either in money ("fines" or "damages") or in kind (legal rulings restricting the behavior, including the continued existence, of the firm in question). It is violence in the same sense in which armed robbery is violence.[2]

In its cruder forms, expropriation through threats continues to be prac-ticed in many less-developed countries today. But its less blatant role in the overall structure of modern government regulation has not been well developed. That is the motivation for development of the rent-extraction model in this book. The possibility of expropriation validates a strategy of extraction, a point that has not been sufficiently integrated into modern models of governmental action, including regulation.

Although it may have normative implications, the rent-extraction model is a positive one. It attempts to explain actual behavior in the real world, rather than suggest what behavior would or ought to be found in some ideal economy. But to qualify as a work of positive economics, the notion of political extortion proposed here must do more than just model rent extraction abstractly.[3]

A positive model must, first, generate hypotheses or implications that are inconsistent with or different from hypotheses and implications already deducible from existing models of political behavior. It must be shown that government acts in ways predicted by the rent-extraction model but not predicted by other models of regulatory action. As discussed earlier, the rent-extraction model seeks in particular to explain political behavior that is not explained by, and is often inconsistent with, existing models of rent creation or other regulatory behavior. The notion of rent extraction does not deny that regulation often creates rents, but insists that much political behavior concerning regulation cannot be understood as involving rent creation.

The second dictate of positive economics concerns empirical testing of the hypotheses (implications) generated by the model. Those hypotheses must be empirically testable and falsifiable, and actually be validated by statistical tests.[4] The positive social scientist effectively says, "If I am right, we will observe the following phenomena in the real world—things not predicted by other models. If we do not observe such things, then I am wrong." As will be illustrated in the rest of this chapter, the empirical implications of the rent-extraction model have in fact been tested and been found to corroborate the model.

The Competing Hypotheses

Chapters 2 and 3 explained that perhaps the most obvious way for politicians to extract rents is to propose legislation or institute other regulatory activity that would expropriate private wealth, but then withdraw the proposal—for a price. Politicians routinely do just this. The issue is whether would-be victims still lose wealth in the process—that is, have rents extracted—even though ultimately no legislation is passed or other action taken. If so, private would-be victims are paying money for nothing (no legislation), leaving them poorer, not richer. This is the basic rent-extraction strategy, one incompatible with any notion of rent creation.

It is important to consider alternative hypotheses possibly explaining this same sequence of submission followed by withdrawal of legislation. Political threats to legislate that are subsequently withdrawn may conceivably have less sinister explanations than that offered by the rent-extraction model. It could be that politicians simply err; they propose legislation that they feel is genuinely beneficial for the general public, but they realize in response to pressure from those affected that the legislation would be a mistake in terms of economic welfare.[5] The threat is then removed: either the threat (proposal, bill) is withdrawn, or, if passed, the extractive legislation is then repealed. Either way, the sequence in the end could be benign. Perhaps legislators' motives are public-spirited; maybe mistakes are made despite the best of intentions, but ultimately entail no harm as they are corrected.

Mistake is a commonplace explanation for welfare-reducing political measures, but it fails the test of positive economics. Labeling seemingly wrongheaded policies as driven by mistake says nothing, unless one offers at the same time a theory of why politicians make mistakes. This is particularly true when the policy persists over years, even decades. (Recall the extractive payments to avoid taxation, like the beer excise threats, noted in Chapter 3, that were proposed annually for a generation but not imposed.) Politicians may make mistakes from time to time—who doesn't? But the mistake model loses credence as "mistakes" persist over years, and the supposedly errant actors actually are paid according to the extent and frequency that they err.[6]

There is a second, somewhat more sophisticated, public-spirited justification for politicians' legislative proposals that, though not enacted, would destroy private rents. Perhaps imperfectly informed politicians use these proposals to elicit information from constituents potentially affected by legislation or regulation, in order to increase the effectiveness of legislative attempts to increase economic welfare. Maybe lobbyists are essentially just information providers, arming busy legislators with the facts they need to fine-tune their legislative agendas. PAC funds and other inducements that lobbyists provide might only be advertising devices to direct legislators' attention to lobbyists' information. Those potentially affected by a particular measure would have less incentive to register their discontent until a proposal was submitted or a measure actually passed. But at that point, when affected constituents react negatively overall, then supposedly welfare-driven politicians have the information they need, and withdraw welfare-reducing measures, as is appropriate.

The two alternative hypotheses—politician mistakes and constituent information—differ as to the reason why politicians propose (or legislate) measures that in the end are not passed (or are passed and then repealed). Both hypotheses have the same empirical content, however. If they were either mistakes or demands for information, rather than deliberate attempts at extracting rents, political measures threatening private wealth would entail a loss of wealth at the time they were made, reflecting some positive probability that harmful legislation might be passed and permitted to persist. But ultimately, firms should recover that wealth when the mistake was realized or when the relevant information was received and acted on.

Here, then, is the discriminating implication, the point of difference to distinguish systematic, purposeful rent extraction from mere mistake or acquisition of constituent information. The rent-extraction model makes opposite predictions. Episodes in which government threatens regulation, but ultimately does not regulate, are due neither to politicians' mistakes nor to their regrettable but understandable ignorance. Instead, regulatory threats are intentionally instigated for the purpose—and, more important, with the effect—of expropriating privately created rents. Removal of rent-extractive threats or reversal of rent-extracting legislation would not restore affected private parties' wealth.

In short, one can look at changes in wealth, first at the time a threat is registered and then at the time it is removed, and look to see whether private wealth is lost in the process.[7] The rest of this chapter reports in detail on two such inquiries. The first, by Roger Beck, Colin Hoskins, and Martin Connolly (1992), examines a series of potentially rent-extracting episodes to see whether the wealth lost at the time adverse political events were originally announced was recouped later when the threats of adverse action were retracted. The second inquiry considers the wealth impact on pharmaceutical firms of the Clinton administration's announced plans to impose price controls on pharmaceuticals, an episode discussed in Chapter 3. The appendix presents the statistical details of both analyses.

Rent Extraction from Canadian Firms

Beck, Hoskins, and Connolly (1992) are the first to have discussed and systematically tested the competing hypotheses concerning rent extraction outlined above. Using a sample of Canadian firms, they examine first how announcements of harmful legislative threats affect firms' stock prices, and then how much impact subsequent retraction of these threats has on the affected firms' stock returns. In the end, their evidence supports the rent-extraction model and rejects the alternative public-interest hypotheses.

The underlying premise in any such statistical study is that stock markets are efficient and that prices are unbiased estimates of the current value of stockholders' claims to future cash flows. Beck, Hoskins, and Connolly break their inquiry into two parts, first measuring the stock-price impact of legislative threats and then considering separately the effect of retracting those threats. That method has the advantage of isolating the individual events that constitute the rent-extraction sequence. It has the disadvantage, however, of requiring the researcher to know exactly when threats are registered and alleviated, something that often cannot be known with precision. The analysis of pharmaceutical price control threatened by the Clinton administration therefore uses a methodology that avoids the problem of knowing exactly when threats are made and removed, although that methodology in turn entails problems not encountered in the one used by Beck and his colleagues.

The Effect of Legislative Threats

It is a necessary condition for a rational political strategy of rent extraction, first, that legislative threats reduce wealth.[8] This was the first hypothesis that Beck, Hoskins, and Connolly tested: a threatening announcement would lower threatened firms' stock prices, causing an abnormal drop in stock returns around the time of the threat as investors lowered their estimate of the stockholders' claims to firms' future cash flows. To test this "Hypothesis 1," the authors identified thirty Canadian government actions, each of which at first threatened economic loss to specific firms or industries but was subsequently retracted.[9]

The events are interesting in their own right. One of them became notorious in Canada for its alleged political motivation, and is consistent with Chapter 2's discussion of politicians' threatening price-lowering legislation as a way of extracting rents. In March 1981 an eight-year federal investigation concluded that Canadian consumers had from 1958 to 1973 paid $12 billion in anticompetitive gasoline prices because of oil-company price fixing, and that the practice was continuing. The matter was referred to the Restrictive Trade Practices Commission for a full public inquiry. In June 1986 the commission concluded that the price-fixing charges were wrong and dropped the inquiry. Other episodes from the Canadian researchers' sample likewise exemplify the sequences of threatening government-imposed price reductions, then removing the threat.[10]

Also illustrating a basic rent-extraction tactic, several of the thirty episodes from the Canadian sample involved threats to impose new costs, including taxes. In June 1987, for example, federal Finance Minister Michael Wilson announced that groceries, prescriptions, and medical devices would be subject to a proposed sales tax. Then in December 1987 Wilson announced that these same items would be exempt from the proposed sales tax. That is, certain firms were first threatened with loss, but the threat was later withdrawn, a pattern observed in other instances of threatened taxation.[11]

The tests presented in Table 4.1, in the appendix to the chapter, show that for the portfolio of firms threatened by the various proposals of the Canadian government, the threat's initial unveiling truly did have a negative impact on firms' wealth, as registered by their stock prices. Not all firms were negatively affected, but two-thirds of them were, a sufficient number suffering a sufficient impact that, overall, the threats proved significantly wealth-reducing for the group as a whole. Thus, the necessary condition for rent extraction to work—a credible threat that reduces wealth—was established.

Alternative Explanations of Legislative Threats: The Effect of Retractions

The results in Beck, Hoskins, and Connolly's first round of statistical tests indicate that a primary and necessary implication of the rent-extraction model holds. A sample of legislative threats shows that they do indeed reduce firms' wealth. Politicians, that is, do have the ability to impose losses by the mere menace of legislation. But that finding, while necessary for the rent-extraction model, is also consistent with the possibility that loss-imposing threats are merely mistakes or invitations to constituents to provide further information.

Validating the rent-extraction model therefore requires investigation of a second set of events, the ultimate removal of the threats, and the effects of removal on firms' wealth. This step is particularly important in distinguishing rent extraction from the possibilities of politician error or constituent information, since upon later correction of any mistake or receipt of any relevant information, firms should recover some or all of the wealth lost.

Beck, Hoskins, and Connolly thus propose two hypotheses essential to corroborating the rent-extraction model. Under their stronger "Hypothesis 2A," a threat's retraction would not affect the firm's stock price. Since the prior tests of Hypothesis 1 had established that a threat reduces firms' wealth, the strong form of the rent-extraction model would mean that a threat's retraction would be a neutral event with no abnormal return in the retraction period. Investors would have understood that stockholders' claims to future firm cash flows were permanently reduced in order to persuade politicians to retract their threat.

A weaker form of the rent-extraction model, though one still consistent with it, was what Beck and his colleagues called "Hypothesis 2B." According to that implication of the model, a threat's retraction would increase the firm's stock price, resulting in an abnormal positive stock return for the period around the time of this event. However—and critically—the increase would be smaller than the decrease caused by the original threat, because it still would have been understood that stockholders' claims to future firm cash flows had been reduced (though less than Hypothesis 2A would imply) in order to persuade politicians to retract their threat.

Beck and his coauthors note that Hypothesis 2A predictably would hold either if politicians extracted nearly all the rents that might be lost by implementation of the threat, or if investors believed that a payoff was almost certain and actual implementation of the threat was therefore most unlikely.[12] Failure to reject Hypothesis 2A would provide strong confirmation of the rent-extraction model.[13] On the other hand, failure to reject Hypothesis 2B would still uphold the existence of a political rent-extraction strategy.[14]

Alternatively, the threatening announcement of a burdensome tax or regulation might be made for genuine public-interest reasons and retracted on equally lofty grounds, perhaps because study of the issue persuades politicians that their proposed policy would be harmful to the public interest. For all such benign political motivations, Hypothesis 1 would still apply: the burdensome tax or regulation is still "bad news," regardless of the politicians' motive. However, Hypotheses 2A and 2B would not apply, because retraction did not signal a payoff, and thus retraction constitutes "good news."

This alternative, benign-motivation model generates "Hypothesis 2C." Again assuming (as was demonstrated empirically) that a threat reduces wealth, retraction of the threat would increase the menaced firm's stock price. But under Hypothesis 2C, the increase would result in an abnormal positive stock return for the period around the time of this event similar in size—but opposite in direction—to the abnormal negative return associated with the original threatening announcement.

In other words, Hypotheses 2A and 2B are both consistent with the model of rent extraction through political extortion. Hypothesis 2C, however, is consistent only with more public-spirited motivations for threatening announcements. (As before, the three hypotheses are stated in terms of a threat made against a single firm, but they also apply to a threat aimed at a group of firms, which may belong to the same industry.)

Examining the effects of threat retraction, Beck and his colleagues first test Hypothesis 2A: was there an abnormal positive return associated with threat retraction? If not, the evidence is consistent with the strongest form of the rent-extraction model. If there is an abnormal positive return, however, one would have to choose between Hypotheses 2B and 2C by comparing the magnitude of the abnormal positive and negative returns. If, upon retraction of the menace of harm, investors systematically recovered only some of the wealth lost by the original threat (Hypothesis 2B), the result would still indicate that extraction of some wealth had taken place.

The results of the retractions in the thirty-episode sample are reported in Table 4.2 (in the appendix). Retraction of the wealth-inducing threats has no significant impact on potentially affected firms, however the retraction period is modeled. This result is consistent with the rent-extraction model's strong Hypothesis 2A. The implication is either that politicians were correctly expected to extract nearly all the rents, or that failure to negotiate a payoff was considered to be a remote possibility. The fundamental results of Table 4.2 provide little support for the abnormal-positive-return predictions of Hypothesis 2B, not to mention the implication of Hypothesis 2C that wealth lost when the threat was made would be recovered when the threat was removed.

Threatened Price Controls on Pharmaceuticals

As a candidate for the presidency, Bill Clinton had made it clear that overhauling the American health-care system would be a priority in his administration. Once elected, he moved quickly to accomplish that overhaul. Just after his inauguration, in January 1993 he named his wife to lead a health-care "task force" to begin researching ways to remake the health-care system. As was discussed in Chapter 3, the administration's plan focused to a considerable extent on imposing price controls on various sectors of the health-related economy.

Thus was the stage set for rent extraction. And as one would predict, pharmaceutical companies in particular responded vigorously, waging a remarkable public-relations campaign against the Clinton plan. But the industry also responded with its wallet, pouring untold funds into the congressional pockets to combat the possibility of price controls. In September 1994 the Democrats announced that they were abandoning their plan to pass health-care legislation in that congressional session. Weeks later, the Republican takeover of Congress effectively precluded any further attempt to regulate health care, at least in the near future.

It is impossible to separate the funds expended for advertising and the like from those simply transferred into politicians' pockets. But for purposes of the rent-extraction model it is important to show, as did Beck, Hoskins, and Connolly, that legislative threats cause the destruction of firms' wealth even when they ultimately are retracted. The Clinton threats provide another "laboratory" in which to test that hypothesis.

The tests are described more fully in the appendix to this chapter. Because it is relatively difficult to identify precisely, first, when the threat was anticipated by financial markets and then, second, when its retraction was foreseen, the methodology used differs from that employed by Beck, Hoskins, and Connolly. But the fundamental question is the same: did the firms threatened by price controls ultimately lose wealth, despite the administration's failure ultimately to make good on the threat?

The regression results presented in Table 4.3 (in the appendix) show that the threatened firms did indeed lose wealth. The losses were incurred between the time of President Clinton's election and the Democrats' announcement in September 1994 that plans for health-care legislation were being dropped for the moment. It is particularly interesting that the November 1994 Republican electoral victory did not restore to pharmaceutical firms the wealth they had lost. In the end, the threatened firms had paid good money for nothing: their wealth was diminished, and no legislation was passed.

Conclusion

The rent-extraction model is based on political extortion: a hypothesized sequence of threatened harmful government action followed by favors given to politicians in exchange for a retraction of the threat. The model predicts an abnormal negative return at the time of the threat and either a smaller abnormal positive return or no abnormal return at all at the time of the retraction. Alternatively, if the threat were retracted to serve the public interest (instead of in exchange for payment from the threatened party), one should find an abnormal positive return at the time of the retraction equal in magnitude to the abnormal negative return at the time of the threat.

Beck, Hoskins, and Connolly's statistical study gives results corroborative of the extortion model set out in prior chapters. Their evidence strongly favors the hypothesis that politicians' presentation and withdrawal of threats to act are motivated by their ability thereby to extract wealth from private firms, not from any desire to correct error or to elicit information. This conclusion ultimately would mean that the basic implications of the theoretical rent-extraction model discussed in Chapter 2 would hold. First, "existing estimates of the social welfare loss from regulation are understated—they ignore the costs of persuading the government not to regulate." And second, "there may be allocative inefficiency from reduction of incentives to invest, particularly in more vulnerable firm- and industry-specific assets" (1992, p. 224).

The statistical results from the Clinton administration's attempt to impose price controls on pharmaceuticals likewise corroborate the rent-extraction model. Once again, political threats were costly to firms that would be affected by price controls. And again also, that wealth apparently was not recovered when the threats were removed.

Appendix: Statistical Tests of Rent Extraction

Rent Extraction in Canada

In the statistical work undertaken by Beck, Hoskins, and Connolly (1992), criteria for the selection of the thirty potentially extractive episodes were as follows:[15]

The government's announcement of the action occurred between July 1, 1977, and December 10, 1987.

Companies affected by the announcements were publicly traded on the Toronto Stock Exchange (TSE).

The cases involved unanticipated announcements of threatened action by politicians, senior government officials, or heads of government regulatory boards.

The events affected national or large regional markets.

The outcome of each of the threats later became known in the market.[16]

The thirty cases came from three sources: *Canadian News Facts,* a monthly publication containing summaries of the news items carried by eleven major Canadian dailies from Vancouver to Halifax; *Canadian Business Periodicals Index,* a monthly index of articles appearing in business-related newspapers, journals, and magazines in Canada; and, finally, a small number of cases from the *Financial Post* newspaper. Beck and his coauthors confirmed each report of a threatening announcement from these sources by comparing it with the news story in the *Globe and Mail,* a national Canadian newspaper.

For each case of suspected rent extraction, a representative portfolio of stocks of potentially affected companies was created. If just one company was affected, or if only a single representative of the industry could be found, single-stock portfolios were used. Otherwise, portfolios were equally weighted with two to four companies. Daily returns for each stock in the portfolio and for those of the TSE 300 index were taken from the

TSE/Western Daily Stock Data recorded on the Financial Data Retrieval System tapes.

Each threatening episode was widely reported. The semistrong efficient market hypothesis (for which there is overwhelming empirical support generally in economics) would therefore mean that the effects of these political threats—none of which ultimately resulted in actual legislation—should be reflected in stock prices. The methodology used to test Hypothesis 1 was typical of that found in the literature using financial-event studies (for example, Schwert 1981). For the *i*th case in the sample, the abnormal share-price performance relative to the threatening announcement or retraction was computed by estimating the coefficients of the following linear regression equations:

$$r_i = a_i + B_i r_m + B'_i r_m d + Y_i d + E_i \tag{1}$$

and

$$r_i = a_i + B_i r_m + Y_i d + E_i. \tag{2}$$

In both Equations (1) and (2), the rate of return of the sample stock or portfolio (r_i) is regressed on the rate of return to the TSE 300 market index (r_m), plus a dummy variable (d) whose coefficient (Y_i) represents the average one-day abnormal return to the stock or portfolio. E_i captures the daily random disturbances. Equation (1) differs from (2) only by including a slope-shift variable ($r_m d$) to cover the possibility that systematic risk changed during the event period.

The estimation period for the cases was 211 trading days, running from 200 days before the announcement date to 10 days afterward. The event period was the time during which the announcement's effect was measured (and so was the period during which the dummy variable was coded 1). Three different event-period windows were estimated: from one day before the announcement to one day after ($-1, +1$); from five days before to three days after ($-5, +3$); and from twenty days before to ten days after ($-20, +10$). The evidence in the economic literature generally suggests that stock prices adjust very rapidly—within a few hours or even a few minutes—to new information. To Beck and his collaborators, that evidence suggested that the shortest event-period window ($-1, +1$) should capture any effects. But they also included the larger windows to guard against the not-uncommon occurrence that traders became aware of the announcement prior to the official announcement time.

Regressions were run to estimate the values of the coefficient of average abnormal returns, Y_i, for each case. The calculations by regression model were summarized, and the following equation used to generate a cumulative average abnormal return (CAAR) for each of the alternative event period windows:

$$CAAR_D = \frac{D}{N} \sum_{i=1}^{N} Y_i, \tag{3}$$

where D is the duration of the event period, and N is the number of cases (thirty).

To test the null hypothesis that CAAR equaled zero—that is, that the threats did not adversely affect the wealth of the sample firms or portfolios—this z-statistic was calculated:

$$Z_D = \frac{1}{\sqrt{N}} \sum_{i=1}^{N} \left[\frac{Y_i}{SE_I} \right], \tag{4}$$

where SE_i is the standard error of Y_i from the ordinary least-squares regression. For each threat and each retraction, six regressions were estimated: Equations (1) and (2) for each of three event periods. Equation (3) was then used to calculate the CAAR for each set of thirty threat regressions.[17]

The results for the thirty threatening announcements are shown in Table 4.1. As expected, the event-period window best supported by the empirical evidence is in fact the three-day window $(-1, +1)$, the shortest period. The CAAR for this time window does show the expected negative abnormal return, and it is significantly different from zero at the .05 significance level using Equation (2) and at the .10 significance level using Equation (1). The CAAR is also negative for the $(-20, +10)$ window and significantly different from zero at the .10 significance level for equation (1). The other estimates are of the expected sign. These results are consistent with Hypothesis 1: negative abnormal returns are associated with announcements threatening harmful political actions.

In each of the thirty episodes comprising the Beck-Hoskins-Connolly sample, the wealth-reducing threat eventually was removed. The issue raised is whether the threat's alleviation left firms' wealth unchanged (Hypothesis 2A), increased it but by an amount less than the original wealth lost (Hypothesis 2B), or increased it by the full amount of the wealth originally lost (Hypothesis 2C). Results consistent with Hypothesis

Table 4.1 Abnormal returns from threatening government announcements

	Duration of event period (days)		
	$(-20, +10)$	$(-5, +3)$	$(-1, +1)$
Equation 1:			
CAAR (%)	−2.57	−.66	−.93
% of cases negative	70	50	67
z-statistic	−1.624**	−.389	−1.652**
Equation 2:			
CAAR (%)	−3.05	−.81	−1.34
% of cases negative	63	50	67
z-statistic	−1.457	−.294	1.932*

Source: R. Beck, C. Hoskins, and J. M. Connolly, "Rent Extraction through Political Extortion: An Empirical Examination," *Journal of Legal Studies,* January 1992, table 1, p. 223. © 1992 by the University of Chicago.

Note: CAAR = cumulative average abnormal return; * = significant at a 95% confidence level; ** = significant at a 90% confidence level.

2A or 2B would corroborate the rent-extraction model; the implications of Hypothesis 2C, if corroborated, would contradict the model.

The effects of the retractions in the thirty-episode sample are reported in Table 4.2. The CAAR is not significantly different from zero at the .10 significance level for any of the six equation/event-duration combinations. This result is consistent with the rent-extraction model's strong Hypothesis 2A. The implication is either that politicians were correctly expected to extract nearly all the rents or that failure to negotiate a payoff was consid-

Table 4.2 Abnormal returns from government retractions of threats

	Duration of event period (days)		
	$(-20, +10)$	$(-5, +3)$	$(-1, +1)$
Equation 1:			
CAAR (%)	−.42	+.51	−.02
% of cases negative	57	47	53
z-statistic	+.037	−.918	+.254
Equation 2:			
CAAR (%)	−.96	+.01	+.24
% of cases negative	60	60	47
z-statistic	−1.358	−.638	−.236

Source: Same as Table 4.1, p. 224.

Note: CAAR = cumulative average abnormal return.

ered to be a remote possibility. The three negative and three positive CAAR'S in Table 4.2 are inconsistent with the positive abnormal return predicted by Hypotheses 2B and 2C.

Rent Extraction in America:
Threatened Pharmaceutical Price Controls

To test the hypothesis that the Clinton administration threat of price controls over pharmaceuticals—ultimately retracted—nonetheless resulted in a wealth loss to the threatened industry, a portfolio of pharmaceutical firms was constructed. The portfolio included all pharmaceutical firms included in the relevant Standard Industry Classification codes (codes 2834 and 2836). Their daily, equally weighted returns (including dividends) were estimated as a function of the equally weighted returns to the market portfolio. Daily returns from June 1991 through November 1994 made up the set of observations.

The regression included two dummy variables, CLINTON1 and CLINTON2, to capture the effects of the Clinton price-control threat and then its retraction. That is, the single equation combines in one regression the two stages of the rent-extraction process estimated separately by Beck, Hoskins, and Connolly. The reason for the different technique is the difficulty of specifying *a priori* the precise days on which the market would have reacted to information about the threats. Predictably, the threat of price controls would be registered with President Clinton's election, given his frequent campaign statements about "reforming" health care. But thereafter there were literally hundreds of pieces of new information (some sixty in the *Wall Street Journal* alone) about what the president's plan would consist of and how it would work.

Rather than speculate about which events had an impact on the market, the entire period from threat to retraction is captured by CLINTON1.[18] The period was a lengthy one. Following Clinton's election (the period of the CLINTON1 variable begins the day before his election), the likelihood of a Democratic health-care bill seesawed back and forth for almost two years. As late as August 1994 the Democrats were talking confidently about passing legislation before the fall elections. But finally, Senate majority leader Mitchell announced in September 1994 that the administration was abandoning health-care legislation for that congressional session. The publication date of that announcement is the closing period for the threat dummy, CLINTON1.

The retraction dummy, CLINTON2, encompasses the period from Mitchell's admission in September that the threat was ended—for that year—through the November elections. The surprising Republican victories, creating majorities in both chambers for the first time in forty years, ended for the foreseeable future any chance of price controls on pharmaceuticals. The second dummy variable, CLINTON2, thus registers the period during which recovery (if any) of wealth lost from the previous threats would have occurred.

The regression results are shown in Table 4.3. Two equations are estimated, one with and another without a variable showing any shift in market returns for the threat period of CLINTON1.[19] In regression I, CLINTON1 is negative and significant at the .05 level. But CLINTON2 is not significantly different from zero. In the period of the price-control threat, that is, daily returns to the pharmaceutical portfolio (with returns to the market portfolio held constant) were significantly lower than before and after the threat period. But there was no recoupment of the lost wealth during the period after the Democrats abandoned their threats and then lost control of Congress to the Republicans (and so any chance of passing price-control legislation in the subsequent Congress).

Table 4.3 Regression results for threats of pharmaceutical price controls (absolute t-statistics in parentheses)

	Regression	
	I	II
Constant	6.09E−05	−5.25E−05
	(.147)	(.133)
Independent variables:		
Market returns	1.695*	1.849*
	(28.69)	(23.58)
Shift in market returns	—	−.342*
		(2.969)
CLINTON1	−.0009513**	−.0006832
	(1.755)	(1.244)
CLINTON2	.0009514	.0011686
	(.771)	(.949)
Adj. R^2	.516	.520
n	884	884
F	189.2*	160.5*

Note: Dependent variable = returns to pharmaceutical portfolio; * = significant at .01; ** = significant at .05.

Regression II adds the market-shift variable to the equation estimated. Unfortunately, the shift variable is highly collinear with CLINTON1, with the result that CLINTON1's reported t-statistic is artificially low. (Even as reported, the coefficient is significant at about the 10 percent level.) The shift variable itself is highly significant and, as one would expect, negative. The specter of regulation lowered systematic risk as well as expected returns for pharmaceutical stocks. And as in the first regression, there is no recovery of lost wealth in the period covered by CLINTON2, which remains insignificant in regression II.

5

Contracting for Rent Preservation: The Durability Problem

> The avoidance of taxes is the only pursuit that still carries any reward.
>
> —JOHN MAYNARD KEYNES

The Durability Issue for Rent-Extraction Contracts

The fact demonstrated in Chapters 3 and 4—that privately created rents and wealth really can be extracted—effectively means that no individual has complete property rights in any of the capital he has amassed or in the wealth he has produced. The state's ability to extract capital or wealth effectively gives the politician the power (or property right) to charge private owners for the right to keep the fruits of what is nominally their own investment or property. The taxing power furnishes perhaps the most obvious demonstration of the ability to extract private wealth, and thus the ability to profit by forbearing from doing so. But other threats—price controls, antitrust cases, licensure, zoning, and so forth—can serve the same extractive purpose. Private owners will pay a politician to be left alone, but only if the amount they pay is less than the value of what the politician would take if compensation were not paid.

Occasionally certain kinds of legislative takings may constitutionally require that the government pay some compensation, a fact that may dissuade the extractor-politician in the first place. The classic example is the taking of real estate in eminent-domain proceedings. When a taking would require compensation, any threat of that taking naturally has less extractive value. But few of the episodes of rent extraction described in the two previous chapters triggered any constitutional takings issue, particularly since the wealth ultimately ceded to legislators was paid over "voluntarily." Apparently the only constitutional protection possibly afforded in situations in which rents or wealth is threatened but (for a price) not taken is the very fragile defense of "unconstitutional conditions."

Constitutionally, the situation is somewhat perverse when it comes to taxation. There is nothing unconstitutional about the process of threatening the returns to private capital but then being bought off for some fraction of total capital value. On the contrary, the extraction process is constitutionally *protected*. Article I of the Constitution grants Congress the power to tax but does not specify any particular amount, form, or targets of taxation, leaving those decisions to congressional discretion. So the power is allocated to politicians to decide whether, how, and whom to tax. This situation sets the stage for contracts with potential targets seeking to pay for costs not being imposed. Would-be victims' ability to make payments to politicians is likewise constitutionally protected, as a matter of First Amendment freedom of speech.[1] In short, politicians can use their discretion to impose costs or not, and a private party can just as legally compensate politicians not to impose costs, all behind the wall of constitutional protections.

Largely untrammeled by the Constitution, then, the politician and the capital owner are left to work out the issue of expropriation versus extraction for themselves. Such an agreement is not a *legal* contract, however, in that it is not legally enforceable. True, the politician ordinarily is just taking money not to do what he has a perfectly legal right to do, and the payor typically is making a legal contribution that leaves her better off.[2] Still, doctrines of contract law would make the agreement legally unen-

Reprinted by permission: Tribune Media Services.

forceable.[3] In other words, rent-extraction contracts are extralegal, outside the judicial system governing most other contracts. Nonetheless, the fact that the extortionate rent-extraction process is essentially (if extralegally) contractual cannot be denied. Thomas Schelling (1963, p. 5) summarizes:

> To study the strategy of conflict is to take the view that most conflict situations are essentially *bargaining* situations. They are situations in which the ability of one participant to gain his ends is dependent to an important degree on the choices or decisions that the other participant will make. The bargaining may be explicit, as when one offers a concession; or it may be by tacit maneuver, as when one occupies or evacuates strategic territory . . . it may involve threats of damage, including mutual damage, as in a strike, boycott, or price war, or in extortion.

Focus on the contractual nature of rent extraction spotlights two interesting problems, both affecting the *durability* of rent-extraction agreements. Both private persons (opting for extractive payments over expropriative legislation) and politicians (opting for receipt of personal payments in lieu of less valuable expropriative legislation) ordinarily will prefer longer-term deals. Both sides, that is, will prefer more durable arrangements for protecting private rents, all other things being equal. Among other things, greater certainty about the future facilitates private planning. As the business press frequently notes, "The Internal Revenue Code changes with maddening frequency, making it hard for companies to map out investment strategies."[4]

Greater durability also reduces deadweight transaction costs of dickering between politicians and private parties. "[I]f the distribution of tax shares is not durable, favored groups will be forced to spend resources in every period to retain their tax preferences, and other groups will repeatedly spend resources to obtain tax reductions or to prevent their current liabilities from being raised" (Shughart 1987, p. 278). Durability avoids these economic losses, as John Maynard Keynes pointed out, as fewer resources are spent moving wealth and income into areas where returns are lower but the tax bite less severe.[5]

Better planning and reduced transaction costs make long-term deals more valuable both to private parties and to politicians. Both factors also make longer-term rent-extraction contracts more desirable socially. If durability in rent-extraction agreements is valuable, it is useful to consider the obstacles to durability.

Two impediments are evident. First, an agreement is less durable as one party to it behaves opportunistically, taking advantage of the other party's performance while holding back on his own.[6] Opportunism is possible because the contracts to which politicians agree are executory. In return for consideration conferred now by taxpayers, the politician will be expected to perform his part of the deal later, forbearing in the future from tax or other legislation not in the interests of the private contributor. Chapter 2 noted, however, that politicians are thereby placed in a situation in which having their cake and eating it too may be attractive. What is to stop an opportunistic politician from a double-cross, taking the money and then expropriating the rents anyway? This problem of political duplicity (or contractual opportunism, in the economic jargon) is the first durability-related issue considered in this chapter.

In addition, an agreement will be less durable as there are greater risks associated with long-term contracts. For example, one party may anticipate that the other party will not be in a position to perform a longer-term deal. Politicians lose elections or retire, as a result of which continued adherence to extraction contracts becomes impossible. As that possibility is anticipated, individuals have less incentive to conclude long-term contracts with politicians.

These two impediments to contract durability, opportunism and greater risk (including the risk of impossibility of performance), are important for understanding political contracting generally. The two issues are analyzed here in the specific context of the rent-extraction model. The issues do not arise just in the rent-extraction context, though, but also with political rent creation. When payments are made for higher prices through cartelization, for example, politicians must be held to their deals. Since cartelization is wealth-reducing overall (that is, consumers lose more than producers who pay for cartelization win), private persons always run the risk that the politician will take their money but then do nothing, so as to avoid losing consumers' votes. Producers must therefore be wary of political double-crossing.

But the issue of contract durability—including both the opportunism and risk aspects of durability—is more important in the rent-extraction setting. If durability cannot be achieved in rent creation, either because politicians act opportunistically or because only short-term deals are made, both private producers and politicians will invest less in working toward creating rents. That is, investments in rent creation will be fewer because the period of profiting from them will be shorter. However, fewer such investments are a good thing for society generally. The investments not made are ones that overall are wealth-reducing in the first place. In the rent-creation model, political opportunism and short-term arrangements, far from being a general welfare problem, are a welfare boon.[7]

The opposite is true in markets in which rent extraction, not creation, is the preferred political tactic. The capital of concern there is private investments in wealth-increasing activities, investments that will not be made to the extent that they (or, equivalently, their value) can be expropriated. The way to avoid expropriation is to pay the rent-extraction "fee" politicians will demand. And since the value of the investment—and thus how much investment will be made—depends on the length of time it will yield a flow of rents (wealth), the ability to make long-term extraction contracts to avoid expropriation is wealth-increasing overall.[8]

To summarize, given that politicians can legally take wealth from the private owners of assets, private incentives to invest in creating those assets and wealth depend on the length of time they will earn returns, all other things being equal. While greater durability of rent-creation deals is wealth-reducing overall, society gains wealth as rent-extraction contracts are more durable. The issue now considered is how this durability, meaning greater avoidance of political opportunism and greater contract longevity, is achieved.

Illustrating the Durability Problem for Rent Extraction: Income Taxation

Perhaps the easiest way of analyzing the opportunism and longevity problems in rent extraction is to look at the process of income taxation. As has been seen, a principal activity in the tax-legislation process is politicians' sale of *non*taxation to those willing to buy it. The process is often played out against the backdrop of what has come to be called, euphemistically, "tax reform." Because changes in income taxation have become so frequent, they offer a useful natural experiment to the analyst interested in studying the difficulties associated with durability in rent-extraction contracts.

A Short History of Federal Income Taxation

Tax change ("reform") has been an accelerating phenomenon. Since its inception, the federal income tax has changed frequently, but a disproportionate number of modifications to the eighty-year-old income-tax system have occurred since 1970.[9] The current federal individual income tax began with a modest bill passed in 1913. It set a top marginal rate of 7 percent on taxable income over $500,000 and supplemented the corporate income tax that had been enacted four years earlier. Almost immediately, tax "reform" became a routine part of Washington politics. From 1917 through 1920 Congress decreased exemptions and increased rates on both individual and corporate income taxes to finance the war. (During this period maximum rates jumped from 7 to 77 percent.) By 1920 the income tax had replaced the excise tax as the United States' dominant revenue source, accounting for approximately 60 percent of all tax receipts. In the 1920s, however, Congress deemphasized the income tax. The Revenue Acts of 1921 and 1924 repealed the excess-profits tax and lowered income-tax rates, but the acts raised the estate tax and added a gift tax. Further tax cuts followed in 1926 and 1928, including decreases in the estate and corporate tax rates.

In the 1930s the direction of tax policy again changed.[10] The Revenue Act of 1932 returned the maximum individual surtax rate to the 1922 level of 55 percent and increased corporate rates as a whole. The Revenue Act of 1934, while raising rates again, focused primarily on perceived administrative shortcomings, capital-gains provisions, and a new tax on personal holding companies. From 1934 to 1945 the Roosevelt administration continued its attack on what it called "an unjust concentration of wealth and economic power," as FDR said in a 1935 message to Congress (see Doernberg and McChesney 1987a, p. 915). During that period Congress passed at least one revenue bill every year, each directed largely at different aspects of individual and corporate economic life.

Throughout the 1940s the income tax became less an imposition on the relatively wealthy, instead raising revenue from all conceivable sources for rearmament. In 1940 Congress imposed an excess-profits tax on corporations and added a 10 percent surcharge for individuals with incomes between $6,000 and $100,000. Further rate increases marked the Revenue Acts of 1941 and 1942. More important, with the Revenue Act of 1942 the personal income tax reached more than 28 million taxpayers, compared with the 13 million covered before. With millions of new Americans on the tax rolls, Congress moved in 1944 to "simplify" the tax system by enacting a graduated withholding system, tax tables, and the standard deduction.

Congress reduced income taxes in 1946 and 1948, overriding President Truman's vetoes. In 1950 Congress reenacted an excess-profits tax to help fund the Korean War. The new tax was conspicuous for the amount of tax relief provided to specific groups: new firms and industries that were growing unusually quickly or unusually slowly; regulated corporations; natural gas, mining, and mineral firms; shipbuilders, railroads, and airlines carrying mail. A year later, the 1951 tax bill raised overall rates for individuals and corporations but also provided many deductions and credits that lowered rates for certain favored groups. Corporately, these included the real-estate industry, mining companies, farmers, ranchers, and the fishing industry. Individually, special treatment went to veterans, Americans living abroad, and the elderly.

For the most part the Eisenhower years were a period of calm for tax legislation, with one large exception. In 1954 Congress fundamentally reorganized the tax code for the first time since 1913. The bill was long and complex, and (as had by then become the pattern) it included provisions that singled out a variety of individuals and organizations. After enactment of the 1954 Internal Revenue Code, however, Congress restrained itself until 1962.

President Kennedy's desire for an increased investment tax credit set the stage for the Revenue Act of 1962. The greater tax credit would be balanced against withholding on dividends and interest. Although the final bill broadened the investment tax credit to cover previously excluded industries and all new capital investment, the withholding provisions for interest and dividends were dropped. The 1962 act was the first major revenue legislation in eight years, but it was insignificant in comparison with what was to come in the 1960s. New legislation in 1964 lowered tax rates across the board. The 1964 act began as structural tax reform but settled for selective provisions benefiting special interests in addition to the general tax cuts. New provisions included a moving-expenses deduction, income averaging, a minimum standard deduction, and a capital-gains exclusion on the sale of homes by the elderly.

In 1968–69 Congress geared up for another run at "tax reform." The Tax Reform Act of 1969 was sweeping, generally focusing on revenue-increasing provisions. By and large, the increased revenue came from the enactment of structural changes, including repeal of the investment tax credit, rather than from an increase in income-tax rates. The 1969 act represented the first significant overhaul of the 1954 code, but, as often happens with tax reform, the final law was not as draconian as the version that initially passed the House Ways and Means Committee. For example, the House Ways and Means Committee did not make good on its threat to eliminate the tax-exempt status of state and municipal bonds.

The 1970s started relatively peacefully with respect to tax legislation, but the pace of change quickened considerably by the end of the decade. The Tax Reduction Act of 1971 reinstated the investment tax credit, liberalized depreciation deductions, and created various export incentives. It also adjusted rates to provide tax relief for individuals. Thereafter through 1974, despite frequent legislative threats of extensive tax "reform," no significant legislation materialized, with the exception of changes in the tax laws governing pensions.

The dam burst, however, with the enactment of the Tax Reduction Act of 1975 and the Tax Reform Act of 1976. As prelude to the massive 1976 legislation, the 1975 act tightened up oil-depletion allowances, increased the investment tax credit, and offered tax aid to profitless industries by extending the loss-carryback provisions. Then, in the Tax Reform Act of 1976, Congress enacted many of the provisions that it had considered during the relatively inactive tax years of 1972–1974. Although the legislation contained some revenue-gaining provisions, its thrust was to extend and create new benefits. By all accounts, the 1976 legislation was long, complicated, and lacking in systematic "reform" of any kind. Perhaps recognizing these deficiencies, the 1976 Congress required a study of the problem of tax simplification.

The pattern in 1977 and 1978 paralleled the 1975–76 sequence: a stopgap bill passed in 1977 presaged more substantial legislation to come. Aware of the incessant growth of federal income-tax provisions, Congress entitled the legislation "The 1977 Tax Reduction and Simplification Act." One of its major features was a new-jobs tax credit, with a complexity typical of the rest of the bill. The Revenue Act of 1978 began with the usual tax-reform rhetoric of simplification, equity, and stimulation of investment. By the time the bill was passed, however, any cohesion in the original proposal had been lost.

The next important enactment was the Economic Recovery Tax Act of 1981, a major tax-reduction bill. The principal features included lower tax rates across the board, inflation-indexed tax rates, increased depreciation deductions, more generous transfers of tax benefits, larger research-and-development deductions, a building-rehabilitation investment tax credit, and a deduction for a family's second earner. Overall the 1981 act gave taxpayers the largest tax cut in American history.

The dust had hardly settled from the 1981 changes when the Tax Equity and Fiscal Responsibility Act of 1982 eliminated part of the previous year's tax reduction and also tightened up on compliance. In 1984

Congress again rearranged the tax furniture by enacting the Tax Reform Act. It froze some provisions from the 1981 legislation scheduled to reduce taxes and tightened up perceived loopholes in the corporate tax area and in the treatment of certain debt instruments. The 1984 Act, however, was less notable for any new direction in tax policy than for its reach into virtually all areas of taxation, as the 1,300-page conference report suggested.

Hard on the heels of the 1984 changes, the House in 1985 passed yet another voluminous tax reform bill. In 1986 the Senate voted almost unanimously for its tax bill, one significantly different from the House bill. Touted as the most comprehensive review of the federal income-tax system since the 1954 codification, or even since World War II, the compromise Tax Reform Act of 1986 occupied center stage for both politicians and those taxpayers with the most to gain or lose as it proceeded to the House-Senate conference committee.[11] In September 1986 the two congressional chambers passed the conference agreement, a bill that borrowed from both the Senate and House proposals and included some new provisions as well. Finally, in October 1986 President Reagan signed the Tax Reform Act of 1986, which modified the prior code to such an extent that it has been redesignated the "Internal Revenue Code of 1986."

So sweeping was the 1986 act, not to mention the political rhetoric that accompanied it, that many tax observers proclaimed it the beginning of a new era in taxation. It engendered optimism, even among those who should have known better, that increased durability had arrived for income taxation. "The Tax Reform Act of 1986 has been characterized as a political miracle," two commentators (McLure and Zodrow 1987, p. 57) noted at the time. One expert proclaimed that, for once, "The general interest prevailed over special interests" (Rabushka 1988, p. 64).

It is remarkable how quickly even the popular press realized that, whether good or bad, the tax legislation of 1986 could not endure (for example, Rosenbaum 1989). Certainly, to any seasoned observer, there was really no reason even in 1986 to think that year's changes had any particular durability. As Milton Friedman (1986) said at the time, "the improvement will turn out to be temporary. Nothing has changed to prevent the process that produced our present tax system from starting over. As lobbyists get back into action, and as members of Congress try to raise campaign funds, old loopholes will be reintroduced and new ones invented."

And in fact the particular version of the Internal Revenue Code produced that year has not been long-lived at all. "When Congress enacted the Tax Reform Act of 1986, which was supposed to stabilize and simplify the code, House Ways and Means Committee Chairman Dan Rostenkowski claimed that he was going to hang up a 'Gone Fishing' sign. But in the five years after that bill passed, Congress made some 5,400 changes to the tax laws through 27 different pieces of legislation" (Wartzman 1993a). To this total of changes made to the version of the tax code produced in 1986 must now be added the Clinton administration changes passed in 1993. And "[n]o one even pretends that this year's [1993] bill precludes future changes"; as one former IRS commissioner said at the time, "There is a universal sense that this thing is out of control" (ibid.).

The Accelerating Rate of Tax Change

This summary demonstrates that Congress routinely contracts over taxation, but only for a certain period. Benefits can only be rented briefly, not purchased for all time.

Moreover, one also discovers, the rental period available on tax relief has been declining over the years; that is, tax "reform" is of decreasing durability. The investment tax credit, for example, has been in and out of the Internal Revenue Code half a dozen times since the early 1960s. This phenomenon of decreasing durability in tax legislation specifically is helpful in analyzing the factors favoring durability of rent extraction more generally.

There is apparently no disagreement that political provision of tax favors is a growth industry. A study by John Witte (1985) focused on 89 "tax expenditures" in effect from 1974 through 1981, regardless of when enacted. "Tax expenditure" is essentially synonymous with "tax break," a special provision that avoids the wealth loss that a firm or individual would otherwise suffer under the income-tax laws.[12] Witte (p. 316) found a relatively even distribution of *new* tax expenditures (breaks) enacted from 1909 through 1981. The annual average for new tax breaks ran as low as .69 (for the period 1920–1945); the average was 1.83 for 1970–1981, the most recent period that Witte studied.

Modifications to *existing* code provisions revealed a different pattern. Of the tax expenditures studied, twenty had never been modified once enacted. But others had been modified almost annually. Overall, the tax expenditures in existence during the 1974–1981 period had been modified 318 times since their enactment. Tax tinkering was relatively uncommon from 1920 to 1945, with only 35 modifications (an annual average of 1.35) for those years. But from 1970 to 1981 there were 164 modifications to the tax breaks studied, an annual average of 13.67 changes. That is, more than half of all the modifications in the seventy-three-year period (from 1909 through 1981) occurred in the last twelve years.[13] Figure 5.1 summarizes the Witte data by showing, for four periods, the number of new tax breaks, the number of modifications to existing breaks, and the ratio of modifications to new tax breaks. Clearly, the relative importance of modifying existing loopholes has grown steadily.

It must be presumed that politicians, as rational maximizers, are not giving away tax breaks that they can sell for contributions, speech honoraria, and the other forms of compensation discussed in Chapter 3. The acceleration in modifying tax breaks represents an accelerating rate of rent-extraction contracts. Tax contracts have grown increasingly fragile; durability in tax-based rent extraction is declining.

But why has the length of legislative tax-relief contracts fallen so substantially? One possibility is that politicians are behaving opportunistically, accepting the payments for longer-term arrangements naturally desired by private parties but then failing to deliver what they promised. Another possibility is that the contracting parties increasingly have agreed on shorter-term arrangements, perhaps because it is increasingly perceived that politicians cannot deliver on longer-term deals.

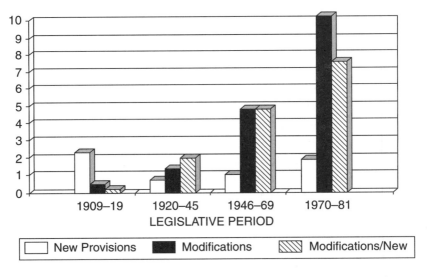

Figure 5.1 Tax modifications vs. new benefits, by legislative period

Opportunism in Rent-Extraction Contracts

Recall from Chapter 2 a prototypical rent-extraction situation faced by a private individual, as represented by the payoff matrix shown on page 38. The matrix highlights two sorts of problems to be anticipated in the rent-extraction situation. The first was whether politicians' threats to expropriate were sufficiently credible to elicit private payments not to expropriate. If not, private individuals might try to call politicians' bluff, hoping to end up in quadrant [A]. But as has been shown in Chapters 3 and 4, politicians threats' are indeed credible and do elicit payments. Now to be considered is the second aspect of the extraction tactic indicated by the matrix: the possibility of opportunism by politicians. Obviously, the politician prefers quadrant [D] to either [B] or [C] separately. In quadrant [D] the politician double-crosses, securing the $10,000 payment from the individual but then expropriating by taxation the $30,000 destined for the Treasury, which is worth an additional $2,000 to him personally, making the value of [D] to him $12,000 overall. The individual then has been duped and does not get what she paid for. Since there is nothing legally to stop the politician from trying to have his cake and eat it too, why does any private individual ever pay for extraction rather than face expropriation? Why not, that is, limit one's losses to the $30,000 in quadrant [C] without throwing good money (another $10,000) after bad? Why are payments for rent extraction actually made? Reciprocally, why does the politician not double-cross the private payors?

The answer is based on several aspects of the players' respective gains and losses. Consider first that while [D] is preferable to [B] for the politician, [B] in turn is preferable to [C] for the politician. That is, [D] > [B] > [C] from his standpoint. If the politician prefers to have money in his pocket for personal use, rather than more money in the Treasury for use by the legislature generally—as must be true by hypothesis when extraction is his desired strategy—then having actually to expropriate is his least-desired outcome. The gains from opportunism thus come at a cost: if private individuals feel they are being suckered and so cease to contribute, neither [D] nor [B] will be available to the politician. He is left with his least-desired outcome, [C].

What can the politician do to avoid this result? This is a standard problem, one that any seller faces in a situation in which reneging on a deal looks attractive: inducing trust (by signaling, bonding, or some other mechanism) that he will actually fulfill his side of the executory contract, once payment has been made. One could seemingly define away the problem by making the deal executory on the side of the private individual: she will pay the politician at the end of the period only if the expropriative legislation has not been passed. But of course, having a contract structured this way just switches the inquiry from one involving political opportunism to one involving private opportunism. The question then becomes whether the buyer can elicit the seller's trust that the buyer will perform her side of the deal, once the seller has rendered the promised performance.

The solution to the problem lies in two aspects of the parties' respective bargaining positions. First, the parties' preferences to some extent match. From the private party's side, the preference ordering is [B] > [C] > [D]. That is, *both* parties prefer [B] to [C]. True, the politician also prefers [D] to [B], but [D] can happen only as long as the private person is willing to pay up. If she does not, both parties are left at [C], which both find inferior to [B].

Thus, the politician needs the private party's "cooperation" to avoid [C] and reach [B]. Reciprocally, the private party needs the politician's cooperation to avoid [D] and reach [B]. This realization somewhat alters the nature of the problem: while the private payor must be concerned about the politician's opportunism, the politician must be concerned about the individual's willingness to pay in the first place. There is a cost to the politician, then, in causing the individual to doubt whether any payment will really purchase forbearance from expropriation.

The question then is what devices are available to ensure that *both* sides are willing to respect the agreement, such that extraction rather than expropriation is the result.[14] The key to the solution is the fact that, second, the players typically are involved in a repeated game. From year to year, the same investors and holders of wealth on the private side for the most part confront the same politicians. Of course, the cast of characters can always change. But wholesale changes in the identities of the parties are uncommon. The same people bargaining to reduce their taxes in 1986—the Marriotts and the Gallos—were dealing with the same taxers—the Packwoods and the Rostenkowskis—who had been there for years.

The repeat nature of the game effectively means that the payoff matrix is altered by the introduction of payments expected to be made over time.[15] The $40,000 payment that the politician prefers in [D] may be available once, but it will not be available repeatedly. Double-crossed private individuals will learn from their mistakes and will refuse to continue playing the game with an opportunistic politician. When they do, the double-crosser is left in quadrant [C], his least-preferred outcome, thereafter. The double-crossing politician unable to establish a reputation as honest may earn $12,000 the first time when he actually expropriates, but only $2,000 per period thereafter. The nonopportunistic politician forgoes the extra $2,000 the first time but earns the $10,000 every period thereafter. Private parties' ability to refuse to play the game next time forces the politician who is in the game over the long haul—and what politician does not plan to be?—to stick by his promises.[16] "Fool me once, shame on you; fool me twice, shame on me!" is the private victim's best response.[17]

The importance of repeated plays in situations of conflict has long been recognized in economics and political science.[18] Its importance goes beyond situations involving the same set of players. With successful repeat plays, the politician establishes a general reputation for abiding by the rules. This means, *inter alia,* that as new private individuals are drawn into the extraction game (that is, as new persons create wealth or come into possession of it), there is less need for the private party to worry about whether the veteran politician will stick by his promises. His reputation as an honest player commits him to abide by the agreement—just to extract, but not to expropriate—so that no uncertainty arises as new players join the game.

Incumbency rates in Congress are high, especially in the House. The typical representative or senator on congressional tax committees has many years' experience. Committee and subcommittee chairs are especially important in the legislative process, and their positions are determined by seniority. Thus, on this basis at least, one would not expect opportunism to be a particular problem for tax-based rent-extraction contracts.

High incumbency and so low predicted opportunism do not mean, of course, that politicians and private parties will always end up in quadrant [B]. The matrix may not represent the actual political payoffs in a given situation. For example, what others are willing to pay the politician to have an individual's surplus extracted and transferred to them—rent *creation*—may be sufficiently high that politicians prefer to do so, meaning that quadrant [C] is preferable to politicians in the first place. (These situations are discussed in Chapter 7.) If so, private individuals would be foolish to pay anything at all to the politician. Moreover, a politician who has played the game repeatedly, and therefore honestly, may suddenly decide to retire, in which case he may feel he can put himself into quadrant [D] with impunity.

Retirement raises the possibility of the "last-period problem," the diminution in incentive that one party has to perform his contractual duties when he knows that he will never have to deal with the other party again. A politician who announces suddenly that he will not run for reelection might then be tempted to breach the earlier taxation contract—seemingly without penalty, since he has already been paid for his services and will not be in Congress to solicit further contracts in the future. Though theoretically of possible importance, empirical evidence indicates no serious last-period problem in fact. Typically, powerful legislators stay on in Washington as lobbyists, and so expect to continue to work (contract) with the same sorts of people and interests that they encountered in office (for example, Easterbrook 1984, pp. 57, 59). Last-period problems that might otherwise exist are likewise minimized by the fact that legislative contracts require complementary voting or forbearance by other politicians, most of whom will not be leaving office. Remaining politicians have an incentive to monitor the actions of a departing politician, to be sure that their own prenegotiated results are attained.[19]

The desire to honor prior deals, even in the face of retirement, is reflected in the efforts of Senator Russell Long, longtime chair of the Senate Finance Committee, during the 1986 tax overhaul. Senator Long was the "master architect" of the version of the Internal Revenue Code that prevailed before the Tax Reform Act of 1986, and so dug in his heels to preserve that version from President Reagan's tax changes. Notwithstanding the freedom from political obligations implied by his impending retirement, Long still fought "to preserve his favorite tax breaks, including those that encourage business investment, employee stock ownership and domestic oil exploration, a business dear to his home state" (Birnbaum 1985a).

Both theory and evidence thus suggest that political opportunism is unlikely to deter politicians systematically from fulfilling rent-extraction contracts. Of course, problems may sometimes arise.[20] But in a situation in which extraction is the strategy chosen politically, the problem of foreseeable opportunism is ordinarily tractable. This is especially true when, as in much of what Congress does (including taxation), both sides are better off cooperating. The same players interact repeatedly, and reputations for abiding by agreements are valuable.

The Risks in Long-Term Rent-Extraction Contracts

Both in theory and in practice, political opportunism seems not to be an important obstacle to the durability of rent-extraction contracts. Thus, the decreasing durability of tax-based extraction contracts may simply reflect a preference by one or both parties for a series of shorter-term contracts to a single, longer-term agreement. Ordinarily, longer agreements are more beneficial to both sides, all other things being equal. So why have parties to rent-extraction deals been opting contractually for shorter-term arrangements?

The answer is that all other things may not have been equal during the period of declining tax-law durability. Longer contracts also have their costs, particularly in the form of increased risk to private parties. Greater longevity increases the likelihood that even a nonopportunistic politician may find it difficult to deliver on his promises, for a variety of reasons now to be considered. Naturally, as risks increase with longevity, risk-averse parties will decrease the length of their contracts. The fact that the risks of contractual nonperformance have increased in the past two decades must explain at least in part the accelerating rate of tax legislation.

Impossibility of Performance

The first risk associated with longer-term arrangements is an increased probability that the politician may not be able to perform his part of the bargain. Intentional opportunism by individual politicians may not be as serious a problem for the integrity of long-term tax contracts, as politicians ordinarily expect to be in for the long haul and so a reputation for keeping one's word becomes valuable. But keeping his word requires that the politician be in office; there is always the possibility that the politician will not be in office for the full period covered by the contract.

Even if the politician intends to keep his side of the bargain and does not himself choose to leave office short of the period foreseen by both sides, he may not be reelected after agreeing to some tax policy for some future period. His performance is then impossible. His successor, who is of course not a party to the deal, has no reason to adhere to his predecessor's policy unless he also receives compensation. Private beneficiaries of tax deals then would have to pay again to obtain the performance already purchased from the outgoing politician. New contracts necessarily would follow turnover among political officeholders.

The risk that the politician will not be there to fulfill his side of the bargain obviously increases, the longer the period of performance contracted for. Longer-term deals involve greater numbers of primaries and elections in which an incumbent can lose his seat. One possible reason for the acceleration in the rate of congressional tax reconsiderations, then, is an increase in the rate of legislative turnover among politicians.

If the durability of contracts between special interests and legislators is related to legislative tenure, tax activity and congressional turnover should be correlated—the less durable the legislator, the less durable the legislation. In fact some noticeable correlation does exist. Although in recent years there has been no discernible change in the overall incumbency effect for House and Senate members,[21] the tenure of service on the tax-writing committees has shown some interesting variations. For the Eighty-ninth Congress in 1965–66, a period of relative stability in taxation, the average length of service on the Ways and Means Committee was 4.84 terms. By the time of the Ninety-fourth Congress in 1975–76, when congressional action on taxes was heating up again, the average Ways and Means tenure had fallen to 2.81 terms, a drop in longevity of over 40 percent. The decrease in average length of service on Ways and Means correlates with the acceleration of tax legislation already discussed.[22]

Until the mid-1970s the Ways and Means Committee characteristically selected its membership from safe districts, thereby limiting turnover (Reese 1980). Typical of this process was Wilbur Mills, who presided over the committee almost unopposed at home for sixteen years. The system broke down, however, around the time of the 1975–76 congressional session, following Mills's nocturnal dip in the Tidal Basin with a stripper, his subsequent revelation of alcoholism, and finally his resignation. During the 1975–76 congressional session, the committee experienced unusual turnover. Mills's successor, Al Ullman, held his position for only six years, and Dan Rostenkowski in turn lost his seat in 1994.

Turnover rates on the Senate Finance Committee have followed similar patterns. The average tenure for Finance Committee members in 1965–66 was 5.76 terms. By 1975–76 the average tenure had fallen to 4.22 terms, a drop of over 25 percent. Average tenure fell further to 3.45 terms as of the Ninety-seventh Congress in 1981–82. The Senate elections were especially noteworthy in 1980, as only 55 percent of incumbents were reelected in that Reagan landslide year.

Of course, the average tenure served does not foretell perfectly how long current legislators will serve in the future. But historical turnover provides at least some relevant information to private capital owners trying to gauge the likelihood that their rent-extraction contract, which merely extracts rather than expropriates, will be durable. Fluctuating rates of turnover indicate how much the contract is worth, given likely future changes in levels of rent-protection durability.

For both the Ways and Means and the Finance Committees, average tenure had begun to climb again at the end of the 1980s. In 1985–86 the average tenure on the Ways and Means Committee had risen to 4.39 terms, and on the Finance Committee to 5.10. More recently, length of tenure on the tax-writing committees has fluctuated, falling in the Senate but rising in the House for 1995–96. However, the years of tenure since 1980 have been less important than the fact that in both chambers of Congress there has been a change in the majority party, with the Republicans in 1995 controlling both the House and Senate for the first time in a generation. Further, the most senior Senate Finance Committee member from either party, Senator Packwood, was forced to resign his seat in 1995, less than a year after assuming the chair.

Increasing Internal Complexity

A second set of risks associated with long-term contracts derives from the structure of Congress itself, including the committee system generally and the structure of the House Ways and Means Committee particularly. Constitutionally, tax legislation originates in the House of Representatives and then may be amended by the Senate. In the House, the effective power over taxation has traditionally resided almost exclusively in the Ways and Means Committee. Practically, therefore, the chairs of that committee and of any relevant subcommittees are the most important congressional actors in the tax-contract process.

To secure favorable legislation or beneficial legislative inaction, however, a committee or subcommittee chair must secure the cooperation and votes of others, which requires a series of ancillary contracts. As part of the chair's contract with private interests, then, he has to muster the votes of many legislators on his committee. The involvement of Treasury experts, committee staff, and others brings even more players into the game.

The more players there are in the game, the more risky long-term contracting for tax legislation becomes. Like their prominent committee chair, less prominent but nevertheless influential actors also resign or lose office, and their successors have no obligation to abide by their predecessors' contracts. Turnover, however, is only part of the problem. More important, the sheer number of persons whose cooperation must be obtained makes it more difficult for committee and subcommittee chairs to deliver on their own taxation contracts. This is particularly true for those actors—Treasury experts, for example—who cannot be compensated for producing favorable tax legislation the way legislators can be.

If over time the number of actors in the process has been increasing and the chair's control over them has diminished, longer-term contracts predictably will become less popular with private payors, and amendments to the tax code will become more frequent. And in fact one does find that various internal changes in Congress have made the system less conducive to long-term tax contracts.

First, numerous changes to the committee system introduced by House Democrats in the mid-1970s had the effect of increasing the number of players and of decreasing the chairman's control. The larger committees in the House were expanded across the board. Ways and Means in particular grew from twenty-five to thirty-seven members. The new system also required that committees establish at least four permanent subcommittees, each with its own chairman. This change greatly fragmented the power previously held by the full committee chairman. Moreover, the entire majority membership of the full committee, rather than just the chairman, began to determine the number and jurisdiction of subcommittees. The changes effectively established a "subcommittee bill of rights," which included the right of various subcommittees to review a single bill simultaneously. This "multiple referral" system resulted in an increase in political infighting for influence over tax legislation.

The proliferation of issues following the rise of subcommittees is reflected in the number of votes in Congress itself. In the Eighty-sixth Congress (1959–60) there were 180 roll-call votes in the House, .7 per day the House was in session. In 1969–70 there were 443 votes, 1.3 per work day. But in 1979–80 there were 1,276 roll-call votes, 3.9 per day; by 1993–94 the total had reached 4.2 votes per legislative day. In the Senate, roll-call votes likewise rose from 1.5 in 1959–60 to 3 in 1979–80, although the number has declined somewhat since 1990 (Ornstein, Mann, and Malbin 1994, pp. 153–157).

The subcommittee system substantially reduced the ability of powerful committee chairs to make good on legislative promises. As one veteran lobbyist (quoted in Easterbrook 1984, p. 61) said in the mid-1980s, "There used to be two to five guys on each side [House and Senate] who had absolute control over any category of bills you might want. All you had to do was get to them. Now getting the top guys is no guarantee. You have to lobby every member of every relevant subcommittee and even the membership at large."

Finally, the difficulty of long-term contracting has grown as the role of nonelected congressional employees has increased over the years. The number of committee employees ballooned from fewer than 400 in 1946 to more than 3,000 in 1980. A significant portion of the increase occurred during the 1970s; increases thereafter have been relatively slight (Ornstein, Mann, and Malbin 1994, p. 127). Along with the growth in numbers, according to some members of Congress, has come a corresponding growth in the influence of these nonelected officials. According to one report (Congressional Quarterly 1982, p. 477), "The growing impact that committee staff is having on legislation has become a subject of concern. There is a feeling among some members [of Congress] that too many decisions are getting away from the persons that were elected to make them." To a considerable extent, the growth of staff is itself due to the desire to diffuse power previously held by the committee chairs. When the subcommittee structure was imposed in the 1970s, for example, each subcommittee chair and each ranking minority member were authorized to hire a staff person for subcommittee work. In the Senate, staff increases were ordered in response to complaints from junior senators, who wanted some of the same help their more senior incumbents had.

Like the rise of the subcommittee system, greater staff numbers are blamed for the increase in the amount of legislation reviewed by committees (Congressional Quarterly 1982, p. 483). An increase in the number of bills, of course, introduces new sources of uncertainty into any long-term promise to provide tax or other sorts of legislative benefits. The uncertainty is particularly pronounced when some of the provisions will embody policy innovations from nonelected staff who cannot legally be paid directly for any legislative promises. The independent role of congressional staffers in whatever legislation results is reflected in lobbyists' increased attention to staff members in addition to elected officials. As one lobbyist, a former administrative assistant to Senator Daniel Inouye, put it, "Until recently many Congressmen played active roles in the legislative detail work. Now they can't. Nobody can. The staff does the detail work, and so you must lobby the staff" (quoted in Easterbrook 1984, p. 75).

Given the advantages of contractual durability to all parties, the mid-1970s collapse of the congressional committee system that had previously facilitated long-term contracting is interesting. Essentially, it entailed the decentralization of power—and, undoubtedly, of the rewards from having power—from a few powerful committee heads to more of the congressional membership at large, followed by rapid expansions in the roles of nonelected congressional staffs. The resulting redistribution of power inevitably has implications for the future of tax deals. If the restructuring of Congress was a onetime event, the flurry of new tax contracts that resulted in the late 1970s and the 1980s may also prove to be a onetime affair. But as the Republicans move into the majority positions on congressional committees, it remains uncertain whether the Democratic-instigated arrangements of the past will continue to govern Congress.

Increasing External Complexity

The decline in legislator tenure and the proliferation of internal congressional changes in the 1970s necessarily created doubt about the likelihood that legislators would perform on longer-term contracts. Another factor that increased the risks associated with long-term deals, and so reduced their number (all other things being equal), was the change in the ways private interests could contract for rent extraction rather than expropriation. The changes were instigated by Congress itself, in the election-law changes voted in the mid-1970s (though altered subsequently by the Supreme Court, in *Buckley v. Valeo,* 424 U.S. 1 [1976]). These changes made longer-term tax deals less attractive to politicians by creating the system, described in Chapter 3, whereby payments to politicians were increasingly arranged by and channeled through large regional or national political action committees (PACs). But the establishment of the new PAC system has taken time. Since the mid-1970s, the new system of PAC-driven contributions has groped slowly toward a new equilibrium in contracts between politicians and private citizens.

The disequilibrium created by the election-law changes has obvious implications for the kinds of political contracts that will be written and the risks that they entail. To a politician contemplating deals with private interests that are binding into the future, a principal disadvantage is the possibility that other interests will later emerge and offer more money for a conflicting deal. To the extent that new private interests are expected to emerge tomorrow with cash in hand, politicians will want to preserve their legislative flexibility by making only shorter-term contracts today.

In fact, growth in the number of payors for legislative favors has been very large, particularly since the legislative changes concerning campaign funding in the 1970s. From 1950 through 1967, the number of registered lobbyists was practically unchanged, growing from 430 to 449. By 1984, however, lobbyists numbered about 6,000. Just a year later, with the clouds of tax change gathering, the figure jumped to 8,000. By mid-1994 the number of registered lobbyists had risen to almost 12,000.

Vigorous growth of PACs has paralleled that of lobbyists, although that growth has slowed. The number of corporate political action committees grew from 89 in 1974 to 1,206 in 1980. The number peaked at 1,795 in 1990 and has since declined slightly, to 1,660 in 1994. But corporate PACs account for less than half the total number. The annual counts for corporate and all PACs are shown in Figure 5.2.

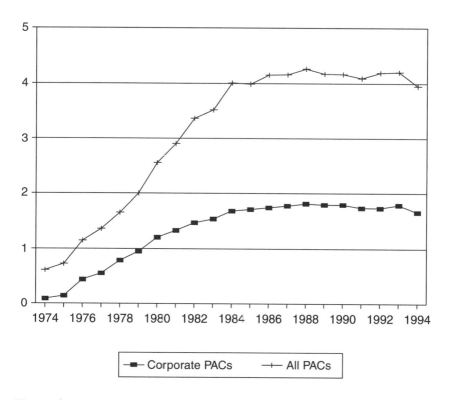

Figure 5.2 Number of PACs (in thousands) annually, 1974–1994
(*Source*: Federal Election Commission, "PAC count—1974 to Present," January 9, 1995)

The figure shows the gradual adjustment to the introduction of the new election-finance laws, as measured by the creation of new institutions to contract with politicians. The legislative changes of the 1970s reduced the advantages to concluding long-term deals with politicians, and so represented yet another reason for the decline in those deals' durability. The data show, however, that the adjustment period is ending, at least insofar as the previous years' legislation is concerned. But election-finance "reform" is a now-perennial item on both Democrats' and Republicans' list of campaign promises. Whether any stability will actually ensue, following the adjustment to the last wave of election-law "reforms," is very much up in the air.

Conclusion

An old saying holds that "an old tax is a good tax" (Cooper 1985, p. 725). However true this may be of taxes, longer contracts *not* to be taxed are certainly good things. The same holds for any rent-extraction contract that avoids even greater expropriation of private wealth.

But in the tax domain at least, durable political contracts are increasingly rare. The problem does not seem to be intentional breach of contract, although the possibilities for political opportunism are always there and undoubtedly sometimes seized. But the risks of longer-term tax deals have risen, perhaps irreversibly. Impossibility of political performance is certainly a perennial concern. Another real difficulty has become the increasing complexity—both inside and outside Congress—that diminishes politicians' ability and desire to deliver long-term deals. In particular, the growing internal complexity in committee structures and personnel and the growth in numbers of organized pressure groups externally create incentives for more short-term arrangements.

Were contracting costless, the problem of repeated short-term deals would be less worrisome. But the costs are important.

The basic point is quite simple. In the current institutional setting, where changes in the tax code are determined by the legislature, repeated efforts at "reform" create a situation in which tax shares are considered "up for grabs" in each and every budgetary period. As a result, the reform process becomes an annual contest among interest groups to preserve existing tax preferences, or to shift tax liabilities to other groups. Realtors, for example, find it necessary in every period to engage in socially wasteful lobbying efforts in defense of the deduction for mortgage interest payments. Similarly, the tobacco industry must continually work against attempts to raise the federal excise tax on its products, and there are frequent efforts by organizations representing individual taxpayers to raise the share of taxes paid by corporations. This list could go on.[23]

The election of Bill Clinton, who ran on an explicit platform of rewriting tax legislation, led to a predictable new set of tax contracts, the Omnibus Budget Reconciliation Act of 1993.[24] With the Democrats' 1970s committee system already in place and with the growth of PACs slowing, the Clinton legislation might conceivably have been the beginning of greater stability in tax contracts.

The elections of 1994, however, brought not only the loss of Ways and Means Chairman Rostenkowski but also a shift in parties controlling both the House and Senate tax committees. As Congressman Bill Archer and Senator Packwood assumed the key positions on the Ways and Means and Finance Committees, could there be any doubt that new tax legislation would soon be coming? Then Packwood himself suddenly was gone. How long is a tax contract with this Congress worth? Will the Republicans be in control long enough to deliver on any long-term arrangements, or will the 1994 election turn out to be like the 1952 blip on the Republican screen?

The Republicans are now in a position to make new tax deals. But as they inherit the system that has evolved in the past twenty-five years, there is no reason to think that their contracts will be any longer-term than those of their predecessors. Someday longer-term tax contracts may be written again. But at the moment the legislative disruptions of the 1970s and 1980s seem symptomatic of longer-run trends by which relatively durable tax contracts are becoming a historical curiosity.

III

EXTENSIONS

6

Extraction and Optimal Taxation: Excises, Earmarked Taxes, and Government User Charges

> Excise—A hateful tax levied upon commodities, and adjudged not by the common judges of property, but [by] wretches hired by those to whom excise is paid.
>
> —SAMUEL JOHNSON

With rent extraction itself now modeled and demonstrated, it is useful to consider the implications of the model in other realms of economics. This chapter discusses some ramifications of rent extraction for the economics of various forms of government taxation.

Perhaps overly simplistically, economic discussions of taxation can be broken into two principal groups. The first is concerned with the maximization of government revenue, a subject that used to be known as "camaralistics" (Tullock 1974b, p. 19). The subject is naturally complex, involving in part difficult estimations of short- and long-run elasticities of various sorts, the difference between the two reflecting in part the ability of the populace to avoid taxes. Also crucial is the tradeoff between current taxation and subsequent growth: expropriations today lower the amount of amount of wealth producible tomorrow, thus the size of the future tax base, and so ultimately the amount of tax tomorrow.

More modern public-finance analysis has tried to integrate taxation into more general concepts of welfare economics. Rather than treating government tax revenues as an end in themselves, the more modern approach sees taxation as a means toward solving other problems entrusted to government, such as reducing externalities or financing optimal production of public goods. Avoidance of taxation's deadweight losses are a principal concern in the welfare model, along with definition of optimal rates and tax bases. Distributional concerns ("tax incidence") are likewise a prominent issue. But many of the same questions studied in the revenue-maximization ("camaralistic") model are raised also in the welfare model, despite differences in the two models' maximands. For example, the welfare model also is critically concerned with elasticities and their changes over time.

Recently the welfare model has been criticized on several grounds. First, it has treated those taxed as passive payors rather than as active, rational avoiders (that is, avoiding taxes up to the point where the benefits of avoidance equal the costs), a point better understood by students of camaralistics.[1] Similarly, the standard welfare model has been criticized for failing to integrate the lessons of public-choice economics into study of the tax-legislation process, meaning that the deadweight losses of seemingly optimal taxation are underestimated (for example, Lee and Tollison 1988; Ramseyer 1993). As Mark Ramseyer (1993, p. 475) accurately puts it, "The only good tax is an impossible tax," once the inevitability of tax politics is added to normative models of taxation efficiency. Finally, one powerful critique laments, the standard approach presents normative rather than positive models of taxation. "The orthodox analysis provides [no] understanding of observed fiscal process."[2]

Introduction of the rent-extraction phenomenon into orthodox models of taxation begins to address all three criticisms. Taxpayers' nonpassivity and demand for avoidance are at the heart of rent extraction by taxation. (So, of course, is politicians' nonpassivity.) Rent extraction imports basic public-choice notions of rational political choice into the world of taxation. And it focuses not just on the model itself but on predicting and explaining observed behavior.

Chapters 3 and 5 presented many examples of payments to politicians to avoid the ravages of taxation. This chapter discusses, more formally and in greater detail, the ways in which a rent-extraction perspective alters conventional views of optimal taxation, particularly excise taxes (including earmarked excises and government-imposed user fees). The ability of taxes to extract private wealth makes politicians' taxation power valuable to them. Necessarily, as well, the ability to use threats of taxation to extract private wealth means that politicians will systematically behave in ways better explained by personal gains to themselves rather than by the economic-welfare models of taxation.

In models of economic-welfare maximization, various forms of government intervention into private markets are typically accepted as necessary, even desirable. Perhaps the most prominent examples of such "legitimate" government intervention involve control of externalities and government production of certain goods and services (so-called public goods). For both, the rationale for government intervention is often lower costs, particularly reduced transaction costs, when government rather than private individuals is responsible for certain transactions. In theory, excise taxes may offer a cheaper alternative to individual contracts or legal actions for controlling externalities; likewise, government production in some markets (roads, for example) can lower the transaction costs associated with holdouts, free riding, and revelation of demand. But maximizing social welfare in either case requires that government impose prices, in the form of either taxes or user charges. Further, taxes and charges are often "earmarked," to be spent only for particular purposes.

The normative economic case for various forms of excises and user charges (whether or not earmarked) seems ironclad, as discussed below. However, the standard discussion of these charges makes assumptions of questionable validity. Most fundamentally, the standard model of user charges depends on government actors' behaving as would nongovernment producers in well-functioning private markets. Moreover, government officials are modeled as maximizing society's welfare, even if doing so detracts from their own well-being. These assumptions, it is now agreed, are generally inappropriate as bases for predicting government behavior.

Once politicians and bureaucrats are treated, like everyone else, as maximizers of their own (not "society's") welfare, certain other assumptions in the orthodox model of user charges are seen to be unwarranted as well. Much real-world government pricing behavior is manifestly inconsistent with the textbook discussion of excises and other user charges. Prices are not set according to cost, as in private markets, but in accordance with predictable political processes. One of these, creating artificially cheap benefits for some taxpayers but then holding them hostage, involves the same rent-extraction strategy analyzed in earlier chapters. When actual government pricing rather than the textbook model is taken into account, there can be no necessary inference that a system of government production with user charges increases societal welfare.

Another source of welfare loss from user charges is the loss entailed in using earmarked taxes. Earmarked taxes typically create a fund for subsequent, not current, expenditures. Once created, however, the fund becomes a hostage of politicians, who have the power to divert the fund to other purposes or to force intended beneficiaries to pay a second time for release of the escrowed funds. The same extraction strategy observed with private capital holders is used once earmarked funds are in existence.

The Standard Model of User Charges and Excises

The welfare economics of user charges is well understood (Due and Friedlander 1973, pp. 90–115; Atkinson and Stiglitz 1980, pp. 457–518) and needs no general explanation here. Certain goods (for example, highways, airports) may be produced more cheaply by government than by private suppliers. Most often, the advantage claimed for government production is government's ability to use its eminent-domain power to amass large holdings of land. The state's ability to take and pay compensation rather than negotiate over each parcel, as any private developer would be required to do, results in lower transaction costs, including avoidance of standard negotiation problems like holding out. When the state subsequently imposes charges for use of the public goods constructed, it recoups its investment in both land acquisition and facilities construction.[3]

Highway construction, for example, requires assembly of large plots of land. The transaction costs of inducing hundreds or thousands of sellers to convey their land may exceed the potential private profit of the project, creating in theory a role for government. First, the necessary resources are obtained by condemnation (eminent-domain) proceedings. Then, once the highway is built, user charges substitute for private prices in rationing the use of governmentally produced goods and services for which exclusion is possible (and thus desirable). Like prices in private markets, governmental prices optimally would be set according to marginal cost.[4] Often user charges are earmarked for special funds that are held for periodic replacement of capital assets that depreciate over time (Buchanan 1963). For example, the highway trust fund (financed by gasoline taxes) exists to disburse funds for road construction. The airport trust fund, financed by the tax on airline tickets, was created to finance airport and related construction.

The orthodox theory of excise taxation is similar to that of user fees. In principle, the classic excise tax is supposed to force private producers to internalize costs (for example, pollution) that would otherwise be external and so not taken into account.[5] More recently, relying on a variant of the classic argument, legislatures have increasingly imposed excises to force consumers to reduce consumption of items (for example, tobacco, alcohol) whose social costs supposedly are not taken into account optimally.[6] But either way, both types of excise are fundamentally just forms of user charges. A pollution tax forces private producers to pay more for the air or water they use and so produce at the appropriate rate, although the compensation is paid to the government rather than to the owner of the resources used. The same is true for tobacco and alcohol, which supposedly are using up productive human capital at an inappropriate rate. (The discussion of excises henceforth refers only to taxes on production activities like pollution, but the argument relating to consumption activities would be complementary.)

Government's task in the orthodox externality model is exactly the same as if it owned the resource (air, water) itself: to impose the correct user's fee. Excise taxes are justified by the same rationale offered for direct government production of goods and services: the transaction costs of excise taxes are supposedly lower than those of individual contracts or lawsuits by private owners compelling compensation for the use of their resources. Like user fees, excise taxes are to be set according to (external) marginal cost. One can therefore speak generally of "user fees" as referring both to excises and to charges for governmentally produced goods and services.

While the general model of user fees (charges or excises) is well understood, two points merit emphasis. First, the welfare case for such fees depends on government's setting the optimal price, as illustrated by Figure 6.1. Suppose that private producers' marginal cost of constructing some

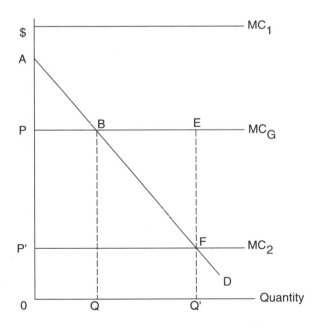

Figure 6.1 User charges and social welfare

good like highways is prohibitive, relative to what users would pay for it: at MC_1, no highways are profitable, since demand D is at every point less than the cost of construction. No highways will be built privately. If government can produce more cheaply, say at MC_G, and it charges P for access to the roads, societal welfare increases by the area of consumer surplus, ABP.[7]

However, if government underprices the public good, it is not necessarily true that public provision increases social welfare. Suppose that although the true resource costs of government production are MC_G, the good is actually priced at P'. Users will purchase Q' of the item, paying only $OP'FQ'$ for resources that actually are worth $OPEQ'$. The welfare loss of BEF from underpricing is greater than the gain, ABP, available when government prices correctly. It would be better not to have the good produced at all, despite consumer willingness to pay a price that would cover the true costs of government's producing it.[8]

In other words, even if government production costs are lower than those of private production, one cannot know whether government provision of goods and services not produced by private markets is desirable, without knowing whether the prices charged are allocatively correct. But in fact many government user fees are suboptimal. Goods and services for which government could charge fees are provided "free" and funded instead out of general revenues.

This is notably true of local government services, such as libraries and city parks. In some cases, like libraries, marginal costs (including congestion costs) may be close to zero over the relevant range. But fixed costs are positive, and the ability to exclude would permit charging a fixed fee for access. Yet such fees typically are not charged. Entry to many national parks likewise is free, although admission fees could easily be charged. Even when prices are charged, they often are conspicuously suboptimal.

> Granted, goods produced from the forests and Yellowstone National Park already entail user fees, ranging from livestock grazing rights to campground and park entrance charges. But these fees are very low compared to [those for] similar activities in the private domain. People are willing to spend $15.00 to $27.50 for a daily ski lift ticket, yet the entrance fee to Yellowstone is now $10.00 for one vehicle for a seven-day stay at the park, raised in 1988 from $5.00. The fee charged for livestock grazing on federal land was recently raised from $1.35 to $1.54 for an animal unit month, still only about one-third of that charged on comparable private land. (Leal 1990, p. 41)

Other examples of suboptimal pricing abound. The existence of limited-access toll roads in several states (as well as similar highways in countries like France and Italy) indicates that a system of direct highway user fees is workable. Yet access to federal highways does not require payment of a fee. Indeed, the Clinton administration itself is calling for greater privatization of highways, supposedly necessary in order to begin charging users for highways (Tolchin 1993). Meat and poultry producers are not charged for federal grading and inspection by the Department of Agriculture, although a fee could easily be levied. The same is true of new drug approvals by the Food and Drug Administration. Litigants are not charged for the use of the courts, including the time costs of judges and juries, although the parallel system of private arbitration illustrates how easily a pricing system could be put into effect.

There are at least three important sorts of welfare loss associated with such undercharging. The first, already noted above, is the overconsumption of valuable resources. As Donald Leal (1990, p. 41) notes of national parks, "underpricing goods on our public lands encourages overconsumption of resources. Hunting pressure on public lands during the deer and elk seasons grows steadily, as more hunters pursue dwindling numbers of animals." The second welfare loss stems from the queuing and related deadweight losses entailed in getting access to the underpriced goods and services. "Arbitrarily low user fees force people to compete for goods through means other than prices. In public campgrounds, this means waiting in long lines or making reservations months in advance" (ibid.). And, third, making up revenue shortfalls from general revenues necessarily produces welfare losses in the excess burdens from the additional taxes required.

The standard model of government excises and user fees fails to account for the repeated instances of underpricing observed. This aspect of the taxation process has puzzled analysts who work with a public-interest, welfare model of excise taxes. Excise taxes have seemed "too low," given the supposed externalities invoked to justify them. The common justification for "sin" taxes on goods like alcohol and tobacco, for example, is the claim that consumption of such goods imposes costs on others. At the same time, it is said that when government imposes excises to reduce externalities from consumption of such goods, the tax rates are systematically too low.[9]

So, why does government systematically misprice? The few accounts that acknowledge that government charges incorrect prices typically ascribe the problem to human error due to a lack of information about the correct price, as it would be registered in private markets.[10] This seems an unlikely explanation, however: in many markets government production competes directly with privately produced goods and services and continues to underprice them. In education, for example, government underprices public schools and funds the revenue shortfalls out of general property taxes. Likewise, government takeover of services provided privately, like fire protection and municipal transportation, results in charges that are insufficient to cover costs, with deficits being funded out of general revenues (for example, West 1967; Pashigian 1976; McChesney 1986). Lack of information can hardly explain underpricing in those cases.[11]

User Fees and Political Gains

The inability of the orthodox model of user fees to explain these phenomena lies in its treatment of political incentives. In the private-market paradigm, it is producers' desire to maximize their profits that drives them to produce the appropriate quantity and sell it at the optional price. Individual gain—Adam Smith's invisible hand—aligns producers' personal rewards with social-welfare objectives. Producers likewise bear the costs of their incorrect price and output decisions.

But once government enterprise replaces private ownership, producers who price efficiently (that is, so as to maximize collective welfare) are no longer rewarded; those who operate inefficiently do not bear the costs of so doing. The orthodox model of user fees fails to take this distinction into account. Standard analyses maintain that, in intervening in or replacing private markets, government "seeks to ensure that firms produce at socially desirable levels," as opposed to private firms, "which seek to produce at their profit-maximizing levels" (Due and Friedlander 1973, p. 97). But there is little incentive for public producers to strive for efficiency or greater social welfare. The politician or bureaucrat who sells Q units at price P cannot keep the profits or social gains he creates; nor does he suffer the losses caused by producing too many units, Q', at too low a price, P'. Nor are there any important constitutional constraints on politicians' decisions how to finance production.[12] With no personal incentives to be efficient, politicians and bureaucrats should not be expected to produce and price optimally.

It is inconsistent, in other words, to treat economic actors as public-spirited while in government but as self-interested outside it. A more consistent and more persuasive model would view economic actors in both situations as motivated by their own welfare. And in fact the self-interest of government actors helps to explain the frequent underpricing of governmentally produced goods and services noted above.

One item of benefit to politicians is votes. Voters will favor those politicians who deliver more benefits to them. Again referring to Figure 6.1, consider two candidates with opposing stands on the operation of a public enterprise. Candidate A, the incumbent, has favored a policy of pricing at P, thus selling Q of the item produced and leaving net consumer benefits of ABP. Candidate B instead promises to lower prices to P', increasing output to Q'. The benefits to consumers of the product rise to AFP'. Thus, intensely interested users of the product will vote for Candidate B. Taxpayers as a whole, including nonusers, must make up the revenue shortfall PEFP', so the politician must design the system so that there will be more consumer-users who vote for the politician than there are general taxpayers who might vote against him.

But taxpayers generally will have little reason to vote against a politician for underpricing. The cost of inefficient pricing imposed on the individual taxpayer is vanishingly small—what is the individual cost to the hundreds of millions who do not ski in Yellowstone to have a few thousand skiers admitted cheaply? With the benefits of underpricing concentrated on a small but intensely interested group, and with the costs diffused over a vast and largely uninterested group, government goods and services predictably would be systematically underpriced.

Thus, empirically, underpricing is found to be the rule. As Sam Peltzman (1971) observed, prices charged for government-produced electricity and for alcoholic beverages (in states where liquor prices are government controlled) are systematically lower than prices charged by private enterprises.[13] The role of politics in underpricing government services can also be seen in the different prices charged voters in different jurisdictions. As Peltzman (1971, p. 114) noted, "Government enterprises may sell to non-voters. If these enterprises benefit voters to secure political support, there is no reason to expect them to benefit non-voters. Therefore, prices should generally be higher to non-voters than to voters." This prediction, too, is borne out empirically. Michael Maloney, Robert McCormick, and Robert Tollison (1984) have examined public-utility prices for electricity and found that prices are higher to customers outside the political jurisdictions in which the utilities are located.

Underpricing of governmentally produced goods and services is useful not just to politicians but also to bureaucrats responsible for administering or selling government output.[14] Low prices ensure that too much of the product, Q' rather than Q, will be produced and sold, necessitating larger bureaucratic budgets and more personnel (Niskanen 1971; Lindsay 1976). Controlling queuing and rationing output in nonprice ways also require greater manpower and therefore larger budgets. So does the need for new taxes in other markets to make up revenue shortfalls when user fees for a particular good or service are too low. Thus civil servants are frequently among the most ardent supporters of government, rather than private, production.[15]

In short, whether government enterprise financed by user charges really is optimal depends on fulfillment of two necessary conditions. Government must be a lower-cost producer than a private enterprise would be, and user charges must be set optimally. But there is good reason *a priori* to expect that the second necessary condition will not be fulfilled. Politicians and their bureaucratic agents face predictable incentives to underprice the goods and services produced by government; examples of suboptimal user charges are ubiquitous. The result is overconsumption of valuable physical resources, waste of valuable consumer time, and deadweight excess-burden losses from the additional taxes needed to compensate for underpricing. Even if one assumes that government is in some cases a lower-cost producer, the inefficiency of its user-charge policies negates any inference that, overall, society is better off when government produces and prices by user fees.

Potential for Political Extortion

The overriding lesson of the rent-extraction process discussed in earlier chapters is that politicians are interested in any stock of immobile capital or wealth from which they can extract a share. The target of expropriation might be the rent triangle representing flows of future returns to already-invested capital, which can be threatened with price controls; or the stock of capital amassed by families like the Gallos, which can be threatened with taxation. *Any* source of wealth, broadly defined, is subject to political threats of expropriation.

This lesson also applies to the process of government pricing. It has already been shown that user fees will systematically be set at suboptimal levels, with the result that government enterprise may have costs (BEF in Figure 6.1) exceeding benefits. But underpricing is not the only predictable source of welfare loss stemming from government user charges. Once a suboptimal price like P' has been set, two other avenues of gain for politicians open up. Both involve extortion of some of the consumer gains that suboptimal prices initially present. As in the examples in earlier chapters, the amounts extorted are not mere transfers but entail additional deadweight losses.

Extortion of Current Gains

In Figure 6.1, underpricing gives consumers of the particular good or service a net gain, measured by PBFP'. The discussion in the previous section treated this area as a simple transfer to users from taxpayers generally. Once the suboptimal user charge is in place, however, an awareness of the basic rent-extraction strategy would lead one to predict that politicians will threaten beneficiaries of the suboptimal prices. Underpricing means that politicians can threaten to reduce the size of benefit area PBFP' by increasing user charges. Higher user charges would flow into the Treasury, to be used by all politicians; payments made to politicians personally *not* to increase fees may well be more attractive. Rather than suffer loss of benefits, beneficiaries will pay a portion of them over to politicians not to impose the higher (optimal) user charges. A portion of the consumer gains is thereby lost, with real resources being expended in the process. What looks like a transfer from one group of taxpayers to another actually would include transfers to politicians themselves, with all the other deadweight costs associated with rent extraction generally.

The prediction turns out to be correct. Politicians do underprice and then allow themselves to be dissuaded by beneficiaries from raising the prices, in effect converting Treasury revenues into personal allowances. Consider again private use of national forest and national park resources. Invariably, attempts to price these resources more correctly meet with powerful political resistance from users. "Until modest fee hikes in 1986 and 1987, the weekly fee per vehicle for Yellowstone Park had been stuck at $2.00 since 1916. When the intention to raise fees in 1986 was announced, there was protest from local merchants and several local recreation groups" (Leal 1990, p. 42). Users of underpriced federal grazing lands are important lobbyists and supporters of friendly politicians who keep prices low. Similarly, the American Meat Institute has been active in lobbying to defeat proposals for a user charge to cover the cost of government meat and poultry inspections (Jaroslovsky 1989). Most health companies "and their lobbyists" fought Bush administration attempts to inaugurate user fees for FDA inspections (Palefsky 1990).

The mention of "lobbyists'" involvement in the political process indicates politely what goes on when users oppose higher (or even positive) prices. Protests against charging or raising user fees are not registered just by letter. Access to politicians—a scarce good, after all—is purchased by contributions. If politicians threaten to raise prices for timber lands or ski areas from P' to P, reflecting government's true costs MC_G, private beneficiaries would pay up to PBFP' rather than have user fees increased.

In other words, politicians have an incentive other than vote-seeking to keep user fees too low: the ability to profit later by threatening to raise them. Politicians who price optimally at P gain nothing thereby. But politicians who price suboptimally then have something of value—continuation of artificially cheap government goods and services—for which users will pay. The lower the user fee set, the greater the personal benefits available to politicians to keep fees low. Moreover, the payments to keep user fees low benefit politicians *personally;* a true user fee would go into general revenues, where the politician has far less control over its subsequent use.

These payments do not represent simple transfers from citizen taxpayers to politicians. Buying lower taxes and user fees requires labor inputs (lobbyists, lawyers), the opportunity costs of whose time are relatively high. Specific investments that are vulnerable to subsequent extortion will not be made in the first place. These opportunity costs must be added to the other costs of user fees.

Extortion of Future Funds

Recognition of politicians' rent-extraction opportunities forces realization that there is yet another cost, heretofore unappreciated, in user-fee systems. That cost involves threats of extorting earmarked funds collected from users. Earmarking establishes a fund that, like the rent triangle or the Gallo personal fortune, is "up for grabs" because politicians can later threaten it.

Superficially, earmarking seems a simple and attractive way to solve a rent-seeking problem. That problem stems from the fact that revenues paid into the Treasury are not allocated to any particular use, and so will cause rent seekers to expend costly resources in attempts to have the funds allocated to themselves. As Dwight Lee (1985, p. 732) has noted,

> The claimants against revenues raised by market prices are generally well-specified, as is the extent of their claims. This is not true with revenue raised by government through political prices. Additional

monies raised by government generally go into the common pool of general revenue. The allocation of these revenues among rival interests is determined through competition for political influence, a competition which requires the use of real resources. To a large extent this represents pure waste, since what is being motivated is zero-sum, rather than positive-sum, competition.

Lee concludes that "the setting within which the distribution of political benefits is determined will typically motivate a significant amount of resource dissipation, rather than resource transfer, and will therefore be waste" (ibid.).

In the orthodox model of user fees, the charges actually paid are treated as transfers to the Treasury. In Figure 6.1, for example, the sum OP'FQ' is the amount paid into general revenues for use of the good or service produced by government. (This is true regardless of whether the price set by government is optimal or suboptimal.) Those revenues are therefore subject to the sort of special-interest competition that Lee describes, although the exact fraction of the sum OP'FQ' that will be dissipated by rent seeking among private interests is difficult to specify *ex ante*.

Socially wasteful competition among transfer seekers explains the apparent social value of tax earmarking. One seemingly could avoid the deadweight losses of general contention for revenues out of the Treasury by earmarking the revenues for specific uses. Earmarking of revenues for some specific future use, like road or airport construction, would keep user charges out of the common pool (that is, the general Treasury). Therefore, earmarked taxes and user charges seemingly would prevent competing rent seekers from obtaining access to the earmarked funds, and so avoid the wasteful dissipation that typifies competition for general revenues.

But the apparent advantage of earmarking is in fact illusory. As was discussed in Chapter 5 concerning taxation generally, it is simply impossible to achieve political durability for any system involving government revenues. Earmarking revenues for some future use gives the supposed beneficiaries no enforceable property rights in those funds. The money is subject to subsequent political expropriation every day the legislature is in session. Defining property rights in some future recipient(s) may defeat rent seeking by other claimants, but only at the expense of creating a pool of future payments to those recipients. The stock of money from which those future payments will come is no different from the rent triangle: as always, it can be extracted politically.

Consider the Social Security system. It is funded by an earmarked payroll tax imposed on employers and employees, ultimately for return as retirement benefits to employees.[16] Over time the fund has grown to enormous proportions, much of it used to meet current obligations but some being held for the future. Currently, "contributions" to Social Security run billions of dollars more than payments to retirees; statutory amendments in 1977 and 1983 raised payroll taxes gradually so as to create an estimated $3 *trillion* reserve by the year 2020 (Porter 1990; see also Roberts 1990). At various other times in the past also, the Social Security system has run large surpluses that created a fund to be held for future needs.

And so throughout its history, as the rent-extraction model would predict, the fund created by the earmarked Social Security taxes has been imperiled by attempts to shift part of the revenues to other uses, threats often described as "borrowing" from the fund. In the early 1970s, for example, Congress considered using Social Security operating surpluses to create a new fund providing loans for college students. Indeed, by law the surpluses must be invested in U.S. government obligations, meaning that the surplus is already being used to fund the budget deficit, and thus other government programs. Creating new obligations like government loans and then using Social Security surpluses to fund them would really be just an accounting transfer on Uncle Sam's books.

But the Social Security fund has never run current surpluses like those expected to accumulate into the twenty-first century. The specter of truly large extractions is thus inescapable. The implications of the huge pool of money, under direct congressional control, in fact have not gone unnoticed. To stave off expropriations, there are frequent calls, by both Republicans and Democrats, for payment of the surpluses into private pension funds, or even for full privatization of fund contributions, by which government-mandated contributions would be made into private funds rather than the Social Security system (Bell 1990; Greene 1990). Supporters list as one advantage the fact that "[i]ndividuals could count on their Social Security taxes being there for them on retirement—a certainty they do not enjoy now, when the money is at the mercy of Congress's spending proclivities" (Porter 1990). As a member of the House Appropriations Committee himself has warned, "it is extremely doubtful that future Congresses would allow a $3 trillion reserve to accumulate untouched" (ibid.).

State-worker pension funds have had similar problems, fighting off state politicians who want to promote pork-barrel investment in local "public

© 1990 by Herblock in the *Washington Post*.

works." As one report (White 1989) notes, institutional investors have become increasingly worried about state legislators' attempts to subsidize public works by requiring pension funds to invest in projects that are popular politically but not yield-maximizing.

> In recent years, public pension funds have been under growing pressures to practice "social investing." That's where pension funds direct some of their money to promote local economic development or other social goals. Popular social investments include home-mortgage programs and local venture capital. The Council of Institutional Investors . . . said such subsidies at the expense of pensioners became more likely if politicians got greater control over pension funds . . . That suspicion is shared by others in the pension industry. Politicians "are interested in closing the budget deficit with public pension assets," [one pension consultant] said in a recent speech.

Some weeks later it was reported that Maryland and Kentucky had "become the latest states to propose using public pension funds for small-business creation. Maryland lawmakers want public pension funds to finance a $15 million venture-capital pool for start-ups" (Gupta 1990).

Of course, none of this would be a problem if pension funds set aside for the benefit of workers performed as well when they were pressured to invest money in certain politically desired "social" ways. But then again, if such investments performed as well as any other, there would be no need for the political pressure on investors in the first place. Thus, one systematically finds state pension funds placed in "social" investments (frequently dubbed "social" only because the investment recipients are in-state) with lower rates of return and embarrassing losses.

> In 1990 the Alaska public employees and teachers retirement system funded loans of 35% of assets ($165 million) to make mortgages in the state. When oil prices fell in 1986, so did home prices and 40% of loans became delinquent or were foreclosed. In the late 1980s the Kansas Public Employees Retirement System was held up as a model for its ambitious ["social"] investments. KPERS has since written off $200 million in ["social"] investments. In 1989 the Connecticut State Trust Funds invested $25 million in Colt Manufacturing Co. to save 1,000 jobs. In 1992 Colt filed for bankruptcy, endangering the whole investment . . . By order of the Missouri Legislature, the Missouri State Employees' System used about 3% of its assets to put

venture capital into small companies in Missouri. Three years and $5 million later, the program was terminated because of unsatisfactory returns and two lawsuits.[17]

Undeterred by the poor results from systematic invasion of state workers' pension funds, President Clinton's secretary of labor has been beating the drum for federal efforts to increase the amount of pension funds' "social" investing (Saxton 1994).

Similar problems beset other earmarked funds. Dan Rostenkowski, the former chairman of the House Ways and Means Committee, proposed the diversion of revenues from the gasoline tax, under current law earmarked for road projects, to various other programs, especially education (Birnbaum 1990). Until Congress banned such levies, municipalities owning airports taxed airline tickets and earmarked the revenues for airport construction and maintenance, but then diverted the funds to other city projects like sewers (Wessell and McGinley 1990). Proposals to start charging user fees for FDA inspections, earmarked for the support of just that function, elicit industry fears even among fee supporters that fees would be "used as a bait-and-switch tactic for other interests such as purchasing B-1 bombers."[18]

Attempts abroad to use special funds run into the same difficulties. Deepak Lal (1993, p. 55) writes, for example, about the experience of underdeveloped countries heavily dependent on exports in using currency reserve funds to buffer exchange-rate shocks:

> One way for the government to insulate itself from the incipient crises that the periodic collapse in export prices generates is to put some of the revenues at good times in foreign financial assets (reserves) to be used to finance fiscal expenditures when times are bad. But for most third-world states this has proved virtually impossible because of the pressures that arise for the State to spend the windfalls, most often by hiring the relatives of its retainers.

The point is simple but fundamental. Just as no person has complete property rights in private capital or wealth—it can always be taken by the state, or its taking threatened unless payments of some part of it are forthcoming—so a public earmarked fund can never truly be the property of its supposed beneficiaries. What is earmarked for one use today can always be diverted to competing uses tomorrow. Realizing this, competing rent seekers invest resources to facilitate such diversions. Then the supposed owners of the funds—pensioners, airport authorities—must compete for the right to receive "their" funds, or else lose them. Even when those to whom the funds were promised actually get to keep some of them, they do not get 100 cents on the dollar. Part of the difference is in the rents extracted by politicians.

Indeed, politicians can practice rent extraction via earmarking even without competition by other groups for the funds. Once deposited in the Treasury as earmarked for future use, politicians may simply refuse to release funds to their supposed beneficiaries without socially wasteful (but personally lucrative) lobbying. Consider the federal trust fund, created with earmarked taxes, to finance the construction of airports and related projects. As the demand for these projects has risen, Congress has simply refused to keep its promise to release the money to finance them. "The trust fund has an uncommitted balance of $7 billion, infuriating airlines, passenger associations and others who want the money spent on aviation projects" (Wessell and McGinley 1990). The supposed beneficiaries of the fund have had to organize several groups to lobby Congress for use of the money as it was intended. As one lobbying group has written,

> Every time you or I fly, we pay an 8% surcharge [now increased to 10 percent] or "ticket tax" to the federal Airport and Airway Trust Fund. By law, Congress has pledged to spend these funds to improve our air travel system. But Congress has failed to keep its promise and more than six billion dollars in unspent transportation taxes sit idle, while safety and capacity projects go unfunded . . . The simple fact of the matter is we pay this ticket tax and we elect our Senators. That gives us the right to demand our tax dollars be used for the purpose for which the tax was created—to improve our air transportation system.[19]

In other words, earmarking cannot shield beneficiaries from congressional threats, nor do taxpayers or supposed beneficiaries have any remedy therefor. Earmarking, if durable, may segregate funds from rent seeking by others. But the supposed beneficiaries of the fund predictably will have to undertake the same kinds of lobbying and other wasteful tasks to obtain the fruits of the fund that private capital owners do. The allocative losses represented by having to repurchase one's own benefits are no different from those of rent seeking by others.

Finally, even when politicians are willing to let earmarked funds be spent for the promised purpose, there is considerable rent seeking among potential recipients of the funds. Earmarking rarely includes specification in advance as to who exactly will get the money or where it will be spent. Thus, potential beneficiaries invest resources to increase the chances that they will get the earmarked money, rather than someone else who also qualifies under the rules of the fund. Part of the difficulty for new airport construction, for example, is competition among politicians to have new projects assigned to their jurisdictions.[20]

Conclusion

The notion of lower-cost government production financed by user charges or of lower-cost government imposition of excises to correct externalities seems unobjectionable in principle. But lower-cost government intervention is only a necessary, not a sufficient, condition for efficiency. Government must also set prices correctly once it intervenes.

In the real world of government user charges, a world in which lucrative rent extraction is routinely practiced, this second requirement is systematically violated. User fees are frequently lower than they should be. As explained here, underpricing is quite rational politically. Politicians and bureaucrats gain little, if anything, from setting allocatively efficient prices. But they gain votes and monetary contributions from setting user charges inefficiently low. The result is overconsumption: both scarce physical resources and user time are wasted when government goods and services are underpriced. Excess burdens from the additional taxes imposed in other markets to cover revenue shortfalls increase the deadweight losses.

These problems have already been identified and studied elsewhere. Of greater importance here is the rent-extraction model's identification of a source of further welfare losses that arise when user fees are set too low. Politicians can and do subsequently threaten to raise user fees, resulting in lobbying and related rent-extracting costs to avoid imposition of the higher charges.

One superficially appealing solution to this problem is earmarking of taxes. Earmarking restricts future uses of tax or user revenues, and so would apparently limit the amount of rent seeking for those revenues. But earmarking entails its own problems. In particular, named future beneficiaries of earmarked taxes actually have no property right to them. Congress can always tax today for earmarked purposes but subsequently refuse to release the revenues unless new lobbying expenses are incurred and payments made. Several examples of this sort of political opportunism have been observed recently. Rent seeking among private contenders for general revenues is replaced by rent extraction by politicians from earmarked revenues.

In the end, then, the economics of user fees is much more complex than has been realized heretofore. The benefits of government production are straightforward and derive from a single source—savings in costs, typically transaction costs. But the indirect costs of reliance on government are considerably more subtle, deriving from several different sources. When the costs of overconsumption, queuing, excess burdens, extortion, and double payment for earmarked funds are all taken into account, there is much less reason for the generally sanguine attitude that economists take toward government production with financing via user charges.

7

Costs and Benefits
of Interest-Group Organization

A government which robs Peter to pay Paul can always depend on
the support of Paul.

—GEORGE BERNARD SHAW

Chapter 6 showed how viewing a familiar institution of public finance
(excise taxes and user fees) from a rent-extraction perspective can yield new
insights and result in better integration of observed phenomena into basic
models. This chapter examines an issue that has bedeviled the standard
economic theory of regulation from its Stiglerian beginnings—how and
why groups organize to obtain government action (that is, action by
politicians)—and presents some solutions offered by the rent-extraction
perspective.

In particular, this chapter investigates the familiar explanation for why
certain groups organize to bring political pressure to bear while others do
not. That explanation usually focuses on increasing free-riding problems
as groups grow larger. Producers are said to be winners from regulation
because, constituting a smaller group than consumers, they face less temptation to free ride. As will be seen, however, the free-riding problem is
neither a necessary nor a sufficient condition to explain interest-group
organization.

Organization in the Economic Theory of Regulation

The nature of political organization in the earliest rent-creating models of
government regulation (Stigler 1971; Posner 1974) was essential. A
group's being organized provided the impetus for regulation in the first
place. Government created rents for producers because they were well
organized, and so could deliver what politicians wanted (votes, money,
and so forth). So, to use the standard portrayal of rent-creating regulation
in Figure 7.1 (embellishing somewhat Figure 1.1), with constant-mar-
ginal-cost supply S, quantity Q_c will be sold at price OE without regula-

tion. If government can be induced to reduce outputs or to fix prices directly, Q_m will be produced and price will rise to OA.[1]

Regulation produces rents of up to ABHE, with price discrimination implicitly assumed to be prohibitively costly. At least some rents will be lost in producer competition for them, including transfers to politicians in payment for the rent-creating regulation. Politicians' personal gains are naturally a function of the rents they create: recipients will pay more for greater rents. (Competition among politicians in the field plus competition between incumbents and challengers for the field push politicians' returns toward competitive levels.)

In this seminal Stiglerian model, consumers are losers in the process because they are disorganized, and so just bystanders.[2] Organizing private groups to bid for surplus is of course costly, and so no interests—consumers or producers—are perfectly organized. But consumers would predictably be less organized. Mancur Olson (1965) had developed the reasons for and implications of consumers' lack of organization generally even before George Stigler posited the economic theory of regulation. Olson

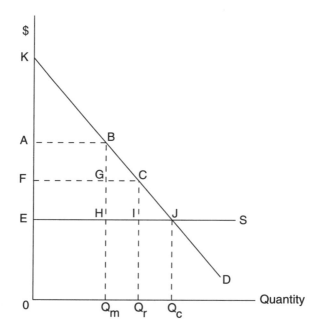

Figure 7.1 The Stigler-Peltzman model of regulation

(ibid., p. 166) noted that "consumers are at least as numerous as any other group in the society, but they have no organization to countervail the power of organized or monopolistic producers." Initially those developing the economic theory of regulation, including Stigler (1971, p. 21) himself, adapted some of Olson's insights about interest-group organization to explain aspects of regulation specifically.

The difference between consumer and producer organization does not arise because the total amount of consumer surplus potentially affected by regulation is less than the size of producer surplus. To the contrary, with deadweight welfare losses taken into account, consumers always lose more than producers gain (a point discussed further below). Rather, consumers' failure to organize fully is conventionally ascribed (for example, Peltzman 1976, p. 213) to free riding and related information-transaction costs. The number of parties who consume any given product typically exceeds the number who produce it, making the free-rider problem of organizing consumers into lobbying groups greater than that of organizing producers. No one consumer at the margin will have much, if any, impact on any political outcome, reducing to approximately zero her incentive to incur the costs (including the value of her time) of participating in any organization. And because their marginal impact is close to zero, consumers also have practically no incentive to incur the costs of informing themselves about the political debates.

This, then, is the point of departure in Sam Peltzman's (1976) and Gary Becker's (1983) amendments to the original Stigler model. To Peltzman and Becker, consumers are not bystanders at the regulatory auction. At the margin, their counterpreference for lower prices will force politicians to reduce the ultimate gains available to producers. As Peltzman (1989, p. 12) later summarized the Peltzman-Becker contributions,

> [The regulatory] equilibrium represents a balancing of marginal pressure exerted by winners and losers . . . The reason is simple: as the regulator moves output away from the efficient level, the deadweight loss increases at an increasing rate. (The marginal deadweight loss is the difference between the heights of the demand and supply function, which gets bigger the further the quantity is pushed from the efficient level.) Deadweight loss is nothing more than the winner's gain less the loser's loss from the regulation-induced change in output. These gains and losses are what motivate the competing pressures on the political process. So rising marginal deadweight loss must

progressively enfeeble the winners relative to the losers. The pressure the winners can exert for each extra dollar's gain must overcome steadily rising pressure from the losers to escape the escalating losses.

In other words, as shown in Figure 7.1, Becker-Peltzman consumers do not buy off the entire price increase that producers would want, from OE to OA, but they are able to buy off some of the increase, from OF to OA. Consumers would bid up to ABCF in order to push price from the proposed OA down to some intermediate level, OF. This amount is more than producers would pay (ABFG) for the increase to OA, but not as much as producers would pay (FCIE) for a partial increase from OE to OF. Hence the ultimate price in political equilibrium is the intermediate one, OF.

Consumers as Voters

There are obvious gaps in this amended model. First, there is no real consideration of exactly how the "pressure from the losers" is registered. That is, exactly what has changed between the Olson-Stigler and Peltzman-Becker world to allow consumer-losers to become players in the regulatory game? The answer originally given was "voting." Even in the Olson-Stigler model, the one thing that consumers demonstrably are willing and able to do is vote. Economists are not sure why individuals, as electors, rationally ignore or overcome the obvious free-rider problem in voting, but there can be no denying that many of them in fact do.

Thus, in the Peltzman-Becker model consumer pressure is registered indirectly, by voting. Consumers exert their power at the polls, giving voter-members increased influence over political outcomes "by changing the revealed 'preferences' of enough [other] voters and politicians" at the margin.[3] This aspect of the model was criticized, as Chapter 1 noted, on the grounds that politicians seek more than votes.[4] But it had the advantage, at the time, of at least introducing losers into the model without having to account very precisely for how they got there. Voting is an individual act, requiring no organization, and is something that consumers clearly do undertake. Introducing the consumer-voter into the economic theory of regulation thus entailed no important modification of the Olson-Stigler model.

But introduction of consumers as mere voters really only pushes the inquiry back a notch. Suppose that consumers really do enter the game only periodically, on election day. Why do they care enough to vote so as to keep prices at OF, but not enough to throw out the rascals who would raise prices above OE in the first place?

Free Riding and Consumer Organization

Modeling consumers as mere voters presents another problem. The usual Olson explanation—consumers face greater costs of organization because of free riding—is incomplete in the regulatory context. It depends solely on differential *costs* of organization between consumers and producers. But there may also be differential *benefits* to organizing. Once these differences in benefits are taken into account, it is seen that free riding by consumers is neither sufficient nor necessary for any tendency of producers to organize more completely than consumers.

Greater free riding by consumers is not sufficient to conclude that they will organize less, because the benefits to consumers from organizing may also be greater. *Ceteris paribus,* the benefits from organizing (the consumer surplus reclaimed) actually would increase as consumers move price back from OA to OF to OE. At each level of price reduction, the size of the surplus trapezoid reclaimed increases. If organization sufficient to hold prices only to OF is possible (that is, if OF is an equilibrium price), the costs of organizing must be not only increasing, but increasing faster than the rising benefits. No theoretical reason or empirical showing has been offered to justify a belief that consumers' organization costs increase faster than their benefits.

Indeed, under slightly different assumptions about production costs, the benefits to consumer organization are even greater than typically discussed. As compared to the constant marginal costs shown in Figure 7.1, let industry supply now be upward-sloping (probably the more common case to begin with). At a given moment, private producers have invested in various forms of physical, reputational, or other capital and have stocks of entrepreneurial ability. With producers owning substantial tangible and intangible capital, returns to those capital assets (quasi-rents) are represented by producers' surplus.

With upward-sloping supply, transfer of consumer surplus to producers through legally imposed higher prices is no less attractive to producers. But the opposite regulatory transfer, of producers' surplus to consumers, is now possible—and is frequently observed. Monopsonistically organized consumers are observed to achieve prices below marginal cost in regulated utility industries (Buchanan 1975; Wenders 1986b). In addition, politically generated transfers to consumers' surplus may come not just at the expense of producers but also at the expense of other consumers.[5] What-ever their differential free-riding problem, consumers are more likely to be organized as the benefits of organization increase. Larger stocks of pro-ducer surplus represent greater potential transfers to consumers, and so predictably will induce greater consumer organization.

In sum, free-riding explanations are insufficient to account for the lesser extent of consumer organization in the standard model of regulation. Even if consumers do face greater free-riding costs in organizing, the benefits of organization endogenous to the model can also be greater. In any given situation, free riding may well account for consumers' failure to organize as completely as producers, *ceteris paribus*. But free riding alone is an insufficient explanation when the benefits of organization rise along with the costs.

Nor is the free-riding rationale offered in the standard (Olson-Stigler) model of regulation a necessary condition for greater producer organiza-tion. There are exogenous benefits, unrelated to seeking surplus transfers, for which producers organize. Some of the benefits are personal—the chance to meet others who do the same thing for a living. But other benefits affect production itself. For example, organization permits beneficial information exchanges that reduce production costs; it facilitates development of industry codes, standards, and advertising campaigns that create brand-name producer capital and increase overall demand. By low-ering production costs and increasing demand, organized producers in-crease their net benefits from production. Consumers share too in the benefits of increased reputational capital and information exchange.

Private producer organization is therefore Pareto superior. Producers are benefiting, not by regulatory transfers from existing consumers' sur-plus, but by increasing the total amount of consumer and producer sur-plus. Producers create their own stocks of capital and thus their private rents, in effect by actually creating the demand curves they face. An industry with a reputation for fair dealing or a lengthy record of satisfying consumers faces a higher demand curve, *ceteris paribus*.

There are few (if any) analogous interdependencies among consumers that would allow organization to increase their private surplus. Consumer demand depends on factors that are beyond the control of consumers (for example, the price of substitutes and complements) or that are unaffected by the extent of organization (individual tastes). Consumption of a few items may entail interdependent utility functions, but examples of those phenomena (concerts, restaurants) are not numerous.[6] Moreover, even if one's consumption utility from a dinner or concert is greater when others also join in, joint consumption hardly requires long-lasting, dues-paying organizations; a few telephone calls usually suffice.

In short, just as consumer free riding and related organizational problems (costs) are not sufficient conditions to explain the greater extent of producer organization in the standard economic model of regulation, free-riding costs are also unnecessary for explaining consumers' relative lack of organization. The benefits of consumer organization are political only, such as lobbying for monopsony prices in government regulatory matters. Because producers reap both private and political advantage from organization, but consumers have only the latter benefit, producers will always be better organized than consumers. This is true, independent of any greater free-rider problem afflicting consumers.

Producers' greater organization to lower production costs has an important implication for the costs of lobbying, however. Once the fixed costs of organizing are sunk, producers can also lobby at lower marginal cost for transfers of others' surplus. Lobbying is a relatively inexpensive by-product (to use Olson's term) of organization for nonlobbying purposes. As Robert McCormick and Robert Tollison have noted,

> [Organization costs] are like start-up costs. Once they are borne, they do not affect marginal costs (though if the "firm" is to survive, they must be borne over time). Groups that have already borne these start-up costs, for reasons unrelated to lobbying, will have a comparative advantage in seeking transfers and will therefore be more successful in procuring transfers as a result. This is simply a point about jointness in production. Some groups will be able to produce political lobbying as a by-product of performing some other function, thereby avoiding start-up costs for lobbying. There are many examples of such groups in the economy, among which are labor unions, trade associations, corporations, and the like.[7]

This difference between producers and consumers, that is, lies not in their respective organization costs but in the difference between fixed and marginal costs for each group in the lobbying and nonlobbying activities they undertake. For producers, the fixed costs of organization have been incurred in prior periods, and the organizations thereby founded continue to provide benefits (exchanges of information and so forth) routinely. For consumers, the pro rata benefits of organization are fewer *ex ante,* and so the fixed costs of organizing are less frequently incurred. Then, as various regulatory issues affecting their welfare come along, producers are able to join the regulatory auction as a by-product (that is, to spread their past fixed costs over more activities). Consumers, not having incurred the fixed costs in the first place—and having less reason to do so—cannot participate in the auction as a by-product but must gear up specially to play in the game each time.

Moreover, consumers' incentives to incur those costs is less than represented in the standard economic model of regulation. The Olson-Stigler story of consumer apathy in the face of regulation is based on consumers' rational ignorance and free riding on one another. But as will be discussed later in the chapter, there is another aspect of free riding that has gone unnoticed, one that allows and even encourages consumers to free ride, not only on one another but also on producers.

In summary, the incentive structure confronting producers and consumers entails more than just an incentive to free ride. Models based on differential organizational costs by definition overlook differences in benefits that would also explain observed patterns of producer versus consumer organization. The differences in benefits and costs cut different ways on the question whether consumers would find it worthwhile to organize to any significant extent.

Ultimately, then, the magnitude of consumers' organization is an empirical question. And in fact, however costly organization by consumers may be, the costs certainly are not as prohibitive as they are typically treated in both the Stiglerian and post-Stiglerian versions of the economic theory of regulation. One observes that although the number of consumer organizations falls well short of the number of producer trade associations, there are many organized consumer groups, and they are active politically. The role of consumer groups in regulated utility proceedings was noted above. A national survey found that 16 percent of those polled had contributed time or money to a consumer group; contributions also rise with income levels, validating the common perception that the extent of consumer organization has risen as income has.[8] The advent of the personal computer has made the organization of hundreds of thousands of electronic-billboard subscribers very cheap and effective. (Manufacturers have begun to use the same system.)[9]

Both theory and empirics therefore indicate that consumers should be included, not just as voters, but as counterbidders to producers in any regulatory auction.[10] But doing so raises again the question already discussed above: how can government action transfer consumer surplus to producers, if consumers are willing to pay to keep it and their losses are greater than any gain to producers? In connection with Figure 7.1, it was asked why voters would succeed in pushing threatened price OA (with regulation) back only to OF instead of all the way to OE (no regulation). That question is even more vexing once the losers are allowed into the auction and it is also found that (like the winners) they are organized.

To recast the problem more generally, focus on pressure-group organization leads ineluctably to the issue of why regulation is imposed in the first place—that is, why consumers do not organize to block all regulation (Wenders 1987). The losses to buyers at any level of regulation exceed the gains to producers. Consumers predictably would and demonstrably do organize, just as producers do. So why does regulation happen?

The Rent-Extraction Perspective

Recognizing the phenomenon of rent extraction is helpful in trying to resolve the puzzle. The process of consumers' buying off politicians described in the Peltzman-Becker model should seem familiar. The core of the basic Becker-Peltzman process modeled in Figure 7.1 is just one type of rent extraction, although that fact has not been generally recognized. In the rent-extraction model generally, the regulatory auction results in one group's repurchasing its own surplus. In the Peltzman-Becker model specifically, consumers faced with credible political threats to transfer their surplus to producers are able to reclaim some or all of the surplus threatened, but at a price. In other words, placed in the proper context, the Peltzman-Becker model represents just one subset of all extraction strategies available to politicians.

The basic proposition should by now seem quite uncontroversial: *the bidders for a given group's surplus always include the group itself.* In effect, the rent-extraction model differs hardly at all from that of Peltzman (1976, p. 212): "There is essentially a political auction in which the high bidder receives the right to tax the wealth of everybody else." But in the rent-extraction model, the highest bidder may well be the current surplus holder, in which cases she is forced to pay an off-the-books tax to retain her own wealth. The taxman is the politician himself.

Indeed, without transaction costs, the current surplus holder will *always* be the highest bidder, and so the one taxing the wealth of everybody else will always be the politician—for his own personal gain. With zero transaction costs, current surplus owners will never offer less for their own surplus than the amounts offered for it by competing claimants. In Figure

7.1, price-fixing producers gain only the rent rectangle at any price above OE, and their maximum gain is ABHE. But consumers would offer up to the surplus trapezoid (ABJE) to avoid regulation.

The same is true if other political threats are considered and other industry demand and supply conditions posited. In Figure 7.2, a tax of OC (raising the industry cost-supply curve from S to S′) yields only the revenue rectangle HIEB, while each of the groups taxed would again offer amounts up to the total of its surplus trapezoid threatened (HIAF for consumers, FAEB for producers) to avoid taxes.[11] The assumption of zero transaction costs logically means that politicians could price discriminate in transferring a group's surplus, making the entire trapezoid available to competing nonowner aspirants. But even in this case, existing surplus holders could never be outbid.

So, as explained in Parts I and II, politicians need not implement regulation to benefit themselves. If credible, mere threats to undertake any of the surplus-transferring policies will elicit extractive payments from potential victims to forestall the expropriation of their surplus by regulation. The initial model of surplus extraction concentrated on extraction of producers' rents. But consumer surplus in principle offers opportunities for extraction

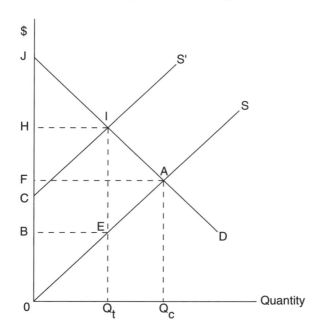

Figure 7.2 Transfers vs. extraction in excise taxation

no less attractive than those presented by producer surplus. If threatened price controls succeeded in extracting rents from pharmaceutical companies, threats to increase prices should extract surplus from consumers.

Indeed, threats of price increases often do elicit direct monetary and in-kind transfers from consumers. The National Rifle Association, an organization of millions of gun users, regularly pays politicians, who regularly threaten but then do not institute gun control.[12] Even if producers do not organize and pay politicians for rent-creating regulation, politicians have an incentive to threaten regulation if consumer interests can be made to pay for removal of the threat. Therefore, producer rent-seeking is not necessary to induce consumers to pay politicians. Politicians have an incentive to act as if producers are seeking regulation, even if producers are not.[13]

Thus, in a political world without transaction costs, there would be no regulation, except that needed tactically to make threats to regulate credible. As in a world of private contracting with negligible transaction costs, resources (or rights to use them) ultimately are owned by those who value them most highly. Without transaction costs, the highest bidders are those who would receive the surplus without regulation. The economic theory of regulation, based as it is on regulation's actually being imposed, is just a subset of the wider phenomenon of rent extraction. Actual occurrences of regulation represent political market failure. They occur only when the process of contracting with politicians to keep one's own surplus—for a price—fails for some reason.

A Coasean Model of Regulation

Politicians' Transaction Costs

The moral is the one emphasized by Ronald Coase in other settings (1937; 1960). The interesting regulatory issues involve specifying the nature of the relevant actors' transaction costs, which alone can explain the observed pattern of regulation, and eventually quantifying them (Shelanski and Klein 1995). Only a Coasean model—one in which political outcomes concerning redistribution are driven by positive transaction costs—can explain the manifold forms of government redistribution observed. "A discussion of wealth transfers by a representative government must be predicated on the existence of certain information and transaction costs. Without the existence of such costs wealth would never be willingly given up."[14]

As in any Coasean analysis, the issue becomes one of identifying the relevant transaction costs. The relevant costs include—but are not limited to—private parties' costs of organization, as in the Olson-Stigler model. The rent-extraction model draws attention likewise to *politicians'* transaction costs, including those of negotiating with private parties over the terms of the regulatory contract.

Politicians are rational maximizers of their own welfare. They operate under constitutional constraints—not all forms of taking are allowed, for example—but the Constitution has become less confining over time, as discussed in Part I. More important, like all other actors, politicians operate under budget and time constraints. Taxation and other regulation require costly bureaucratic agencies to administer the law (that is, to collect payments out of surplus and pay them over to successful bidders). Even when surplus is not ultimately transferred, but allowed to reside with current owners who pay for the privilege of retaining it, threats of expropriation must be credible, requiring politicians to incur costs (for example, by writing, submitting, and then withdrawing or permitting the defeat of bills). There must be negotiation over whether to expropriate and transfer, or whether to extract, and in either case negotiation over the amounts and kinds of payments to be made to the politicians.

Negotiation and related transaction costs are an important part of the rent-extraction model, though not part of the orthodox economic theory of regulation. As rational maximizers, politicians are not interested in transfers that benefit private interest groups but not themselves. To get the benefits available to them, politicians must engage in costly negotiation with private groups over the amount and form of consideration to be paid for regulatory action or inaction. Anyone doubting this phenomenon need only read about how politicians spend the bulk of their time. Brooks Jackson reports on one politician who spent "an hour in the morning and another hour in the afternoon, every day, calling anyone who might be good for a contribution. It was too little; successful fund-raisers spend much more of their time personally soliciting donations."[15] They also hire full-time aides who specialize in raising money (Kuntz 1995). While the politician is increasingly a personal fundraiser, the actual business of running the legislative office is more and more left to others.

As with any exchange, high transaction costs reduce the expected gains from trade for both parties. Politicians thus have an incentive to minimize the transaction costs of threatening or transferring surplus. In some situations, lowering costs will entail allowing private beneficiaries themselves—for a political fee—to collect transferable surplus directly. In Figure 7.1, for example, legalized price fixing permits producers to collect consumer surplus directly, rather than have bureaucrats collect it through a tax that is then paid over to producers.[16]

Like all entrepreneurs, that is, politicians operate a Coasean firm. Services produced at lower cost internally will be undertaken by the political firm (that is, the state) itself; those available more cheaply in the market will be contracted for, as in government-sponsored cartelization and price fixing. The collection and payment of surplus will predictably be done by the group that can transfer any given surplus at least cost. And, operating under the various constitutional and budgetary constraints, politicians will spend more time regulating or threatening markets where the amount of surplus net of the transaction costs is greatest.

This means the net surplus that politicians will threaten or transfer is, in turn, a function of the extent of private-group organization. Individuals can affect regulation as atomistic voters, or they can organize for additional influence. Any private group will be more effective the better organized it is. Greater organization allows a group to make higher pecuniary offers to politicians. It also lowers politicians' costs of negotiation: a politician will find it cheaper to negotiate with an organization (the NRA) representing millions of persons from whom it has already collected the money, rather than with those millions (of gun owners) individually.

The model thus implies that politicians would invest resources to encourage (subsidize) otherwise unorganized groups' attempts to organize, so as to lower politicians' costs of negotiating. And in fact such political subsidies are regularly provided. For example, the Magnuson-Moss FTC Improvements Act of 1975 created funding for consumer-group participation in Federal Trade Commission rulemaking proceedings. Appearance by taxpayer-funded groups organized specifically for the particular proceeding in question became a standard feature of the late-1970s spate of rulemakings at the FTC. Politicians continue to subsidize the organization and activities of consumer and other groups, in a process that James Bennett and Thomas DiLorenzo refer to as Congress "twisting its own arm" (Bennett and DiLorenzo 1985; 1987). The United States does not practice this strategy alone; in the United Kingdom, the National Consumer Council is funded by the government.

Regulation as a Function of Organization

The preceding discussion of political transaction costs reveals two other limitations of the standard economic model of regulation. First, the model is static, treating the existence of a regulatory auction in a particular market as a given. Yet many markets in fact remain unregulated; the various constraints that politicians face mean that they cannot be active everywhere. The interesting dynamic issue is which markets offer the greatest net surplus to politicians. The amount of surplus that is available, net of transaction costs, is itself a function of the extent to which current surplus owners are organized. Because private organization facilitates higher offers to politicians at lower negotiation costs, politicians have greater incentive to threaten regulation of organized groups.

Politicians in effect make two choices: *whether* to regulate or threaten a particular market so as to benefit themselves; and *how* to regulate, by expropriating and transferring surplus or by threatening to do so but selling surplus back to its current owners. Decisions whether and how to regulate are not independent, however. Whether to be active in a particular market is a function of the total amount of available surplus, net of the transaction cost of transferring or extracting it. The total amount of net surplus available is itself a function of the extent of interest-group organization. Greater organization increases the risk to group members that politicians will choose to be active in that market. All other things being equal (including the extent of groups' organization), credible threats of transfer will elicit greater rewards than actual transfers, since current owners will pay more to keep their surpluses than other groups will pay for transfers. Therefore, if current surplus owners are as well organized as potential transferees, that market is more attractive to politicians than an analogous one in which surplus owners are not organized, *ceteris paribus*.

A second limitation in static models of the regulatory auction is their single-minded focus on the consumer-producer battle over a given fraction of consumers' surplus. Consider again Figure 7.1, portraying a conflict as to whether the market price will be that preferred by producers (OA) or consumers (OE). The static issue in that case is how much of surplus area ABJE consumers will lose.

But if surplus can be successfully extracted by politicians themselves, the *entire* amount of organized consumers' surplus (EJK), not just that imperiled by higher producer prices (ABJE), is at risk. To return to the National Rifle Association, the typical political proposal is not merely to increase the price of gun use. Rather, various proposals seek abolition of certain gun use—in effect, by setting a price at which the quantity consumed would be zero. The result would be complete eradication of consumer surplus for those products.

But again, politicians' ability to extract all consumers' surplus in the typical regulatory auction depends on the extent of organization. Consumers can remain unorganized, letting producers successfully bid for higher prices and destroy up to ABJE of consumer surplus. Or consumers can organize, perhaps successfully repurchasing some or all of ABJE, but perhaps having an even greater area (up to EJK) extracted. The effect of organization itself is as before. It increases the amount of net surplus exposed to politicians, and so is more likely to attract political attention to that particular market.

The more dynamic Coasean model thus generates yet another explanation—one independent of any free riding—of why consumers would organize less frequently than producers. Organization to effect favorable outcomes also exposes groups to a greater likelihood of an unfavorable result: extraction of their own surplus. One previously unrecognized cost of organization is exposure of greater amounts of surplus to extraction, making it more worthwhile for politicians to try to extract them. And the risk that being organized will result in extraction increases more, the smaller the individual amount of surplus held by each member. At the margin, then, greater organization entails greater risk of surplus loss for groups of consumers. This last point can be developed more rigorously.

Consider a costly regulation or a tax that would increase the prices each consumer pays by ten cents. The regulation might imperil millions or billions of dollars of total consumers' surplus but would not elicit payments from unorganized consumers to avoid the regulation. Transaction costs are prohibitive: even without free riding, it costs more than ten cents for each potential victim and the politician to negotiate removal of the threat in exchange for payment of some of the surplus threatened.[17] Surplus still might be taxed, or producers allowed to cartelize and transfer consumer surplus to themselves.

But each of these strategies would yield lower total amounts transferred than consumers would pay if organized and able to negotiate for their own surplus; the trapezoid including deadweight consumer loss is larger than the transferable rent rectangle, and the entire preregulation triangle of consumer surplus is larger still. The political returns to regulating the industry are lower than if regulation could merely be threatened and consumers made to pay to retain their own surplus. At the margin, then, the industry is less likely to attract politicians' attention in the first place when consumers are unorganized.

As consumers organize, however, politicians' set of profitable opportunities expands. In the aggregate, a well-organized group represents more amounts of extractable surplus than disaggregated individuals did. Once it is organized and its ability to raise funds is proved, a consumer group like the NRA represents to politicians a lower-cost way of collecting surplus. Appreciating this, politicians are more likely to resort to extraction strategies in the first place. Potential producer rent seeking is not a sufficient reason for consumers to organize. Even if there is no free riding and organization is otherwise costless as well, it may be strategically wiser for consumers to refrain from organization and to limit their role to voting. Politicians may be able to extract even more surplus from organized consumers than would be lost to successful producer rent seeking if consumers did not organize.

This point is illustrated in Figure 7.3, where the costs and benefits to politicians of regulatory activity (threatened or actually imposed) are measured vertically and the amount of activity horizontally.[18] Assume that the legislative costs of transferring surplus (for example, the costs of writing a transfer bill and getting it passed) are the same as those of credibly threatening surplus but not transferring it (for example, the costs of writing the same bill but getting it killed). The only costs relevant to the politicians' choice thus are the transaction costs of securing extractive

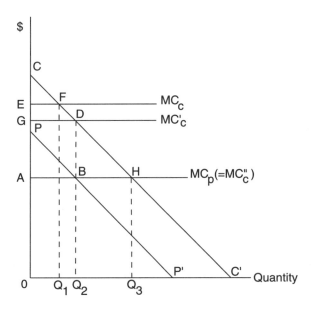

Figure 7.3 The rent-extraction costs of organizing for rent creation

compensation to allow current recipients (consumers) to keep their surplus, versus the costs of negotiating compensation for rents received by surplus transferees (producers). The choices are mutually exclusive; consumers' surplus cannot both be guaranteed to consumers and then transferred to producers. Stated otherwise, no postcontractual opportunism occurs; politicians and private interests are repeat players, and regulatory contracts are honored. Politicians' transaction costs are assumed constant in Figure 7.3; scale economies in negotiation could be assumed without altering the main conclusions.

Assume that there has never been any regulation or regulatory threat, perhaps because the industry was constitutionally protected, but that protection has now eroded, allowing politicians to consider regulation. The issue is whether they will actually regulate or will be bought off by existing surplus holders. Let politicians' benefits be a positive fraction k $(0 < k < 1)$ of the amount of surplus retained by current recipients or transferred to new ones. Since consumers (current surplus owners) will always offer more from their trapezoids than producer transferees would pay for any rectangle transferred, the marginal political benefits from threatening consumer surplus (CC') are always greater than those from surplus transfers to producers (PP'), *ceteris paribus*. That is, the total size of the consumer surplus trapezoid is greater than the surplus rectangle transferable to producers: $CC'0/k > PP'0/k$. These curves representing marginal benefits to politicians decline, on the assumption that politicians rationally will undertake regulation affecting more surplus before that affecting less surplus.

The decision whether to allow consumers to keep their surplus or transfer it to producers depends on these marginal benefits and on the relevant transaction costs of reaching agreement with the affected group. Politicians' costs of dealing with producers (MC_P) are lower than those of negotiating with consumers (MC_C), since producers are already organized for exogenous reasons (information exchanges, setting of standards, creation of brand-name capital, and so forth) prevailing before the constitutional change. Consumers initially are unorganized. Given the cost of negotiating with consumers, politicians can credibly threaten only Q_1 of regulation, extracting up to CFQ_10 from them at a transaction cost to them of EFQ_10, leaving triangle CFE as politicians' net gain. Alternatively, politicians can actually impose Q_2 of regulation, being paid PBQ_20 by producers to do so, and netting gains of PBA after transaction costs of ABQ_20 are deducted.

Given these different transaction costs, maximizing politicians will regulate, since the net gains to them of doing so are greater than the gains of allowing the industry to go unregulated: PBA > CFE. True, consumers would offer more to remain unregulated than producers would pay for regulation; the trapezoids are bigger than the rectangles. But the incremental transaction costs of negotiating a no-regulation solution with unorganized consumers exceed the incremental gains.

Suppose next that consumers organize to repurchase the surplus now being transferred to producers. With Q_2 of regulation in place, consumers might organize just enough to lower the costs of political negotiation to MC_c'. But here, relative transaction costs leave politicians indifferent between negotiating with consumers for deregulation and with producers for continuing regulation (CDG = PBA). Since continuing regulation requires no new (costly) legislation but removing it would, consumer organization sufficient to lower transaction costs to MC_c' will not secure deregulation.

Suppose therefore that consumers organize to the same extent as producers, such that negotiating with them for deregulation now confronts a politician with identical transaction costs: $MC_c'' = MC_P$. For removal of Q_2 of regulation, consumers can offer more for deregulation net of the transaction costs (trapezoid CDBA) than the net gains from producers to continue regulation (PBA). It might seem therefore that this would be the negotiated outcome.

But as Figure 7.3 shows, threatening only Q_2 of regulation is no longer an equilibrium solution. Having organized, consumers represent greater net benefits to politicians who can credibly threaten their surplus. Politicians will not stop at threatening regulation of Q_2, but will threaten regulation of Q_3, since that strategy offers the greatest net gains of all, triangle CHA rather than trapezoid CDBA. Once organized, that is, consumers represent transferable surplus for which politicians can exact compensation at lower cost. At the margin, as the costs of threatening surplus decline the extent of regulatory threats will increase.

Intuitively, Figure 7.3 demonstrates that politicians will find it more profitable to threaten (but not pass) more gun-control legislation, the better organized gun users are. It is expensive to extract payments from millions of gun owners individually when they are not organized; it is relatively cheap to do the extracting from the National Rifle Association. At the margin, lack of organization has the advantage of discouraging politicians' extractive strategies. And the risk that being organized will result in extraction increases more, the smaller the individual amount of surplus held by each member. As a group's surplus is distributed among more members, the difference between MC_C and MC_C'' is greater. All other things equal, greater organization entails greater risk of surplus loss for such groups, including consumers.

Treated endogenously, lack of organization represents a strategy of refusing to negotiate, of refusing to join the chicken game that possession of expropriable surplus would entail. If a party fears being forced to bargain over conceding some of his surplus, one strategy is to put himself intentionally in a position where he cannot bargain. Thomas Schelling (1963, p. 26), for example, discussed the strategic use of communication difficulties as a way to maintain a stance of refusing to enter into bargaining that will lead to concessions. A person who is incommunicado "cannot be deterred from his own commitment" to stay out of the game by any entreaty of the other party. Analogous tactics have been analyzed in other contexts where it can also be useful not to be able to organize.[19]

This not to say that consumer organizations like the NRA do not provide net benefits to their members overall. Their continued survival indicates that they must. The point is simply that, *ex ante*, organization imposes an expected cost that reduces the expected net benefits of organizing. Although net benefits are undoubtedly positive for those groups that actually have organized, at the margin the expected costs identified in the Coasean model here will cause other groups not to organize at all.[20]

Free Riding Revisited

What does this analysis add to what is now understood about organization to influence regulation? Under existing models, greater interest-group organization is unambiguously good. But this interpretation is incorrect, or at least incomplete. As the Peltzman-Becker model implicitly recognizes, much regulatory activity results in extraction of a group's own surplus, as politicians sell back to the group the surplus it would have received in the absence of government. Group organization lowers politicians' transaction costs. The resulting lower costs of extracting surplus mean that more extractive regulation will be threatened, and so more surplus lost.

Organization thus represents a tradeoff. Organization increases the ability to add to the group's surplus by becoming a transferee of others' surplus. But once organized, a particular group will always offer more to keep its own surplus than competing groups will pay to have it transferred;

organizing therefore gives politicians greater incentives to threaten a group's existing surplus. Organization, that is, increases the odds of getting another group's surplus but also increases the risk of having one's own surplus threatened and expropriated.[21] The relative expected gains and losses will differ for different groups, and so different degrees of organization should be observed, *ceteris paribus.*

The tradeoff from organizing requires one final look at the consumer free-rider issue. In the richer model of regulation that includes a rent-extraction strategy, politicians not only create political rents but also threaten private rents and forbear for a price from expropriating them. The fact that extraction is practiced creates an incentive for consumers to free ride not on one another, as in the Olson-Stigler model, but on producers. Consider again the excise-tax example of Figure 7.2. As costs rise, producers lose their surplus (rents) to the extent that purchasers lose theirs (consumer surplus). Unlike the rent-creating version of economic regulation, the rent-extraction model notes that producers and consumers are often affected alike by threats to regulate. As already-organized producers repurchase more of their own surplus by buying off legislators' threats of taxation, they are simultaneously repurchasing consumer surplus for their buyers. Without organizing, that is, the buyers obtain a benefit from organized producers, a circumstance that reduces their incentive to organize in the first place.

One thus would predict that, in such a situation, producers would attempt to enlist the aid of their consumers. Producers would attempt to overcome the problem of free riding on sellers' attempts to repurchase producers' (and inevitably consumers') surplus from politicians. And so they do. Attempts at extraction via taxation frequently cause producers to enlist consumer pressure on politicians not to expropriate. Threatened excises on beer and alcohol, for example, cause brewers to place forms in stores, making it easy for their customers to write to Washington to protest the threatened taxes.[22] More directly, they have established—subsidized—consumer organizations of their own, which stand ready to oppose tax increases when they are proposed. Beer Drinkers of America is one such organization. As of 1990 it had 400,000 members in thirty states and sponsored programs on 500 college campuses. Although members pay ten dollars to join, the organization really "depends on money from brewers . . . But there's more to it than tossing back a few cold ones. The group is also an aggressive lobbyist. When tax increases on alcohol are threatened, the organization quickly, and successfully, mobilizes its members in letter-writing campaigns. [In 1989] the group fought proposed increases in beer taxes in New York, New Jersey, Florida and Arizona, winning all but New York."[23] Similar campaigns to bring consumer pressure to bear in Washington have been waged by firms hurt by politicians' extortion from trust funds. The airlines, trying to get user-fee money that supposedly exists for their benefit out of politicians' hands and applied as promised to upgrading airports, have also been conspicuous in their use of consumer pressure on politicians.[24]

With consumers and producers affected alike by some threats of regulation, it is not necessarily the case that producers will incur the costs of overcoming any consumer proclivity for free riding. The extent to which one group loses more or less than another depends on the elasticities of supply and demand. Where producer' surplus is slight compared to consumers' surplus, the opposite outcome is more likely: producers are more likely to free ride on consumers. Consider again statutes that would abolish the use of guns. Producers' surplus would of course be destroyed by such a statute, but so would vast amounts of surplus held by millions of intensely interested gun enthusiasts. Not surprisingly, although consumer and producer interests are aligned in resisting gun control, the National Rifle Association is primarily a consumer-user organization, with several million dues-paying members.

Conclusion

This chapter has sought to develop certain points pertaining to pressure-group organization. These points have been neglected in the standard economic model of rent-creating regulation, but they emerge clearly once politicians' rent-extraction strategy is recognized.

The theoretical gaps may stem from semantic imprecision. Rents are not "created." They represent transfers of existing surplus from current recipients (consumers, in the standard model) to new recipients (producers).[25] The same surplus could be transferred to others outside the industry, for example by levying an excise tax whose revenues were then given to those outsiders. But again, no rents are created; existing consumer surplus is simply transferred.

Transfers will actually occur only in a world of second-best political contracts. The essence of the Peltzman-Becker model is that "[p]oliticians and bureaucrats are assumed to carry out the political allocations resulting from the competition among pressure groups" (Becker 1983, p. 396). But in a zero-transaction-cost world, such political competition would usually result in regulation's being threatened but not imposed. The typical way to avoid this problem is to consign consumers to a role as mere voters in the model, to declare that they face insuperable free-riding problems, or both. As discussed here, however, free-riding problems are neither necessary nor sufficient to explain observed disparities in interest-group organization or regulatory outcomes.

The Coasean model presented in this chapter focuses instead on a different asymmetric factor, the transaction costs of political negotiations with different groups, and on the gains available to politicians from different regulatory strategies. In a Coasean world, politicians choose between transferring and threatening a group's surplus. The choice depends on the relative gains to politicians, net of the transaction costs of securing them. The transaction costs depend on the beneficiaries' and victims' degrees of organization.

The gains and losses from organizing pressure groups in this model are different from those postulated in the simpler model in which politicians only transfer surplus. In particular, organization is seen to have a hitherto-unrecognized cost. Organization reduces the probability that one's own surplus will be lost, given a political agenda that includes regulation. But organization also alters the agenda, increasing the likelihood that politicians will include threats of regulation in their schedules.

As more and more groups possess substantial amounts of surplus, increasingly complex political strategies become feasible. Regulation can be used to transfer producers' surplus to factor suppliers, or suppliers may have their surplus transferred to producers (Benson and Faminow 1986; Shughart, Tollison, and Higgins 1987). Likewise, both consumer and producer surplus can be transferred simultaneously to others outside the industry through an excise tax. But behind the complexity of outcomes are two simple facts about the process: politicians must be compensated for every transfer or forbearance from transferring, and their compensation will predictably be a positive function of the surplus at issue, net of transaction costs.

In appraising the overall importance of rent extraction, it may be useful to consider that the orthodox economic model of regulation is but a special case of the rent-extraction model. The orthodox model has been of undeniable and immense importance in the economics and political science of the past twenty-five years. Nevertheless, the model has approached regulation from the wrong theoretical angle. *In the absence of transaction costs, all regulatory activity would be rent extraction.* Existing owners of rights to future capital flows or present wealth will always pay at least as much, and usually more, to keep what they have rather than have it transferred away. Regulation ensues only when the transaction costs of avoiding expropriation—of achieving a rent-extraction contract—prove prohibitive.

Because that point has not been fully appreciated, models based on the economic theory of regulation too often explain only why one group of beneficiaries is (was) willing to pay for regulation. While certainly interesting, such models are not enough to explain why regulation happened. To say that regulation occurred is to say that someone who valued the resources more—their owner in the current period—failed to acquire them for the subsequent period. In other words, regulation is proof of failure in the market for political contracts. That regulation represents political market failure is terribly ironic; not so long ago economists were analyzing regulation as a result of *private* market failure.

8

Improving the Model:
Worthy yet Unanswered Questions

Politicians are interested in people. Not that this is always a virtue.
Fleas are interested in dogs.

—P. J. O'ROURKE

At this point it is time to stop and take stock. What does the model of rent
extraction add to what we think we know, and what remains to be
explained?

Review

Despite criticisms made in earlier chapters of the standard economic theory
of regulation, one must acknowledge its capabilities. Thanks to that model,
our understanding of government regulation has progressed markedly in
the past two and a half decades. The notion that government regulates in
some disinterested, "public-interest" fashion to repair market failure has
crumbled. Too much regulation is demonstrably at odds with the general
welfare for any such public-interest explanation now to be taken seriously.
Noting "the paradigm shift that has clearly occurred" in this respect, one
analyst (Poole 1986) has written that no one "would today advance the
simplistic notions of disinterested public servants carefully weighing the
pros and cons of the public interest to derive the optimal social policy,
notions that were still common in text books just a few years ago." The
economic model seems to explain much better the reasons for and effects
of government regulation. "The economic theory of regulation," another
source observes, has "put public interest theories of politics to rest" (Kalt
and Zupan 1984, p. 279).

But for all its superior explanatory power, the economic theory of
regulation as rent creation has proved incapable of explaining many aspects
of government regulation. Moreover, analysts (with a few exceptions) have
not even attempted to integrate into the economic model perhaps the
most obvious and pervasive sort of government regulation: taxation. This

156

must be counted a major omission. Unlike most sorts of regulation, which are focused on specific industries or transactions, taxation affects virtually every aspect of production and exchange. A model of regulation that does not encompass taxation—including both taxes imposed and those threatened but not imposed—misses a significant part of what government is about.

Aside from its inability to explain some of the most visible activities of government, the current version of the economic model of regulation fails to integrate satisfactorily the role of the politician. While much attention is paid to private demands for regulation, relatively little thought has been given to the determinants of the supply of regulation provided by politicians. And almost no consideration has been given to the various ways in which politicians themselves can benefit from acting as suppliers. The nature of politicians' compensation for brokerage services is not fully specified and is often simplistically treated in terms just of votes.

Those deficiencies are the point of departure for the model of rent extraction set forth in this book. The rent-extraction model focuses more specifically on politicians than do most other studies of regulation. Politicians are seen not as mere brokers redistributing wealth in response to competing private demands, but as independent actors making their own demands to which private actors respond. The economic theory of regulation has thereby been extended to show how politicians reap benefits by first threatening to extract the returns to private producers' capital already in existence, and then being paid to forbear from doing so. These private returns, as opposed to regulation-created rents, represent returns to their owners' entrepreneurial ability and private capital investments. The consideration that private capital owners will pay to keep politicians from expropriating the returns to their capital is measured not so much in votes as in cash.

After the many demonstrations in previous chapters, the process of rent extraction should now be well understood. Any number of further examples could be studied in detail. For instance, one instinctively suspects that increasingly prominent environmental regulations, which allow politicians to benefit from the "not-in-my-back-yard" (NIMBY) phenomenon, have become a rent-extraction playground. Bruce Yandle (1989) reports, for example, that threatened location of the toxic-waste cleanup sites required by the 1980 Superfund legislation caused those in threatened locales to lobby legislators hard against having the new sites dumped in their backyards.

Given the ubiquity of rent (wealth) extraction, as Chapters 3 through 5 demonstrated, it might then be asked why rent extraction is not yet part of the orthodox economic treatment of government. One reason noted in Chapter 4 is the relative paucity of sophisticated empirical work on rent extraction. Several other reasons probably account for economists' greater interest in rent creation than in rent extraction.

First, as noted in Chapter 1, economists are naturally disposed toward analysis of *exchange*-related processes. But economists are conditioned to think of exchange as a process of Pareto improvement, one in which the interests of both sides are advanced and so wealth is created. In that respect, the political creation of rents seems superficially akin to private exchange: private interests provide votes and money in exchange for rents, making both sides better off. There are of course crucial differences.[1] Nonetheless, by leaving both private and political contracting parties better off, rent creation resembles familiar economic models of contract.

What has been missing, however, is the natural corollary. The realm of contract does not capture the entire set of even private parties' relations among themselves. In addition to contracts, torts (including intentional ones) and crimes (like theft) unfortunately are also routine parts of social interaction. In these aspects of human association, the parties are worse off overall, even if one gains something at another's expense.

Extortion and its variant, blackmail, are further examples of processes that, like theft, benefit one party at the expense of another. The analogy between extortion and rent extraction is particularly close. As in the ordinary extortion setting, politicians can and do benefit themselves by threatening to reduce wealth but then forbearing, for a price, from doing so. The process is essentially contractual, albeit extralegal. But these are vastly different sorts of exchange from economists' usual model of contract.

A second reason for economists' general failure to include rent extraction in their overall model of politicians' behavior is undoubtedly the absence until recently of a formal microeconomic model of the process. Chapter 1 noted that economists had vague notions of what eventually became formalized as the economic model of regulation before George Stigler's (1971) inaugural contribution. It was not Stigler's concept that was new, so much as his ability to fit observed behavior into a standard microeconomic model of rational, maximizing behavior. With Stigler's rudimentary but integrated model set forth, economists got out their toolboxes and went to work, resulting in enormous progress in the economics of political behavior.

The model of rent extraction posited in Chapter 2 is no more sophisticated than Stigler's. Still, the model does what perhaps has been required for economists and other social scientists to begin systematic consideration of rent extraction by politicians. It integrates rent extraction into a familiar theoretical microeconomic/public-choice apparatus that has already shown much explanatory power in other realms of political behavior. Moreover, the model is able to explain both anecdotally (Chapter 3) and more sophisticatedly (Chapter 4) episodes of political behavior that are otherwise inexplicable under the more standard economic theory of regulation. Why else would rational, maximizing politicians routinely submit bills ("fetchers," "cash cows,") and then withdraw them or let them die, all the while enriching themselves in the process?

Outstanding Issues

The rent-extraction model thus seems to have satisfied the requirements of any positive science, social or natural. It rests on a coherent body of theory, yields testable implications, and has been vindicated (so far) by the tests. But the rent-extraction model also raises at least as many questions as it answers.

The Victims of Rent Extraction

Foremost among these questions is why some groups' rents get extracted while others do not. This question is really just the converse of the one raised (but hardly answered) in the standard economic theory of regulation: why are some groups (or industries) regulated while others are not? Sam Peltzman (1989, pp. 14–16) discusses the problem in his review of the development of the economic theory.

> Most of the development of the ET [economic theory of regulation] concerns the behavior of established regulatory bodies: whom they will favor and how and why their policies will change. But the question of why the body was established in the first place cannot be ignored. The ET's answer to that question is about what one would expect from a maximizing theory of institutional behavior: politicians seek politically rewarding fields to regulate and avoid or exit from the losers. The difficulty with the ET as an entry theory is precisely that it never gets much beyond this level of generality . . . one leaves Stigler's model with the nagging question of why minimum rate or

entry regulation of structurally competitive industries is comparatively rare. Peltzman's version is hardly an improvement.

The rent-extraction model adds a third option to the politician's list of choices, and re-asks the question in two parts. First, why are some groups (industries) relatively ignored by politicians while others are not? And second, for those groups of interest to politicians, on what basis is the choice made between rent creation and rent extraction?

To take the second question first, simple economic theory supplies some answers. Chapters 2 and 3 noted, for example, that industry demand and supply elasticities should have predictable effects on politicians' choice between rent creation and rent extraction across industries. As for the first question, the creation-extraction tradeoff model suggests a time profile of political activity within a single industry. New industries (firms) have relatively little capital; therefore, little extraction is to be expected, since there is little to extract. Because the product also is not well established or highly differentiated from substitutes (that is, demand is relatively elastic), there will be little private or political incentive to seek rent creation through the means identified in the now-traditional economic theory of regulation. Given the transaction costs of either expropriating and trans-ferring surplus, or alternatively of threatening and extracting it, politicians are likely to do neither and instead to spend their time more lucratively elsewhere.

But over time, in successful industries (the only ones of interest to surplus-minded politicians) the tradeoff presents itself more clearly. A stock of reputation and physical capital sets up the possibility of extortion; but success of a product (firm, industry) also increases the returns from successful cartelization by regulation. Whether extraction or cartelization becomes the dominant political strategy would depend, empirically, on the relative magnitudes involved, net of the transaction costs of politicians' siphoning their portion. Industries in which competition is the rule, and thus in which demand elasticities are relatively high, can expect extraction strategies. Gambling, for example, which has become established in many states but is highly competitive among states, is now worried about rent extraction. Silicon Valley, with its sharp competition but rapidly increasing stock of capital, would seem a natural target for extraction soon.

Discussion of a creation-extraction tradeoff presupposes, too, that in the choice between rent creation and rent extraction politicians can be ex-pected to be paid either way, though for different reasons. In some (though perhaps not many) instances, this assumption may not hold. Imagine a firm that has, perhaps by dint of a superior product, created considerable profits for itself, such that the government really can do little for it by way of creating rents. It thus has no rent-creation lobbyists and is otherwise uninterested in being involved in politics. Its very profitability plus its lack of interest in paying for rent creation mean that it is more likely, all other things being equal, to face rent-extracting demands.

William Niskanen pointed to this situation in one of the earliest references to rent-extracting political strategies. He discussed (in Manne and Miller 1976, p. 103) an industry "that has never asked for any special favors" from government, in which case "a congressman has an incentive to create special costs, the relief of which then becomes a special favor." As a result, "Congress creates a whole new environment, which poses high special costs in the industry, the relief of which becomes an opportunity for the congressmen to collect some rent from this particular industry." Recent antitrust investigations against firms facing low demand elasticities but also seeking nothing from government also exemplify this phenomenon.[2]

Why Auction Losers Pay

Another issue, one truly vexing for the entire study of regulation and not just rent extraction, is politicians' ability to "work both sides of the street." Politicians often represent geographically both the winners and the losers from any attempt to transfer one group's surplus to another. Since any transfer always results in the losers' losing more than gainers gain, the explanation for any transfers actually imposed was seen in Chapter 7 to rely on the transaction costs of transferring relative to extracting.

But what of the situation in which *both* parties in the regulatory auction are paying the politician—side A paying (in the rent-creation model) to have B's surplus transferred, and side B paying (in the rent-extraction model) to keep its own surplus? There is a story (Kurtz and Peoples 1990, p. 265) about Governor Earl Long of Louisiana:

> Earl and a Roman Catholic priest were having a friendly, casual conversation in his office. Suddenly, a lobbyist walked in and dropped a wad of cash on Earl's desk. "Don't worry about a thing," Earl told the man. "I'll take care of you." A few minutes later, a lobbyist from the other side walked in and left an even bigger wad of cash on the desk. "Don't worry about a thing. I'll take care of you." After the man

left, Earl turned to the startled cleric and bellowed, "Who in hell do those bastards think they are, trying to bribe the Governor of Louisiana? I'm not going to do a thing for either one of those sons of bitches!"

One is reminded also of the Russian judge, in Gogol's play *The Inspector General,* assessing a new source of wealth in his life. He says to the local governor, "I myself came here intending to give you a gift right now . . . I felt I could afford it. Chaptovitch is suing Varkovinsky: a suit that can last the rest of my life. Meanwhile, I can hunt on the estates of both!"

Analytically, the social scientist confronts two problems here. First, the fact that both A and B (or groups A and B) are paying indicates that whatever transaction costs exist have been overcome. So why does group B, the current surplus owner, not always win? Second, if transaction costs are negligible and thus group B is destined to win anyway, why does group A pay at all? More generally, why is it routinely observed that both sides to a political (rent-transfer) issue pay, when only one will win?

To return to an issue mentioned in passing in Chapter 2, consider the "cash cow" of product-liability legislation. For years, the trial-lawyer beneficiaries and the corporate losers from current product-liability laws have squared off in Congress. The prospect of legal change generates large revenues from both partisans (producers) and opponents (lawyers) of change; Ralph Nader calls the issue "a PAC annuity for members of Congress" (Abramson 1990). Every year, bills to reform the law die or lose in committee. And yet every year the debate—and the payments from both sides—begins anew. Why is the issue simply not resolved once and for all, and why are both sides paying when only one side is winning (no legislation has ever been passed)? I have no answer to these important questions, which are as applicable to the world of rent creation as to that of rent extraction.

The Returns from Rent Extraction

Along the same lines, there is an unresolved issue why politicians' returns from rent extraction are so small, relative to the expropriable wealth threatened. The diaries of former Senator Packwood reveal, for example, that he apparently was selling to one constituent tax and antitrust assistance worth millions of dollars, in exchange for his estranged wife's being hired for just several thousand dollars (Simpson 1995). The rents expropriable by threatened price controls in pharmaceuticals (discussed in Chapter 3) were several *billions* of dollars, while the payments to politicians amounted to only a few millions. Why is politicians' take so small?

I am unable to explain why. There is a competitive market for politicians, with the result that the prices they can command is lower than would be the case without competition. That is, returns to politicians presumably are competitive. Committee chairmen with secure seats and others well situated in the political process would seem to be less subject to this competition. Yet even their gain is rather small, relative to the amounts they credibly imperil.

Accounting for the relatively low returns to politicians, however, is not a problem unique to the world of rent extraction. Many, led by Gordon Tullock, have noted that in creating rents by actually regulating, politicians also garner amounts that are trivial compared with the surplus they transfer.

> There is a good deal of talk in the popular press, as well as in the public choice literature, about campaign contributions, both by individuals and by political action committees (PACS). There is no doubt that these outlays influence congressmen. There is also no doubt that such outlays are very small compared to the value of gifts that congressmen distribute.[3]

In perhaps the only empirical estimate of the returns to rent seeking, John Jackson, David Saurman, and William Shughart (1994) found that politicians got about 5 percent of the wealth they were transferring.

The amount of gain to politicians seems only a small fraction of the amount of surplus at stake, meaning that politicians get only a small amount of the equivalent of the "gains from trade" in an ordinary contract. The situation is reminiscent of the relative gains to bidding and target firms in corporate takeovers, in which the former profit by only a small fraction of the total amounts at stake, relative to the gains to targets (Jensen and Ruback 1983; Jarrell, Brickley, and Netter 1988). There, too, competition on the one side (bidders) is the usual explanation for the relatively low returns. Recently, more complex models have also been offered to explain the low returns to politicians, relative to the benefits they confer on rent seekers (for example, Rasmusen and Ramseyer 1994; Wirl 1994). The implications of these models remain to be derived and tested.

The Relative Attraction of Rent Extraction

Once the dual phenomena of rent creation and rent extraction are recognized generally, a question naturally arises as to their relative importance.

As the money changes hands, is a politician engaged more in selling rents created politically, or just in selling private parties the right to keep wealth they have created themselves? In his pathbreaking article on rent creation via regulation, Stigler opined that creating new rents was the primary regulatory activity of politicians.[4] That is, of course, an empirical claim for which no supporting evidence has been presented. Nor do I have any compelling evidence to the contrary. Yet despite the centrality of rent creation in the economic literature, there is good reason to think that selling wealth protection explains more of what is going on in the United States.[5]

Consider the prime engine for raising money in America in the past twenty years, the political action committee, and its principal beneficiary, the Democratic Congressional Campaign Committee. Throughout the 1980s, the DCCC was much more successful at raising money than its Republican counterpart. For what were its donors paying? According to its longtime chairman, Representative Tony Coelho of California, it was not rent *creation*.

> Rather, he said, lawmakers withheld proposals that would offend donors. "Take housing. Take anything you want. If you are spending all your time calling up different people that you're involved with, that are friends of yours, that you have to raise $50,000, you all of a sudden, in your mind, you're in effect saying, 'I'm not going to go out and develop this new housing bill that may get the Realtors or may get the builders or may get the unions upset. I've got to raise the fifty thousand; I've got to do that.' That isn't a sellout. It's basically that you're not permitted to go out and do your creativity. I think that's bad."
>
> Whatever the Realtors or the Home Builders or the unions disliked, the lawmakers no longer even considered . . . Too often, moneyed interests prevail by blocking legislation they don't want. (Jackson 1988, pp. 108–109)

The relative importance of preserving privately created wealth, rather than generating new political wealth, is perhaps best indicated by who gets the PAC money. In the House of Representatives during the 1980s, the Ways and Means Committee—the tax writers—received the most money (Jackson 1988, p. 90). Donors of course are typically paying not to be taxed. Data on federal corporate and personal income-tax changes from 1909 to 1981 show that more of the tax modifications made benefited taxpayers than hurt them (Witte 1985, pp. 315–318; see also Doernberg and McChesney 1987a, p. 923).

Rent Extraction and the Law

All the issues discussed so far in this chapter relate to making the model of rent extraction as complete and as internally coherent as possible, as part of a broader approach to analyzing government regulation. But recognition of the ubiquity of rent extraction (over time and over space) should also begin to raise questions outside the confines of what is traditionally thought of as "regulation." If regulatory threats are useful to a politician in eliciting payments not to follow through on them, one predictably would see other government officials using the same tactic in other settings. The rent-extraction model suggests several issues concerning the law and politics generally.

Illegality of Victimless Crime

Potential for rent extraction may help to explain, for example, why certain transactions, often called "victimless" crime, are in fact made illegal. Economists have been surprisingly uninterested in the whole issue of victimless crime, often content just to dismiss criminalization of drugs, prostitution, and the like as normatively unjustified.[6] If both buyers and sellers in contracts for things like drugs and prostitution are made better off thereby, why are such transactions so often outlawed legislatively—indeed, criminalized? Outlawing victimless acts seems particularly unjustified when it leads to crimes with real victims (for example, murder). Little positive analysis of the reasons for criminalization has been undertaken.

Surely part of the answer must be that outlawing mutually beneficial transactions affords an opportunity for rent extraction from buyers, sellers, or both. It is standard practice for police organizations to come out in favor of maintaining the illegality of victimless crime, even though it increases their exposure to danger—a seeming paradox. But making victimless conduct illegal is quite understandable in terms of the extractive potential inherent in criminalizing certain acts of mutual gain to buyers and sellers.

The current obsession with drug-related crime is a good example. The illegality of drugs has proved to be a boon for police budgets.[7] Not only does the illegality of drugs increase taxpayer-provided budgets, but police have been allowed to keep the proceeds of assets forfeited as a result of drug-enforcement activities, increasing their discretionary budgets (Benson, Rasmussen, and Sollars 1995). Not surprisingly, police have responded to their ability to practice extraction legally with greater numbers of drug-related arrests (ibid.; Rasmussen, Benson, and Mast 1994).

As important as these gains are, budget increases do not measure the personal gains available to police from keeping drugs and other victimless activities illegal. Police shakedowns of drug dealers and prostitution rings for cash are scarcely newsworthy any more, no more unusual than schoolyard extractions of lunch money in exchange for not getting beaten up. Journalistically, the "honest but weak" legislator who turns to extortion by regulatory threats has an exact analogue in the "good cop gone bad" who sells protection from the law.

Almost anything can be made illegal, then used as the basis for rent extraction. Another example of the value of keeping victimless crime illegal was the transvestite "Miss All-America Camp Beauty Pageant" and similar drag beauty contests of the 1960s. The All-America Pageant was a national contest of considerable underground renown.

> The organizer was Jack Doroshow, also known as Sabrina, who held 46 contests a year from 1959 to 1967 through his company, the Nationals Academy, which in its heyday had 100 employees on the payroll. Mainstream America didn't know it, but the nation had a flourishing drag subculture, and not just in the major cities . . . Since local laws often prohibited cross-dressing, Mr. Doroshow would meet with officials and propose a donation to some unspecified charity. In return, the town would pass a variance allowing the contest to take place. (Grimes 1993)

Making things illegal—drugs or drags—just to be paid to allow them is easily practiced. In that sense, our seemingly sophisticated society is no different from more blatantly corrupt Third World countries. Victimless crime seems an area in which further positive investigation along rent-extraction lines would prove fruitful.

Law Enforcement and Rent Extraction

A subject of related interest is enforcement of the law against "true" (other than victimless) crime. A priori, the political model described here implies that resources used in enforcing laws against murder, theft, and so forth would be positively related to rent-extraction possibilities. In a state where politicians can extract for themselves, they predictably will have less incentive to tolerate crime (for example, theft) by others, since the overall wealth reduction necessarily entailed reduces the stock of expropriable capital. Thus, as Tullock observed (1974b, p. 20), where governmental power is sufficient for politicians to extract from their own citizens, one would expect that power to be used also to stop crimes among private citizens. At the time, Tullock pointed to the Soviet Union as an example of the state that was highly effective both in extracting for itself and in preventing crime among the governed. Some twenty years later, events in Russia seem to corroborate Tullock further, as private theft apparently waxes while the potential for political extraction wanes. The links between the state's functioning simultaneously as rent extractor and crime fighter remain largely to be explored.

Indeed, the analysis can be taken a step further. There has been little systematic consideration of the more general relation between the use of the state to increase wealth (by combating crime and by enforcing contracts and other property rights) and the power of the state needed to do so. Some economists (for example, Haddock 1994) are beginning to make progress on this question. The fact that so far the question has interested only a few perhaps reflects the profession's slow progress in elaborating fully the various activities undertaken by governments and integrating them into familiar models. If so, recognition of the apparent importance of rent extraction may speed development of fuller models of the overall role of government in increasing or destroying private wealth.

Rent Extraction and Elections

Another theme deserving greater study is the possible relationship between rent-extraction potential and electoral outcomes. There is some anecdotal evidence that a relationship does exist, simply because greater potential for extraction increases the amount of money at a politician's disposal, and so the possibility of her election. According to reporter Brooks Jackson, perhaps the most thorough chronicler of the massive rent extraction now endemic to the federal taxation process, the rent-extraction strategy has caused a major shift in the political ties binding politicians to their electors. No longer are a politician's "constituents" only (or even mainly) the inhabitants of the district or state he represents. Rather, they include the various interests potentially affected by legislation before the congressional committees on which the politician sits. It is increasingly the case, particularly for the more senior (and therefore more powerful) members of Congress and its committees, that most of the money collected for political campaigns comes from the special interests across the country, rather than from "the folks back home."[8] Moneyed interests become more important as the cost of mounting a campaign increases.

The growing importance of this new constituency is of interest in itself. By definition, politicians' voting decisions become more complicated as they represent increasing numbers of interests whose preferences on various issues will naturally differ at times. But there are other implications of this trend that are not so obvious. For one thing, the ability of senior politicians to attract large amounts of cash from the new constituency alters electoral choices that local residents have in the first place. As a senior incumbent draws more and more money from outsiders, he becomes less vulnerable to challenge at home. Thus, politicians whose campaign coffers bulge with money extracted by the threat of expropriation have been increasingly able to use the size of their bank accounts to discourage challengers, to whom any race has seemed futile.[9]

The importance of rent extraction, operating in considerable part through constant reconsideration of the tax code, is apparently growing. Tax "reform" is onerous for the great masses who must fill out the forms and alter their investment portfolios. But the great masses do not contribute to politicians; those with exceptional wealth do, because they are the more attractive targets. The ability to use the specter of tax change (and other rent-extraction threats) permits politicians to milk those moneyed interests for "contributions" that will alleviate the threat. The rent-extracting value of tax and other legislation has become so great that the extortion money paid to avoid taxes now helps determine who will win elections—particularly because the cost of winning is now so high as to demand large sums of the candidates. And because the extracted sums affect who will win, they also determine the very identities of the candidates a party will field for particular elections.

Rent Extraction in a Second-Best World

The way rent extraction alters the very process of democracy leads to perhaps the ultimate economic question about political extortion. Would the world be a better place if extortion payments were punished legally or somehow made more difficult? Contribution limits, often coupled with proposals for public funding of candidates, are often offered as a way out of the current morass in which politicians can shake down private parties for contributions in lieu of expropriating even more from them. But would such things as contribution limits really solve the problem? Given politicians' ability to threaten privately created rents and so, ultimately, the creation of wealth, the answer to the question might at first seem to be yes.

But of course, as Chapter 7 showed, the situation is more complicated, even if one makes the large assumption that a ban could be enforced on political threats and/or payments to alleviate them. True, restricting private owners' ability to buy off threats reduces politicians' incentive to threaten extraction in the first place. In that sense, an effective ban on rent extraction would seem to be like increased constitutional protection for property generally. It seemingly would afford a way for capital and wealth owners to refuse to be drawn into the political game.

But—again assuming perfect enforcement of the hypothesized ban on political extortion—there is always that other margin along which politicians would adjust. Rents that cannot be threatened and extracted could still be expropriated and transferred. Payments to mitigate the extent of political extractions being made, by definition, avoid even greater harms that politicians could inflict. And so in the second-best world of politics—that is, the real world—extraction payments are actually beneficial—not just to the payor, but societally. As Gary Becker and George Stigler explained about payments (which they called "bribes") to avoid certain rent-extracting measures, "bribes that reduced the effectiveness of many housing codes, of the laws in Nazi Germany against Jews, or of the laws restricting oil imports, would improve, not harm, social welfare" (Becker and Stigler 1974, p. 6; see also Fabella 1995). That is, nonpayment would result in the state's simply taking that which it could always expropriate anyway, leaving victims even worse off. If there were no credible threat to expropriate, there would be no extraction to worry about in the first place.

"Fine," it then will be said. "Let us outlaw not only threats and extraction, but also the actual taking and transferring of rents and wealth." Then, eliminating politicians' ability to extort need not increase the amount of actual transfers. That claim may be true, depending again on the heroic assumption of perfect enforcement—and now, enforcement against not just one but two types of political activity, both threats and expropriation (extortion and bribery, rent extraction and rent creation).

But outlawing both kinds of political activity is essentially to reduce the state to its optimal scale, where politicians undertake only measures that are truly wealth increasing, and even then only if losers are optimally compensated. Outlawing actual transfers (rent creation) and payments to buy off threats of transfer (rent extraction) therefore means nothing less than abolition of what politicians ("government," "the state") spend much—perhaps almost all—of their time doing. More simply, it means abolition of the state's *power* to do almost everything it currently does.[10]

In a more game-theoretic model, therefore, whether more-restrictive rules on payments to politicians to avoid expropriation really would reduce the overall amount of government-related wealth destruction depends on the other assumptions made at the same time. Taking existing levels of state power as given, effective abolition of political threats to wealth (or of the returns from threatening) would only increase the amount of wealth actually expropriated. Inability to be compensated for removing threats would naturally result in the enactment of more expropriation. Rent extraction would give way to more costly rent creation (surplus transfer) and the rent-seeking that inevitably would follow.

That is the second-best world in which we currently live. But assume instead that government also loses the ability to transfer wealth. This entails moving toward a first-best world, one in which politicians' ability to gain personally both by taking and by threatening is reduced. The assumptions necessary for limiting all payments to politicians, however, obviously take us well out of the world in which we live.

In that sense, Gary Becker (1983) was right. The regulatory outcomes observed today—including use of rent-extracting payments to avoid even more costly rent transfers—are in fact efficient in a second-best world. Attempts to make that world a better place by imposing this or that constraint on the system, to mitigate or end only one aspect of the problem, can only exacerbate some other problem. The one unambiguous solution for reducing rent extraction is reducing the size of the state itself and its power to threaten, expropriate, and transfer. The enormity of *that* task should cause anyone to hesitate before embracing the facile solutions so frequently offered that would only alter the bargaining between politicians and private parties, without reducing the size of what politicians have to sell.

Notes

References

Index

Notes

Introduction

1. Langley and Jackson (1986). More recently, bond dealers have collectively agreed to discontinue the previously common practice of making large contributions to political campaigns. See, e.g., Fuerbringer (1993).
2. Bacon (1993). As noted in Chapter 3, most of Citicorp's lobbying activities are aimed simply at getting politicians' permission to compete in various markets, not at obtaining special favors.
3. See Coffman (1992). Another fictional, truly apocalyptic portrayal of political extortion is found in the Clint Eastwood movie *High Plains Drifter*. Eastwood rides into Lago, a remote western mining town. Earlier, three thugs hired by the town's citizens had murdered Lago's marshal; to keep the killers from squealing on them, the citizenry then trumped up a separate charge against the three men to get them sent off to prison. When Eastwood arrives, the three killers are about to be released, having vowed to return to devastate Lago. Observing that Eastwood is a rather tough hombre himself, the town's citizens implore him to undertake their defense. He agrees, on condition that the townspeople do everything he orders and give him everything he wants. When the mayor acquiesces—promising "a free hand in this town . . . help yourself, go ahead"—Eastwood strips the mayor and the sheriff of their jobs and so obtains total political power. At that point his objectives become clearer: to avenge the marshal's death, Eastwood will fend off the killers, but only by destroying practically everything in Lago in the process. He rides out at the end, the marshal avenged, leaving the town "saved" but a smoking ruin.

   In Eastwood's fictional world, his pleasure (utility) comes from annihilating others' capital, both physical assets and human relationships. In the real world, of course, most people would rather transfer riches to themselves than just destroy them; thieves rarely steal just to cause others pain. So it is with politicians, who in many spheres possess the legal power to demand payments in return for not taking or destroying others' wealth. "Property is taken from some, not so that they will lose, but so that others, who control the political process, will win" (Epstein 1993, p. 4).

1. Background

1. This analytic reductionism has been called "normative analysis as a positive theory" (Joskow and Noll 1981). It is similar to the now-famous "nirvana fallacy": markets are imperfect; therefore, government will do a better job. See Demsetz (1969).
2. See, e.g., MacAvoy (1970). Perhaps the most influential early articles were Averch and Johnson (1962) and Stigler and Friedland (1962).
3. "Stigler had important predecessors . . . The lasting significance of Stigler's 1971 article is less in its specific conclusions or elements than in the question it poses—the why of regulatory behavior—and in the structure of its answer" (Peltzman 1989, p. 6).
4. Government cannot do so costlessly, of course, but the costs are borne by taxpayers, not by cartel members. Nor can government do so perfectly. In some situations, the problems that make private cartels unstable will also prevent government from cartelizing effectively (Hoffman and Libecap 1995).
5. In keeping with standard terminology, the term "rent creation" is used in this chapter. As explained further in Chapter 7, however, this term is a misnomer. Politicians cannot create rents other than by transferring some group's surplus (consumer surplus, producer surplus) to another. Nothing is really "created" in the process. To the contrary, something is always lost.
6. Additional welfare losses would occur because of the wealth effects in markets for normal goods, whose demand curves would fall with the increased spending in the monopolized markets; but economists have not investigated extensively the implications of this phenomenon.
7. Of course, the value of the rents (and so the amount producers will spend to acquire them) depends on the risk and uncertainty of being successful in attaining monopoly. If there is only a 50 percent chance of actually earning $1,000 in rents, their expected value is only $500, and a risk-neutral producer will spend only up to $499.99 in seeking rents.
8. Posner (1974, p. 335). Migué (1977, p. 214) also discussed regulations that are "difficult to reconcile with the economic theory of regulation."
9. For early demonstrations, see Kaun (1965); Williamson (1968). The fixed costs of regulatory compliance mean that regulation often affects smaller firms disproportionately. A recent study found that small companies spend 80 percent more per employee in complying with federal regulation than do larger firms (Sele 1995).
10. Technically, some of the returns to private individuals are true economic rents (e.g., the returns to entrepreneurial ability, artistic talent, or athletic ability), while others are more properly termed "quasi-rents" (the returns to prior

capital investments). See Friedman (1962, pp. 115–118). Often, however, the differences are of little operational significance. See, e.g., McCloskey (1982, p. 294): "Producers' Surplus Is Economic Rent Is Quasi-Rent Is Supernormal Profit." It is not the type of rent but its source—political versus nonpolitical behavior—that is of interest here. Also, the term "capital" as used in the model refers to both human (including entrepreneurial) and other types of capital—tangible as well as intangible.

11. McChesney (1987, p. 103, n. 9) cites several examples.

12. When the deadweight loss to regulation's victims is included, a dollar transferred actually costs the victims more than a dollar. Chapter 7 considers this point further.

13. "Regulation is . . . an instrument of wealth transfer—the extent of which is determined in a political market—where interest groups demand regulation and politician regulators supply it" (Migué 1977, p. 214).

14. Welch (1974, p. 84). See also Jackson, Saurman, and Shughart (1994, p. 258), which notes in the context of state lotteries that "it is not always the political pressure brought to bear by external interests expecting to benefit from legal change" that explains legislative enactments. In some cases (including those studied by Jackson, Saurman, and Shughart), "the legislature [stands] to gain the most."

15. Peltzman (1989, pp. 6–7; emphasis added). Peltzman then criticizes his own analysis but also repeats the notion that both consumers and producers are beneficiaries in the regulatory game: "This result—that all groups will share in the rents at the regulators' disposal—is as essentially empty as any similar result of constrained maximization analysis . . . [It] gives no guidance on expenditure shares, that is, whether the producers, the consumers, or neither group typically gets the lion's share of the rents" (ibid., p. 7).

2. Rent Extraction

1. Indeed, since the losses to consumers must be greater than the gains to producers, the regulatory contract is not even Kaldor-Hicks superior, which is the same as saying that regulation, unlike private contracts, is on net wealth-reducing.

2. Telser (1980); Klein and Leffler (1981). Of course, an agreement to make payments to avoid imposition of harm could be called a contract, in the same sense that responding to the choice "Your money or your life," offered by one wielding a gun, could be deemed a gift. Both popularly and legally, however, such a transaction—whatever option is chosen—"is still regarded as a robbery even though the participation of the victim was necessary to its completion, for the victim is compelled to choose between two alternatives, both of which are his as of right" (Epstein 1983, p. 556).

3. Gunning (1972, p. 20). For an early recognition of the bribery/extortion

distinction in explaining campaign contributions, see Aranson (1981, pp. 250–254).

4. On bribery versus extortion generally, see Lindgren (1993). One additional practice often distinguished in the literature is blackmail (requiring payment in order to keep secret certain information that otherwise would be disclosed). Since revelation of the information would make the payor worse off, blackmail is just a subset of extortion: "Coercive extortion is often called blackmail, particularly where hush money is involved, but few blackmail statutes remain on the books. Usually, blackmail behavior is covered under extortion, theft or coercion statutes" (ibid. at 1696).

5. That is, depending on the form of regulation to be imposed, the politician can offer up to the capitalized value of area P_cP_mBA in Figure 1.1 or of the net increase in rents (area I minus area II) in Figure 1.2.

6. Landes and Posner (1975). Since more durable rent contracts are in the interest of both private parties and politicians, the intervention of third-party institutions predictably would be sought to hold legislators to their deals. The judiciary, for example, may help guarantee congresssional rent-creation contracts, since courts can overrule legislators' attempted revisions of earlier contracts by holding the changes unconstitutional. Executive veto of attempted changes in legislative deals is another way to increase the amounts private parties would spend for rent creation (Tollison and Crain 1979). But neither guarantee system is perfect: "there will be some expectation that an independent judiciary will not support all past legislative contracts" (ibid., p. 167). In addition, newcomers to both the legislature and the executive office have less stake in continuing bargains made by their predecessors (Crain and Tollison 1979, pp. 561–566).

   More durable contracts to neutralize political threats are also more desirable to both politicians and would-be victims, as discussed in Chapter 5, where differences concerning durability of rent extraction versus rent creation are also considered.

7. For more on the distinction between good and bad rents, see Buchanan (1980); Tullock (1993, p. 22).

8. Just how much politicians will charge for rent creation is a subject on which little empirical evidence exists. One careful study of a particular rent-seeking episode (Couch, Atkinson, and Shughart 1992) found that politicians' "brokerage fee" for creating rents was about 5 percent of the rents created.

9. Of considerable interest, but ignored here, are standard public-choice issues involving collective legislative action: how to assemble political coalitions when each politician maximizes his own interest, how to divide the gains from rent extraction among individual politicians, the role of committees versus the entire legislature, and so forth.

10. On the importance of firms' specific capital, see Telser (1980); Klein and Leffler (1981). On advertising as a depreciating capital investment, see Peles (1971); Ayanian (1975).

11. "Buzzwords," *Newsweek,* November 20, 1989, p. 6.

12. Lindgren (1993, p. 1700). For example, Foner (1988) presents many examples of how the growth of government following the Civil War spawned political corruption in the Grant administration, corruption involving both rent creation and rent extraction. Foner notes, however, that the two were difficult to distinguish: "Coupled with the vast sums now handled by officials and the new functions assumed by the state, the increasing cost of political organization helped produce the political scandals of the Gilded Age. Much of the corruption of the Grant era involved payments to public officials by businesses seeking state aid, and in the Reconstruction South it often proved difficult to tell where bribery left off and extortion began" (ibid., p. 486).

13. Indeed, it may be difficult to distinguish governmental extortion, with negative implications for social wealth in the long term, from governmental enforcement of contracts and other activities with positive wealth effects. Both require the state to threaten, and often to take when private parties do not react appropriately (Gunning 1972, p. 25). As Tullock (1974b, p. 19) amplifies:

    We thus have two "models" of government. One is a cooperative venture by individuals to reduce the extent to which they are compelled to play a negative sum game. Facing a prisoner's dilemma, they turn to coercion of each other to behave in a "cooperative" manner.

    The other model is that of an exploitative group that simply has the power and is attempting to maximize the returns it can obtain by the use of this (same) power. Some elements of each of these models are present in almost any real government.

14. The fact that private parties' participation is "forced" does not contradict that they do so as part of a contract. An agreement to make payments to avoid imposition of harm is a contract, like the choice forced upon a robbery victim confronted by the choice between "your money or your life." Once again, however, this is not a legal contract—handing over one's money and then being shot would not subject the criminal to an action for breach of contract! Nonetheless, it is an extralegal contract; the victim has an incentive to hand over his money only if he thinks that the criminal will then leave him alone. If he thinks he will be shot anyway, the would-be victim will resist. Of course, that is why the robber offers the contract—the choice—in the first place.

15. Jackson also reports (1988, p. 69) on the campaign launched by Rep. Tony Coelho of California, chairman of the Democratic Congressional Campaign Committee, to interest business PACs in Democratic candidates by stressing candidates' business backgrounds and interests. "Coelho didn't rely wholly on the supposed business credentials of his candidates, however. He announced he would record names of those who didn't support candidates he deemed worthy. It was as though a traffic cop were stopping cars to sell tickets to the police-union ball."

16. Jackson (1985a). Further instances of how politicians pressure PACs for money are found in Sabato (1984, pp. 111–114).

17. "[P]otential victims of threats will want to reduce their vulnerability to threateners; they can do this in two ways. First, they can diminish the scale of the activities that expose them to risk . . . Second, a person can take precautions to lower the likelihood of threats given the scale of his activity" (Shavell 1993, pp. 1879–80).

18. Tullock (1967, p. 229, n. 11). For a demonstration of this same point graphically, showing how the threat of expropriation leads to a diminution in production and an increase in (nonexpropriable) leisure, see Tullock (1974b, p. 18).

19. See Posner (1993, pp. 1818–20): "blackmail is, and should be, forbidden because, although ostensibly a voluntary transaction between consenting adults, it is likely to be, on average, wealth-reducing rather than wealth-maximizing . . . [Extortionate threats] are intended to transfer wealth from the person threatened to the threatener. Such a transfer does not, on its face, increase social wealth; indirectly, it diminishes social wealth by the sum of the resources employed by the threatener to make his threat credible and of the victim to resist the threat. So, prima facie at least, it is a sterile redistributive acitvity, like (simple) theft."

20. This chapter's discussion of information problems inherent in the rent-extraction game is admittedly incomplete, in that it omits the problems faced by private parties in correctly anticipating politicians' actions. The amounts that private parties are willing to offer to avoid even greater losses in extracted rents depend on certain identifiable variables, among them (1) how long the deal not to extract rents is to continue, and (2) how likely it is that tomorrow the politician will stand by his promise today not to extract. These points are considered further in Chapter 5.

21. Observing the extortion of wealth by unwanted stoplight windshield-washers, Laband (1986, p. 408) finds that "they tended to select vehicles on the basis of perceived affluence of driver, as proxied by type of vehicle driven."

22. Henderson (1985). See also Abramson (1991): "Detroit's purse strings have also been loose when it comes to political contributions. The industry and related trade organizations have poured more than $20 million into the campaigns of federal lawmakers since 1984, when the fuel-efficiency issue was first seriously debated."

23. One study of the Federal Trade Commission, for example, discusses "Congress's inability to deter FTC action, even when considerable congressional pressures are exerted" (Clarkson and Muris 1981, p. 26). But for evidence of systematic congressional influence over FTC actions, see Weingast and Moran (1983); Coate, Higgins, and McChesney (1990). See also Rose-Ackerman (1978), who discusses in detail the role of political corruption at the agency level.

24. In that sense, rent extraction is different from private blackmail or extortion in one way. A private blackmailer or extortionist can increase the credibility of his threat—and therefore the amount needed to buy him off—by persuading his victim that he actually derives independent pleasure from depriving the victim of her reputation or wealth, i.e., that his utility function is negatively interdependent with hers. (This is the situation portrayed in the Eastwood film *High Plains Drifter*.) A politician is less likely, however, to try to convince his victims of any personal animus toward them, since they have other ways of imposing costs on him in the next period: withdrawal of votes, telling other voters about his dislike for them and its consequences, and so forth. (In *High Plains Drifter*, Eastwood's game was played in a single period; there would be no repeat dealings.)

    With respect to private extortion, Shavell (1993, p. 1880) appears mistaken on the effect of an extortionist's negatively interdependent utililty function. Calling the extortionist T and the victim V, and assuming that they both have relatively good information about each other's valuations, Shavell writes: "suppose that it will give T pleasure to carry out his threat. Then T will carry out his threat whether or not V accepts his demand, so again V should reject it; he would gain nothing by accepting the demand." But of course, if T's utils from carrying out the threat are greater than V's losses, then there is no reason for T to threaten in the first place; he will undertake the action harmful to V regardless, since the latter will offer no price sufficient to buy T off. On the other hand, if T's utils are less than the losses prospectively suffered by V, then V will still be able to buy T off—but at a higher price, to compensate T for the foregone utility of harming V. Posner (1993, p. 1839) adds that the "spiteful" blackmailer (i.e., one whose utility is negatively interdependent with his victim's) may be a more credible threatener.

25. See generally Neely (1991). According to Lindgren (1993, pp. 1696–97, n. 7), the earliest reported legal action for acts of extortion (referred to in the case as "bribes") involved a constable who in 1600 "levied more soldiers for musters than were required, and after by the way agreed with some of them for bribes and turned the men home again."

26. In the ordinary blackmail/extortion situation, the incidence of such threats is a function of the legal rules against the threats. "Rules that penalize the making of threats and their execution will generally increase the expected cost of making threats, and thus reduce the number of occasions in which a threatener will decide to make a threat" (Shavell 1993, p. 1883). But merely legislative rules cannot contain politicians' rent extraction, since they themselves establish those rules. Thus, the protections against politicians' extractive threats must be of a higher, constitutional, nature.

27. To return to the bribery/extortion analogy, one who solicits bribes from some people to increase their welfare is hardly precluded thereby from demanding payment from other people not to decrease theirs.

28. Stigler (1971, p. 3). As discussed in Chapter 8, however, Stigler did not

believe that rent-extracting regulation was very important in the overall economic model of regulation.

3. Observing Extortion

1. "Lobbyists' Price to Persuade Congress Hits $49 Million in '85," *Atlanta Journal,* June 5, 1986, p. 8.
2. Not all payments are made to avoid rent extraction; some are made for the creation or preservation of rents, or even for altruistic reasons, as noted in the Introduction.
3. Finance Committee Chairman Packwood (should that have been PACwood?) led his fellow committee members in almost all categories of financial activity for 1985: PAC receipts ($965,517), total receipts ($5,137,569), expenditures ($1,877,125), and year-end cash on hand ($3,545,970). He also received $34,750 in honoraria during 1985. Senator Dole was close behind, with direct PAC receipts of $595,750 and another $417,976 for his own PAC, Campaign America. The campaign contributions, however, were dispersed among all committee members. Further, the 1985 figures do not reflect 1986 contributions made while the Finance Committee was considering the tax bill. Similar patterns emerge for the House Ways and Means Committee, although the payments to then-Chairman Rostenkowski were slightly more subtle. Directly, he showed only $5,500 in outside PAC contributions. His own PAC, the Chicago Campaign Committee, however, raised $378,321 in 1985 and reported year-end cash on hand of $410,544. Overall, fourteen of the thirty-six Ways and Means Committee members collected more than $100,000 from PACs during 1985. For further discussion and sources for these figures, see Doernberg and McChesney (1987a, pp. 926–940).
4. Abramson and Rogers (1991, p. A6). According to Jackson (1988, p. 44), House incumbents' cost of retaining their seats had already risen steadily to $87,000 by 1976. (This amount is a mean, but probably not the median, since so many House seats are virtually tenured positions, with reelection rates above 90 percent.) "But the average cost of winning rose by 46 percent, to nearly $128,000, in the 1978 campaigns. That included modest sums spent by many old-time incumbents who still got re-elected buying little more than some billboards and bumper strips." For challengers, of course, the amounts required were much higher; they "simply could not hope to win without spending sums that had seemed extravagant, even sinister, only a few years earlier" (ibid.).
5. For further details on "bundling" as a way of skirting the donation limitations, see generally Jackson (1988).
6. "When former Gwinnett [County] Commission Chairman Lillian Webb reimbursed the county in 1989 for improper expenditures, she used campaign funds instead of her own money" (Sherman 1993).

7. For further discussion, see Doernberg and McChesney (1987a, pp. 940–941).

8. Noah (1993). The article described one three-day outing to an exclusive resort near Washington, with all room, food, alcohol, and entertainment expenses paid. "[A] congressional staffer who stayed the full three days received amenities that, had he or she paid his own way, would likely have totaled more than $1,500—and that is assuming the aide stayed in the very cheapest rooms, skipped lunch, carried his or her own golf clubs and was a teetotaler to boot."

9. See, for example, the stories surrounding the extortion conviction of state senator Joseph Montoya of California, who "gave the appearance of a politician who was squeezing both sides of the same fruit for 'juice'—a term that became familiar to jurors"; Dan Bernstein, "Montoya's Impossible Job," *Sacramento Bee*, Feb. 4, 1990, pp. A1, A22. Part of the testimony against Montoya came from the owner of a company that would have been put out of business by a particular bill, who "testified she felt she was being shaken down for campaign contributions by Montoya's former top aide"; Dan Bernstein, "I Didn't Sell Votes, Montoya Insists," *Sacramento Bee*, Jan. 23, 1990, p. A10. At the same time Montoya was taking money (plus free eyeglasses) from the California Optometric Association.

10. For example, Seabrook (1994) discusses a bill to place caps on home-equity loan interest rates, fought by the banking industry, that was killed in committee.

11. The Magnuson-Moss Federal Trade Commission Improvement Act of 1975 included an order to the FTC to initiate within one year "a rulemaking proceeding dealing with warranties and warranty practices in connection with the sale of used motor vehicles"; 15 U.S.C. sec. 2309(b). For the FTC's initial rule, see 16 C.F.R. sec. 455 (1982).

12. The FTC announcement of the veto appears at 47 Fed. Reg. 24542 (June 7, 1982).

13. Akerlof (1970). See, e.g., "Can Regulation Sweeten the Automotive Lemon?" *Regulation*, September/October 1984, p. 8: "Both intuition and empirical data suggest that the used-car market attracts lemons . . . A number of market mechanisms serve to alleviate these problems. The most visible solutions take the form of dealer guarantees and warranties, which recently have been beefed up with extended coverage backed by national insurers. Indirectly dealers invest in brand-name maintenance (local television ads, for instance), which makes it more costly for them to renege on a reputation for quality. The reputation of the parent automakers is also laid on the line. All four domestic car manufacturers have certified the quality of the better used cars sold by their dealers. Two generations of Chevrolet dealers, for example, have designated better used cars with an 'OK' stamp of the dealer's confidence in the car's marketability." See also Genesove (1993), which finds only weak evidence of any adverse selection in the used-car market; and Bond

(1982), which likewise reports no systematic "lemons" problems in the used-truck market.

14. See, e.g., "An Open Letter to President Clinton from 565 Economists from All 50 States on Healthcare Reform," *Washington Post*, March 16, 1994, p. A15; "Dear Mr. President . . . ," *Wall Street Journal*, Jan. 14, 1994. See also Driscoll (1994): "President Clinton has proposed an elaborate system of price reviews, blacklists and mandated rebates that establish price controls in effect, if not in name." Describing the pharmaceutical industry's public-relations campaign against the Clinton plan, one company executive said, "If we get 30 minutes, we talk about price controls. If we get 30 seconds, we talk about price controls" (Wartzman 1994b).

15. Insurance interests, for example, "oppose 'flat community rating,' whereby they wouldn't be allowed to charge people higher premiums based on factors such as age and smoking habits . . . The group also opposes government-imposed caps on how much insurers could raise their premiums each year, labeling these limits 'artificial controls on price'" (Wartzman 1993b).

16. An interesting question not considered here is the process by which (and the reasons why) the executive branch launched an initiative to enrich the legislative branch. There seems little doubt that the health-care proposal badly hurt Clinton's popularity; in any case, he did not apparently share in the outpouring of wealth from those whose prices would have been controlled by his plan.

17. "Requiem for Reform," *Wall Street Journal*, Oct. 14, 1994, p. A10.

18. Seelye (1994). Since the congressional action has proceeded principally through threats of new taxes, only sometimes passed, the principal recipients of tobacco money have been an interesting combination of politicians from tobacco states and others who merely wield influence to stop the taxes (former Representative Rostenkowski from Illinois, former Senator Dole from Kansas).

19. See also Fischel (1985). Fischel discusses instances of relaxation of zoning regulation conditioned on payments by property owners, a phenomenon he calls "zoning for sale."

20. As Epstein (1993, p. 183, n. 15) points out, in *Nollan* there were forty-three other plaintiffs facing the same extractive demands from the Coastal Commission. Every property owner except Nollan capitulated to those demands.

21. The situation is reminiscent of Yandle's "bootleggers and Baptists" strategy (Yandle 1983). The Baptists want taxes on legal alcohol in order to reduce its consumption; the bootleggers, operating illegally without paying taxes, also want higher taxes. Politicians can appeal electorally to both groups by putting taxation of legal alcohol on the political agenda.

22. See Brownell (1994). The politics and economics of taxing activities regarded as pleasurable by some but wrong by others is addressed in Shughart (1997).

23. For numerous episodes in addition to those recounted here, see Jackson (1988).

24. See Rabushka (1988). For a dissenting opinion, with citations to other enthusiasts of the 1986 legislation, see McChesney (1988).
25. See, for example, Krueger (1974); Johnson (1975). Krueger's study was particularly important, coining the term "rent-seeking" to describe the phenomenon first identified by Tullock (1967).
26. See Lal (1993, pp. 46–57). Lal discusses the revenue-maximizing "predatory state" in underdeveloped countries and the various forms of wealth transfers that politicians inflict on their populations.
27. The king's concern is maximizing his return, so he is indifferent whether money is paid to him personally or into the treasury, which he owns. (Obviously, this perspective is far removed from modern welfare-economic models of optimal taxation.)
28. Shleifer and Vishny (1993, p. 603). Shleifer and Vishny's article is one of the very few formally to integrate corruption into neoclassical economic theory. However, what they call "corruption" does not really distinguish between bribery and extortion. They refer, for example, to a case in which "bureaucrats prohibit imports of goods on which bribes cannot be collected without detection, and encourage imports of good on which they can collect bribes" (ibid., p. 614). However, the "bribes" here are being paid not for rent creation, but to avoid the wealth destruction that a bureaucrat can cause by denying entry to the imports. To most people, this is pure extortion, not bribery. A similar failure to distinguish bribery from extortion is found in Becker and Stigler (1974, p. 4), discussing "bribes" to avoid anti-Jewish laws in Nazi Germany. For further discussion by economists of bribery, however defined, see Pashigian (1975) and Rose-Ackerman (1978).
29. One story, for example, tells of an arrested person who "was released only after paying a large cash bail and giving authorities the title to his home"; "Vietnam's Prisoners, Iran's Dead," *Wall Street Journal,* June 12, 1992, p. A14.
30. See, e.g., Stone (1993). In one instance recounted there, a Singapore businessman in China had extorted from him "more in bribes than for the land, labor and capital needed to set up his venture."
31. For example, on the diminution of rent extraction from the destruction of India's former "license raj," see Murphy (1993).
32. Brooke (1992, p. 42). "Since that one-time shock remedy, consumer prices have increased 13,000 percent."

4. Validating the Model

1. Greif, Milgrom, and Weingast (1994, pp. 745–746). Tullock (1974b) refers to the two faces of Leviathan as the "cooperative" and the "exploitative" state.
2. See also Sowell (1980, pp. 115–116).

3. For further discussion of the methodology of positive economics and citations to principal contributions, see McChesney (1992).
4. Technically, the statistical tests cannot prove the hypotheses tested, but can only fail to refute them.
5. See Figure 2.1 and the related discussion in Chapter 2.
6. Mistake models are not only antiscientific but also futile. History demonstrates that seemingly "mistaken" policies followed by politicians through the years will eventually be recognized as purposeful actions by informed politicians, actions of benefit to them personally. See McChesney and Shughart (1995), chap. 19.
7. A similar methodology is used in other lines of inquiry. Mitchell and Maloney (1989) examined the effects on airline-firm wealth of an airline crash, followed by official determinations whether the airline itself was at fault. They found that the stock market discriminates between crashes that are not the fault of the airline (in which case the wealth lost at the time of the crash is eventually recovered) and those for which the airline is determined to have been at fault (in which case lost wealth is not restored).
8. Wealth losses from legislative threats are not a sufficient condition, however, since (under the mistake and the constituent-information hypotheses) the wealth lost would be restored at the time the threat was withdrawn.
9. I am grateful to Roger Beck for personal discussion of his research generally, and for further details of the specific episodes that make up his sample.
10. In 1978 the Canadian federal government announced an investigation of the food-processing and -retailing industry following a significant increase in food-processing prices; four months later it was annnounced that the investigation had found nothing untoward. Likewise, the House of Commons ordered an investigation into bank profits in February 1982; in July 1982 it determined that profits were not excessive. In late 1980 the government announced that exporters of natural gas would not be allowed to raise prices to cover a new excise tax; that policy was reversed in early 1981.
11. In February 1987 the Canadian government announced a new sales tax on snack foods, microwave ovens, and VCRs. In December the government announced a lowering of the proposed tax. A new tax on insurance policies announced in June 1987 was abandoned at the end of that year.
12. Politicians' extraction of all the rents parallels the general result concerning extortion described by Shavell (1993, p. 1882): "[if the threatener] has accurate knowledge of the harm that V [the victim] would suffer, he will demand exactly this amount, extracting the maximum from V."
13. Of course, constituents' transmission of information to politicians may be costly. But if the information-transmission process costs as much as the wealth threatened by the harmful legislation, such that upon retraction no increase in wealth results (Hypothesis 2A), then constituents have no incentive to provide the information in the first place. It is no more costly simply to allow the threat to become reality.

14. "Both hypotheses 2A and 2B are consistent with McChesney's rent extraction model" (Beck, Hoskins, and Connolly 1992, p. 219).

15. "Since McChesney proposed his model in a legislative context, it is appropriate that twenty-five of the thirty threats in our sample came directly from legislators—who were almost always cabinet ministers" (ibid., p. 220). Only two threats came directly from theoretically independent regulatory agencies, and three from enforcers of Canada's antitrust law. These last three were the only threats involving accusations of illegal behavior.

16. Not all events in the Beck-Hoskins-Connolly sample were harmful *socially*, only harmful to certain firms affected. For example, in May 1978 changes were proposed to allow easier entry into bank markets by both Canadian and foreign firms. The proposals were criticized by the Canadian Bankers Association and relaxed in October. The implications of other events were ambiguous in social-welfare terms (e.g., a proposed weakening of copyright laws to allow greater uncompensated copying of computer programs) but unambiguous in their threat to the firms affected.

17. The same methodology was used later for the thirty retraction regressions, as described in the text.

18. One disadvantage of this approach is that all pharmaceutical-specific events during the period are ascribed to the Clinton administration's threats. However, during this period there were relatively few *Wall Street Journal* stories specific to the pharmaceutical industry that did not concern its political difficulties. One can be relatively confident that the events included in the CLINTON1 dummy period were mostly the political ones.

19. In both regressions, one- and two-day lagged values of the dependent variable were included as regressors (the Koyck distributed lag model). Both were significant in each regression.

5. Contracting for Rent Preservation

1. The seminal case is Buckley v. Valeo, 424 U.S. 1 (1974).

2. It is this aspect of ordinary extortion, including blackmail, that has made such arrangements analytically thorny for legal scholars (e.g., Epstein 1993, pp. 58–63; Lindgren 1993; Posner 1993; Shavell 1993). Ordinarily, Mr. A has a perfect legal right to call Mr. B's wife and tell Mrs. B about Mr. B's infidelity. Alternatively, A has the right not to tell Mrs. B. If so, why is it (or should it be) illegal for A to agree with B not to tell Mrs. B, if Mr. B pays A not to do so?

3. Most obviously, the offer is constructed along the lines of the classic "Your money or your life." Thus, the private party's acceptance is made under duress (from the politician) and is legally unenforceable. The agreement would also be void for lack of consideration, since the politician is merely allowing private parties to enjoy ("your life") what supposedly is already theirs to enjoy.

4. Wartzman (1993a). Wartzman notes that although companies would prefer tax stability, all other things being equal, they also "lobby feverishly for special exemptions" once tax change is on the table. For a more detailed discussion, including reference to the continuing debate among tax scholars over tax longevity, see Ramseyer and Nakazato (1989).

5. For a general discussion and history of politicians' expressed concerns about tax avoidance, see Cooper (1985). For a review of the economic literature, see Spicer (1990).

6. The term "opportunism" is used here in the sense used in the literature of contracts and industrial organization, indicating postcontractual behavior to take advantage of one's contracting partner (e.g., Klein, Crawford, and Alchian 1978; Telser 1980; Klein and Leffler 1981). A separate strain of literature uses the term to refer to a politician's voting that does not reflect his constituents' wishes. For a summary and critique of that literature, see Lott and Davis (1992).

7. This is true as long as the lack of durability in political contracting was taken into account *ex ante*. See McCormick, Shughart, and Tollison (1984).

8. Again, this statement describes the real, second-best world in which the private producer's choices are between extraction and the more severe expropriation. The first-best alternative, the world in which the politician is content to sit by, without expropriating or threatening to, is utopian.

9. For an excellent study, on which this summary is based, see Witte (1985). See also Doernberg and McChesney (1987a, 1987b).

10. Ironically, growing reliance on the income tax paved the way for the end of Prohibition. Shortfalls in income tax caused by the Depression increased the relative attraction of restoring the excise tax on alcohol, necessitating repeal of Prohibition. In 1932, "The Democratic Party's platform had a very un-Keynesian theme: 'If only given a chance, Americans might drink themselves into a balanced budget'" (Yelvington 1997).

11. See, for example, Pechman (1987, p. 11), claiming that the 1986 legislation was "the most significant piece of tax legislation enacted since the income tax was converted to a mass tax during World War II"; Birnbaum (1986), describing coming tax changes as "the most dramatic and far-reaching measures in decades."

12. "The term 'tax expenditures' means those revenue losses attributable to provisions of the Federal tax laws which allow a special exclusion, exemption, or deduction from gross income or which provide a special credit, a preferential rate of tax, or a deferral of tax liability"; Congressional Budget Act of 1974, Pub. L. No. 93-344, sec. 3(a)(3), 88 Stat. 297, 299. Essentially, Congress has forgone revenue by creating a special provision that lowers someone's tax liability.

13. The percentage of changes occurring recently would be larger if 1969 had been included in the most recent period, since that period would then include the Tax Reform Act of 1969, a major piece of tax "reform."

14. Again, if the chronology of payments had the private party paying after the politician's performance, the private individual would have to find ways to guarantee her performance.
15. The repeat nature of any game alters importantly the ability of the players to attain better outcomes. See generally Axelrod (1984).
16. Even if the politician himself does not see sticking to his promise as his optimal strategy, perhaps because he has decided not to run for reelection, his party will still be part of next session's game, and will devise ways to increase the likelihood that the individual politician will keep his word.
17. In this sense, the best strategic reaction in the face of possible opportunism when there are repeated games (or repeated rounds of the same game) is the "tit for tat" strategy shown to be superior in the prisoner's dilemma game. See Axelrod (1984). In other words, although the "chicken" (opportunism) and prisoner's dilemma games are structurally different, players' optimal strategies in the two are similar as long as the games are repeated.
18. See generally Schelling (1963), especially chap. 2. As Schelling points out, one way for private parties to avoid ending up in quadrant [D], in the event they fear opportunism by the politician, is to break a single transaction down into a series of smaller ones whose payoffs are dependent on honesty in the preceding round. Rather than pay the full $10,000 for forbearance in an entire legislative session, the private individual might agree to pay $1,000 per month for the first six months, with another $4,000 coming at the end. The first six payments would establish the private owner's bona fides; desire for the last payment would likewise motivate the politician to honor his side of the bargain.
19. For an insightful analysis of how congressional voting is structured to ensure that legislative deals already struck are observed at voting time, see Crain, Leavens, and Tollison (1986). For evidence that no change in their behavior arises when politicians are in their last period, see Lott and Bronars (1993).
20. In addition to the problems already noted, there is always a possibility that a politician will try but fail to deliver on his no-expropriation promises; other politicians may favor actual expropriation and outvote the politician who has taken the extraction payment of $10,000. This outcome, however, is just a nonequilibrium problem of miscalculation. The next time around, private individuals will be less willing to pay that politician and will move on to those who have superior clout.
21. The term "incumbency effect" refers to the high likelihood that an incumbent seeking reelection will be returned to office. For the period 1946–1994 the percentage of House incumbents successfully seeking reelection has ranged from 80 to 98 percent. For Senate incumbents, the percentage has generally been slightly lower. See Ornstein, Mann, and Malbin (1994).
22. Figures concerning average time of service on the Ways and Means and Finance Committees are derived from information reported in successive volumes of the *Congressional Index* and the *Congressional Directory*.

23. Shughart (1987, pp. 274–275). See also Brennan and Buchanan (1980, p. 190).
24. This legislation is not to be confused with the legislation signed by George ("Read My Lips") Bush, the Omnibus Budget Reconciliation Act of 1990.

6. Extraction and Optimal Taxation

1. This may be changing, however, as new tax models have begun to recognize the importance of politics. For example, Hettrick and Winer (1988); Kiesling (1990); Gradstein (1993).
2. Brennan and Buchanan (1980, p. xii). Even those discussions that have begun to include politics in the tax process have typically done so only at the level of theory, not empirics; e.g., Hettrick and Winer (1988); Gradstein (1993). For an exception, see Anderson, Shughart, and Tollison (1989), which provides a model and empirical tests of states' use of excise taxes.
3. For other public goods, if consumption is nonrivalrous and exclusion from consumption is not possible, a free-riding problem (without government coercion) would arise from failure to pay for that consumption. National defense is the standard example. The government's transaction-cost advantage lies in being able to force those who consume (benefit) to pay.
4. For simplicity here, constant marginal costs are assumed. Of course, in many markets in which government is active, high fixed costs and declining marginal costs mean that second-best pricing solutions often should be adopted; Atkinson and Stiglitz (1980, pp. 458–470). That complication does not alter the analysis here.
5. This is the now-standard analysis made famous as a matter of welfare economics by A. C. Pigou and later criticized by Coase (1960). As a positive matter, many excises (such as those on life-insurance policies and long-distance telephone calls) have nothing to do with externalities but are simply ways of raising revenue and redistributing income; see Shughart (1997).
6. A major concern with alcohol use, for example, is whether users are too young to measure optimally the long-term costs involved; see, e.g., Kenkel and Ribar (1994). That there are costs to some consumption activities seems increasingly clear, but the existence of costs does not decide the issue, since there are also present benefits. It is safe to say that the real issue, whether rational maximizing is at work even among a particular group (the young, the addicted), has not been resolved. It may not even be resolvable, since what is "optimal" is subjective, depending on the personal discount rate determining future losses, which must be balanced against present gains. Assumptions of different (unobservable) discount rates alters many of the conclusions. See Becker and Murphy (1988, p. 683). See also Pogue and Sgontz (1989, p. 242): "determining alcohol tax rates on the basis of efficiency criteria—the optimal tax framework—does not in itself greatly limit the range of tax rates. Either taxation near the present level or very high taxation may be optimal,

depending on the values of key parameters." Even if some alcohol users demonstrably abuse it, it still does not follow that a tax levied on *all* alcohol purchases, including those made by moderate users, is the optimal way to control external costs. See Wagner (1997).

7. The analysis for excises is slightly different, since the tax is to control a bad (a negative externality) like pollution, rather than to produce a good like a road. Acting optimally in the externality situation, government would price the activity at its costs to third parties (e.g., in lost use or investment value from pollution).

8. Again, with a bad (the negative externality like pollution) rather than a good (the road), the analysis is slightly different. In such cases, government can cause welfare losses both by under- and by overpricing, leading to either over- or underproduction of the externality-causing activity.

9. E.g., Pogue and Sgontz (1989). As the authors also note, however, there is disagreement whether any costs of such "sins" are truly "social" (i.e., external) or whether they are effectively internalized. For an excellent discussion of this point, and the way that the "social cost" argument often has more to do with politics than with economics, see Anderson (1992).

10. See, for example, Atkinson and Stiglitz (1980, p. 480), discussing how "optimal pricing" by government enterprises requires information that it typically does not have. The information problem is often endogenous, however. It may be true that with public goods for which exclusion is impossible or impractical (such as national defense), government actors will have difficulty discerning consumers' true demands. In such cases, "The political process may result in serious misallocation because it may fail to interpret preferences correctly" (Due and Friedlander 1973, p. 99). But no such problem exists for goods for which exclusion, and thus the imposition of user fees, is possible. Government disinclination to obtain information, rather than the difficulty of doing so, is the true problem in those instances.

11. Once again, part of the problem is endogenous, even if there are no private competing enterprises by which government could be guided. The very fact that government enterprise is known typically to be an underpricer will keep competition out. Since government enterprises are not profit maximizers and they have access to general revenues to fund losses from pricing below cost, their threat to price predatorily is much more credible than that of any private firm. See Lott (1990).

12. "A safe answer to the question of how a majoritarian government may raise money to build or maintain roads and other projects is to say that it has many options and that it can do pretty much as it pleases . . . governments could use special assessments and user fees more than they currently do, but little is known about why and when these devices are used" (Levmore 1990, p. 290).

13. Evidence consistent with that of Peltzman is presented in De Alessi (1975), showing that public electric utilities buy power at higher wholesale prices and

sell it at lower prices than comparable private companies do; and in De Alessi (1977), explaining why public power companies make less use of optimal peak-load pricing than do private companies.

14. For discussion of the reasons for bureaucratic preference for government enterprises, and of how those firms operate, see Lott (1990). As was noted in Chapter 2, there is some debate over whether and to what extent bureaucrats' own desires enter into government production decisions, versus to what extent they are merely agents of elected officials. That debate is of less concern for understanding government underpricing, however, since both legislators and bureaucrats apparently have an incentive to favor underpricing.

15. As Buchanan (1963, p. 467) notes in his analysis of tax earmarking, a bureaucrat's objective is "primarily that of expanding the size and importance of the public sector." For historical examples of bureaucratic preferences for "free" government services, see West (1967); Pashigian (1976); McChesney (1986).

16. This statement admittedly oversimplifies the way Social Security works. Social Security is essentially a "pay as you go" system, with current revenues from workers going to pay current obligations to retirees. But in addition Congress has required overcontributions in the current period to create a fund supposedly available for the heavier withdrawals expected in the future.

17. Saxton (1994). The Kansas experience with politically driven investments of public pension money has been particularly disastrous (White 1991). Several more systematic academic studies (e.g., Romano 1993) also show that these anecdotal reports in fact portray the overall result of "social" investing by public pension funds. Overall, those investments are riskier and earn lower returns.

18. Palefsky (1990). A slightly more subtle diversion occurs when the earmarked funds merely replace money that would have been appropriated anyway. State lotteries, for example, often are required to earmark their net proceeds for a certain purpose, such as education. But education was already an important component of state spending before lotteries were adopted. It is thus reported (e.g., Borg and Mason 1988) that adoption of a lottery allows a state to shift money *out* of education, where it would have gone but for the lottery, and into new channels.

19. Letter from the Partnership for Improved Air Travel, November 28, 1989, asking members to contact politicians and demand release of trust-fund money. One growing problem for trust funds and their supposed beneficiaries is concern about budget deficits. When budgets must be balanced, trust funds that hold money, rather than spending it as promised, free up dollar-for-dollar revenues available for other government spending.

20. See, e.g., Christensen (1990), discussing competition among congressmen for aviation trust funds to build airports to compete with Atlanta's Hartsfield International Airport.

7. Costs and Benefits of Interest-Group Organization

1. In Figure 7.1, Q_m corresponds to the monopoly profit-maximizing quantity, determined by equating marginal revenue (not shown in the diagram, but intersecting the supply schedule at point H) with marginal cost.
2. "The general problem with rent-seeking analysis as exposed, for example, by Posner is that it focuses almost entirely on the cost of resources spent by sellers in attaining, and competing with one another for, monopolizing regulation. Those who purchase the output of the industry in question seem to be assumed to sit idly by and await the outcome while sellers scrap over monopoly profits and rents. This is indeed a heroic assumption" (Wenders 1986a, p. 2).
3. Becker (1983, p. 392). For further discussion of consumer votes as a counter to producer payments to politicians, see Denzau and Munger (1986). For an empirical demonstration of consumers' influence as voters, see Becker (1986).
4. Hirshleifer (1976). Politicians should be modeled as wealth, not vote, maximizers. "If wealth is the ultimate goal, majority maximization can only be an instrumental and partial aim" (ibid., p. 241).
5. Buchanan (1970, pp. 66–67) has suggested that some consumer groups organize to lobby for regulations impeding production of lower-quality goods, so that producers will produce more of the higher-quality goods that group members themselves purchase, lowering their price. There is some empirical support for this model (McChesney 1990). This sort of regulation is analytically analogous to the phenomenon of generating rents for some producers at the expense of rival producers by "raising rivals' costs" or "cost predation," discussed in Chapter 1.
6. See Becker (1991); Karni and Levin (1994). More generally, see Liebowitz and Margolis (1994).
7. McCormick and Tollison (1981, p. 17). "The common characteristic which distinguishes all of the large economic groups with significant lobbying organizations is that these groups are also organized for some *other* purpose. The large and powerful economic lobbies are in fact the by-products of organizations that obtain their strength and support because they perform some function in addition to lobbying for collective goods" (Olson 1965, p. 132).
8. Louis Harris & Associates (1983, p. 60). For those with incomes over $50,000, the figure was 30 percent.
9. See, e.g., Davis (1987, p. 33): "activists, lobbyists and politicians have begun to mobilize subscribers of such computer services. 'Using the new technology, activists who hit a hot-button issue for subscribers and make it easy for them to volunteer can create an instant organization,' says Larry Sabato, a University of Virginia professor." The National Association of Manufacturers communicates via NAMnet, its own electronic news service, to keep members informed on issues in Congress (ibid.).

10. As shown by Rowley and Tollison (1986) and by Wenders (1987), buyers can be included directly as bidders against producers in the auction.

11. The conclusion that current surplus owners will bid more to avoid regulation—in this case, EIA more—holds even when potential welfare losses from regulation exceed the trapezoid, a possibility modeled in Baysinger and Tollison (1980).

12. See, for example, Kurkjian (1986). In a congressional vote to "weaken federal controls over the sale and registration of firearms," the article describes how congressmen and senators who backed the NRA received most of the money—close to $1 million in each chamber—donated by the "gun lobby."

13. See Appelbaum and Katz (1987). In their model, regulation is a three-sided game among consumers, firms, and the regulator; the regulator has different "threat strategies" available. In certain conditions, "the regulator is shown to use the firms to extract rents from consumers. Firms, as a group, neither gain nor lose in this case" (ibid., p. 698).

14. McCormick and Tollison (1981, p. 16). As long as the costs of contracting (transaction costs) are zero, there will never be any regulation; "efforts to achieve monopoly through regulation would never be successful because the losers could always outspend the gainers" (Wenders 1987, p. 459). But there is much regulation. Thus, the task for economics "is to explain how the various degrees of asymmetry in regulatory influence between buyers and sellers result in balances at the margin that produce the observed degree of regulation" (ibid.).

15. Jackson (1988, p. 193). Birnbaum and Murray (1987) also provide many examples of personal negotiations between politicians and private parties seeking their help.

16. This implication is general and testable: all other things being equal, there will be fewer excise taxes imposed in cartelized industries, where lower-cost means of surplus transfer already operate. Industries that go from regulated to unregulated likewise can expect imposition of new excises, *ceteris paribus*.

17. As was discussed in Chapter 2, another consideration is the extent to which consumers can switch their purchases to substitute goods more cheaply than it would cost to buy off politicians. This ability to substitute, reflected in demand elasticity, parallels the value of producers' capital mobility in avoiding rent extraction.

18. Though used routinely, the notion of a "quantity" of regulation is admittedly imprecise. As Aranson (1990, p. 247, n. 1) says, "It is not apparent how one should 'measure' the extent of regulation or year-to-year changes in its pervasiveness. Regulation is not like other government policies, whose explicit expenditures provide simple indicators." An additional complication is the extent to which efforts to regulate are onetime or recurring events, and thus the period over which "quantity" is to be measured. Compare McCormick, Shughart, and Tollison (1984) with Cherkes, Friedman, and Spivak (1986).

19. See, e.g., Schwartz (1988, p. 173): "[Numerous] passive shareholders could do better when facing prospective buyers [of the firm] than single owners of the same assets would do. An intuitive example of this result exists: everyone knows that in some negotiations the ability to sit sphinxlike and let the other person make a series of proposals can yield useful information about the other person's views." Schwartz's model relies on ignorance of opposing parties' valuations and the costs of becoming informed. In the Coasean model used here, regulators are perfectly informed of groups' surplus values but face positive costs of inducing them to pay either to retain their surplus or to effect a transfer of another group's surplus. But the models are fundamentally similar in showing that in either private-group or regulatory bargaining it can pay one group to be unorganized.

20. If an item like availability of guns is regarded as a good by some consumers but a bad by others, the prices that politicians charge for transferring or not transferring surplus will be different. This complication, however, does not change the fundamental points discussed here.

21. An interesting example of having one's cake and eating it too is provided by Greif, Milgrom, and Weingast (1994, pp. 754–758). They relate how in medieval times foreign merchants were often at the mercy of local thieves and so turned individually to the local ruler for protection. It was of course in the ruler's interest to maintain commerce, but sometimes the ruler failed to provide the protection promised. At that point the foreign merchants organized in order to boycott the countries where problems with the ruler had arisen—but they organized the boycott *in their own country,* where their rents and wealth would not be vulnerable to the ruler. Thus the benefits of organization to countervail the force of the sovereign were obtained, without exposing the organization itself to any rent extraction.

22. One such form read as follows:

    I NEED YOUR HELP, SENATOR

    _____

    (Print Senator's name here)
    U.S. Senate
    Washington, D.C. 20510
    Please stop new liquor taxes. I already pay a higher tax rate on liquor than on *any* other product. More taxes could mean higher prices for me and could put people in the liquor business out of work.

    Lines for the customer's name and address followed. Attached was an identical form for the other state senator, plus one for the customer's representative in the House.

23. "A Brew in One Hand, a Petition in the Other," *Wall Street Journal,* April 27, 1990, p. B1.

24. The Partnership for Improved Air Travel, chaired by the chairman and president of Southwest Airlines, was created in the late 1980s to oppose increasing airport user fees and, especially, to lobby for release of money from

the Airport and Airway Trust Fund. Though established by an alliance of airlines, airports, and other aviation-related businesses, it then enrolled hundreds of thousands of frequent flyers, who received kits (similar to those used by alcohol interests described above) to help consumers contact Washington on various issues of political interest.

25. Calling redistributions of surplus "transfers" does not imply an absence of deadweight losses. For a complaint that the Chicago school of economics often argues that regulatory transfers entail no welfare loss, see Crew and Rowley (1988).

8. Improving the Model

1. See Chapter 7. Politicians cannot create wealth, only transfer it. Gains to one private group entail losses to another. Unlike private contracts, political bargains are not Pareto superior; indeed, since the losers' losses outweigh the gainers' gains, political rent creation can never be even a Kaldor-Hicks improvement.

2. The extraction opportunities presented by antitrust investigations are shown in Faith, Leavens, and Tollison (1982). A good example of government attempts to extract rents from a successful firm was the antitrust action threatened against Microsoft in 1993 (by the FTC) and 1994 (by the Justice Department). Microsoft has attained something approaching a natural monopoly; its sole potential competitor, Apple, has hurt itself by not licensing its software, and so has failed to slow Microsoft's market dominance. Thus there is little the government can do for Microsoft, by way of creating rents, that it cannot do for itself.

   Since extraction is the only way for the government to make money in this situation, it has tried hard to do so. Under repeated pressure from both politicians and Microsoft's rivals to "do something" about the success enjoyed by the developer of MS-DOS and other successful computer software, the government antitrust agencies threatened Microsoft with various forms of wealth loss. The firm refused to capitulate, and eventually it was the government that recoiled: in return for an innocuous consent order agreed to by Microsoft, no antitrust suit was filed. The numerous press reports of this confrontation do not mention any lobbying or other costly effort by Microsoft, other than arguing the merits of its case before the federal agencies involved. See McChesney and Shughart (1995, chap. 19).

   A similar scenario seems to be unfolding in the Justice Department's investigation of West Publishing Company for its numbering system of case-law citation widely used in the legal profession. Because the system is popular but copyrighted, other firms complain that they lose business from being unable to use West's copyright. The Justice Department is investigating. See O'Brien (1994).

3. Tullock (1993, p. 38). See also Tullock (1989).

4. "A central thesis of this paper is that, as a rule, regulation is acquired by the industry and is designed and operated primarily for its benefit. There are regulations whose net effects upon the regulated industry are undeniably onerous; a simple example is the differentially heavy taxation of the industry's product (whiskey, playing cards). These onerous regulations, however, are exceptional" (Stigler 1971, p. 3).

5. Although no data have been developed to separate the two empirically, Aranson (1981, pp. 252–253) has suggested that "bribery" (rent creation) may not be as important as "extortion" (rent extraction). "The metaphor of bribery may seem overly simplistic. Some would argue that the real market for contributions is one of 'extortion' by those who hold a monopoly on the use of coercion—the officeholders . . . examples of this [extortion] interpretation of campaign contributions are not uncommon."

6. Moreover, the few analyses of victimless crime that have been done usually focus on enforcement of the law rather than the reason for making the conduct illegal in the first place. See, for example, Becker and Stigler (1974, pp. 3–4).

7. Benson and Rasmussen (1997) note that the process of making drug use illegal in this country began with attempts to tax it. But taxation proved difficult to enforce, and so—incongruously, some would say—the use of various substances was simply outlawed.

8. Jackson (1988) develops this theme in several places, including his chap. 8.

9. By the fall of 1986 Senator Robert Packwood had amassed such large amounts of money—selling tax breaks in 1985–86 prior to the 1986 tax legislation—that those who had been expected to challenge him declined to run. Eventually the Democrats were able to field only token opposition. "For all practical purposes, he had won a year before voters went to the polls, by collecting special-interest donations given in the hope of influencing the shape of the bill" (Jackson 1988, pp. 131–132).

10. For one view of the legal functions that still would legitimately be undertaken by such a minimal state, see Epstein (1995).

References

Abramson, Jill. 1990. "Product-Liability Bill Provides Opportunity for Long-Term Milking of PACs by Congress." *Wall Street Journal,* June 21, p. A16.

———. 1991. "Car Firms Kick Lobbying Effort into High Gear in Bitter Fight over Fuel-Economy Legislation." *Wall Street Journal,* Sept. 20, p. A14.

Abramson, Jill, and David Rogers. 1991. "The Keating 535: Five on the Grill but Other Lawmakers Help Big Donors Too." *Wall Street Journal,* Jan. 10, p. A1.

Akerlof, George A. 1970. "The Market for 'Lemons': Quality Uncertainty and the Market Mechanism." *Quarterly Journal of Economics,* 84: 488.

Alchian, Armen A. 1987. "Rent." In John Eatwell, Murray Milgate, and Peter Newman, eds., *The New Palgrave Dictionary of Economics,* vol. 4. New York: Stockton Press. P. 141.

Alm, James. 1985. "The Welfare Cost of the Underground Economy." *Economic Inquiry,* 24: 243.

Anderson, Gary M. 1992. "A Sober Look at the Costs of Intoxication." *Contemporary Policy Issues,* 10: 111.

Anderson, Gary M., William F. Shughart II, and Robert D. Tollison. 1989. "Political Entry Barriers and Tax Incidence: The Political Economy of Sales and Excise Taxes." *Public Finance/Finances Publiques,* 44: 8.

Anderson, Terry L., and Peter J. Hill. 1980. *The Birth of a Transfer Society.* Stanford, Calif.: Hoover Institution Press.

Appelbaum, Elie, and Eliakim Katz. 1987. "Seeking Rents by Setting Rents: The Political Economy of Rent Seeking." *Economic Journal,* 97: 685.

Aranson, Peter H. 1981. *American Government: Strategy and Choice.* Cambridge, Mass.: Winthrop Publishers.

———. 1990. "Theories of Economic Regulation: From Clarity to Confusion." *Journal of Law and Politics,* 6: 247.

Aranson, Peter H., and Melvin J. Hinich. 1979. "Some Aspects of the Political Economy of Election Campaign Contribution Laws." *Public Choice,* 34: 435.

Atkinson, A. B., and Joseph E. Stiglitz. 1980. *Lectures on Public Economics.* New York: McGraw-Hill.

Averch, Harvey, and Leland L. Johnson. 1962. "The Behavior of the Firm under Regulatory Constraint." *American Economic Review,* 52: 1052.

Axelrod, Robert. 1984. *The Evolution of Cooperation.* New York: Basic Books.

Ayanian, Robert. 1975. "Advertising and Rate of Return." *Journal of Law and Economics,* 18: 479.

Bacon, Kenneth H. 1993. "For Citicorp, Which Has Largest Lobbying Force in Banking Industry, Victories Are Won Quietly." *Wall Street Journal,* Dec. 14, p. A18.

Barbash, Fred. 1994. "British Tories Face Another Cash Scandal." *Washington Post,* Oct. 21, p. A27.

Baysinger, Barry, and Robert D. Tollison. 1980. "Evaluating the Social Costs of Monopoly and Regulation." *Atlantic Economic Journal,* 8: 22.

Beck, Roger, Colin Hoskins, and J. Martin Connolly. 1992. "Rent Extraction through Political Extortion: An Empirical Examination." *Journal of Legal Studies,* 21: 217.

Becker, Gary S. 1983. "A Theory of Competition among Pressure Groups for Political Influence." *Quarterly Journal of Economics,* 98: 371.

———. 1991. "A Note on Restaurant Pricing and Other Examples of Social Influences on Price." *Journal of Political Economy,* 99: 1109.

Becker, Gary, and Kevin M. Murphy. 1988. "A Theory of Rational Addiction." *Journal of Political Economy,* 96: 675.

Becker, Gary S., and George J. Stigler. 1974. "Law Enforcement, Malfeasance, and Compensation of Enforcers." *Journal of Legal Studies,* 3: 1.

Becker, Gilbert. 1986. "The Public Interest Hypothesis Revisited: A New Test of Peltzman's Theory of Regulation." *Public Choice,* 49: 223.

Bell, Jeffrey. 1990. "Moynihan Plan? A Good Idea, Even If Stolen." *Wall Street Journal,* Feb. 26, p. A8.

Bennett, James T., and Thomas J. DiLorenzo. 1985. *Destroying Demoncracy: How Government Funds Partisan Politics.* Washington, D.C.: Cato Institute.

———. 1987. "How (and Why) Congress Twists Its Own Arm: The Political Economy of Tax-Funded Politics." *Public Choice,* 55: 199.

Benson, Bruce L., and M. D. Faminow. 1986. "The Incentives to Organize and Demand Regulation: Two Ends against the Middle." *Economic Inquiry,* 24: 473.

Benson, Bruce L., and David W. Rasmussen. 1997. "Predatory Public Finance and the Origins of the War on Drugs: 1984–1989." In William F. Shughart II, ed., *Taxing Choice: The Predatory Politics of Fiscal Discrimination.* New Brunswick, N.J.: Transaction.

Benson, Bruce L., David W. Rasmussen, and David L. Sollars. 1995. "Police Bureaucracies, Their Incentives, and the War on Drugs." *Public Choice,* 83: 21.

Berke, Richard L. 1994. "Health Debate Is Filling Campaign Coffers." *New York Times,* April 19, p. A1.

Berkman, Harvey. 1995. "Legal Defense Funds Are Pols' Latest Perks." *National Law Journal,* Dec. 11, p. A1.

Birnbaum, Jeffrey. 1985a. "Sen. Long, an Architect of the Income-Tax Code, Is Ready to Protect Handiwork from 'Reform.'" *Wall Street Journal,* May 7, p. 64.

———. 1985b. "House Committee Seeks Big Support for Tax Bill through Myriad Concessions to Small Interests." *Wall Street Journal,* Nov. 21, p. 64.

———. 1986. "Tax Bill Saga: How a Pre-Emptive Political Step Became a Plan to Restructure Taxation in the U.S." *Wall Street Journal,* June 4, p. 62.

———. 1990. "Rostenkowski Backs Boost in Gas Tax, Would Use Defense Cuts to Trim Deficit." *Wall Street Journal,* Jan. 3, p. A8.

Birnbaum, Jeffrey, and Alan Murray. 1987. *Showdown at Gucci Gulch: Lawmakers, Lobbyists, and the Unlikely Triumph of Tax Reform.* New York: Random House.

Bond, Eric W. 1982. "A Direct Test of the 'Lemons' Model: The Market for Used Pickup Trucks." *American Economic Review,* 72: 836.

Borg, Mary, and Paul Mason. 1988. "The Budgetary Incidence of a Lottery to Support Education." *National Tax Journal,* 41: 75.

Brennan, Geoffrey, and James M. Buchanan. 1980. *The Power to Tax: Analytical Foundations of a Fiscal Constitution.* Cambridge: Cambridge University Press.

Brooke, James. 1992. "Looting Brazil." *New York Times Magazine,* Nov. 8, p. 31.

Brownell, Kelly D. 1994. "Get Slim with Higher Taxes." *New York Times,* Dec. 15, p. 29.

Buchanan, James M. 1963. "The Economics of Earmarked Taxes." *Journal of Political Economy,* 71: 457.

———. 1970. "In Defense of *Caveat Emptor.*" *University of Chicago Law Review,* 38: 64.

———. 1975. "Consumerism and Public Utility Regulation." In Charles Phillips, ed., *Telecommunications, Regulation, and Public Choice.* Lexington, Va.: Washington and Lee University.

———. 1980. "Rent Seeking and Profit Seeking." In James M. Buchanan, Robert D. Tollison, and Gordon Tullock, eds., *Toward a Theory of the Rent-Seeking Society.* College Station: Texas A & M University Press.

Califano, Joseph. 1994. "Imperial Congress." *New York Times Sunday Magazine,* Jan. 23, p. 40.

Carnevale, Mary Lu, and Mark Robichaux. 1994. "FCC Votes to Require Cable Rate Cuts and This Time Claims It Will Prevail." *Wall Street Journal,* Feb. 23, p. B1.

Cherkes, Martin, Joseph Friedman, and Avia Spivak. 1986. "The Disinterest in Deregulation: Comment." *American Economic Review,* 76: 559.

Christensen, Mike. 1990. "Bush's Air Fare Tax Plan May Not Fly in Congress." *Atlanta Journal & Constitution,* Feb. 7, p. A5.

Clarkson, Kenneth W., and Timothy J. Muris. 1981. "Commission Performance, Incentives and Behavior." In *The Federal Trade Commission since 1970: Economic Regulation and Bureaucratic Behavior.* Cambridge: Cambridge University Press.

Coase, R. H. 1937. "The Nature of the Firm." *Economica,* n.s., 4: 386.

———. 1959. "The Federal Communications Commission." *Journal of Law and Economics,* 2: 1.

————. 1960. "The Problem of Social Cost." *Journal of Law and Economics*, 3: 1.

Coate, Malcolm B., Richard S. Higgins, and Fred S. McChesney. 1990. "Bureaucracy and Politics in FTC Merger Challenges." *Journal of Law and Economics*, 33: 463.

Coffman, Richard B. 1992. "Mud Farming and Political Extortion." *The Freeman*, 42: 258.

Congressional Quarterly. 1982. *Guide to Congress*. 3rd ed. Washington, D.C.

Cooper, George. 1985. "The Taming of the Shrewd: Identifying and Controlling Income Tax Avoidance." *Columbia Law Review*, 85: 657.

Couch, Jim F., Keith E. Atkinson, and William F. Shughart II. 1992. "Ethics Laws and the Outside Earnings of Politicians: The Case of Alabama's 'Legislator-Educators.' " *Public Choice*, 73: 135.

Crain, W. Mark, Donald R. Leavens, and Robert D. Tollison. 1986. "Final Voting in Legislatures." *American Economic Review*, 76: 833.

Crain, W. Mark, and Robert D. Tollison. 1979. "The Executive Branch in the Interest-Group Theory of Government." *Journal of Legal Studies*, 8: 555.

Crew, Michael A., and Charles K. Rowley. 1988. "Toward a Public Choice Theory of Monopoly Regulation." *Public Choice*, 67: 49.

Davidson, Joe. 1991. "In Zaire, Corrupt and Autocratic Rule, Backed by U.S., Has Led Straight to Ruin." *Wall Street Journal*, Dec. 17, p. A16.

Davis, Bob. 1987. "Hobbyists as Lobbyists: Computer Users Are Mobilized to Support Host of Causes." *Wall Street Journal*, Sept. 29, p. 33.

De Alessi, Louis. 1975. "Some Effects of Ownership on the Wholesale Price of Electric Power." *Economic Inquiry*, 13: 526.

————. 1977. "Ownership and Peak-Load Pricing in the Electric Power Industry." *Quarterly Review of Economics and Business*, 17: 7.

Demsetz, Harold. 1969. "Information and Efficiency: Another Viewpoint." *Journal of Law and Economics*, 12: 1.

Denzau, Arthur, and Michael C. Munger. 1986. "Legislators and Interest Groups: How Unorganized Interests Get Represented." *American Political Science Review*, 80: 89.

Doernberg, Richard L., and Fred S. McChesney. 1987a. "On the Accelerating Rate and Decreasing Durability of Tax Reform." *Minnesota Law Review*, 71: 913.

————. 1987b. "Doing Good or Doing Well? Congress and the Tax Reform Act of 1986." *New York University Law Review*, 62: 891.

Doerner, William F. 1986. "California's Political Gold Rush." *Time*, Feb. 3, p. 24.

Driscoll, James. 1994. "The Moral Battle Plan." *Wall Street Journal*, Feb. 16, p. A18.

Due, John F., and Anne F. Friedlander. 1973. *Government Finance: Economics of the Public Sector*. 5th ed. Homewood, Ill.: Richard D. Irwin.

Easterbrook, Gregg. 1984. "What's Wrong with Congress?" *Atlantic Monthly*, December, p. 57.

Eaton, Jonathan, and Mark Gersovitz. 1984. "A Theory of Expropriation and Deviations from Perfect Capital Mobility." *Economic Journal*, 94: 16.

Epstein, Richard A. 1983. "Blackmail, Inc." *University of Chicago Law Review*, 50: 553.

———. 1985. *Takings: Private Property and the Power of Eminent Domain.* Cambridge, Mass.: Harvard University Press.

———. 1993. *Bargaining with the State.* Princeton: Princeton University Press.

———. 1995. *Simple Rules for a Complex World.* Cambridge, Mass.: Harvard University Press.

Fabella, Raul V. 1995. "The Social Cost of Rent Seeking under Countervailing Opposition to Distortionary Transfers." *Journal of Public Economics*, 57: 235.

Faith, Roger L., Donald R. Leavens, and Robert D. Tollison. 1982. "Antitrust Pork Barrel." *Journal of Law and Economics*, 25: 329.

Fessler, Pamela. 1986. "Russell Long: Tax Master and Senate Mentor." *Congressional Quarterly Weekly Report*, 44: 797.

Fialka, John J. 1993. "Washington Battle for Health Reform Showed Possible Erosion of Blue Cross-Blue Shield Clout." *Wall Street Journal*, May 6, p. A12.

Fischel, William A. 1985. *The Economics of Zoning Laws: A Property Rights Approach to American Land Use Controls.* Baltimore: Johns Hopkins University Press.

Fisher, Franklin M. 1985. "The Social Cost of Monopoly and Regulation: Posner Reconsidered." *Journal of Political Economy*, 93: 410.

Foner, Eric. 1988. *Reconstruction, 1863–1877.* New York: Harper & Row.

Freda, Ernie. 1993. "9 Lawmakers Accused of Abusing Perks," *Atlanta Constitution*, Sept. 3, p. A10.

Friedman, Milton. 1962. *Price Theory: A Provisional Text.* Rev. ed. Chicago: Aldine Publishing.

———. 1986. "Tax Reform Lets Politicians Look for New Donors." *Wall Street Journal*, July 7, p. 14.

Friedman, Milton, and Anna Schwartz. 1963. *A Monetary History of the United States, 1867–1960.* Princeton: Princeton University Press.

Fuerbringer, Jonathan. 1993. "17 Big Underwriters Bar Campaign Gifts Aimed at Bond Sales." *New York Times*, Oct. 19, p. A1.

Genesove, David. 1993. "Adverse Selection in the Wholesale Used Car Market." *Journal of Political Economy*, 101: 644.

Gradstein, Mark. 1993. "Rent Seeking and the Provision of Public Goods." *Economic Journal*, 103: 1236.

Greene, Marilyn. 1990. "Moynihan Leads Surplus Showdown." *USA Today*, Jan. 16, p. 7A.

Greif, Avner, Paul Milgrom, and Barry R. Weingast. 1994. "Coordination, Commitment, and Enforcement: The Case of the Merchant Guild." *Journal of Political Economy*, 102: 745.

Grimes, William. 1993. "'The Queen' on the Runway Again." *New York Times*, March 27, p. 13.

Gunning, J. Patrick, Jr. 1972. "Towards a Theory of the Evolution of Government." In Gordon Tullock, ed., *Explorations in the Theory of Anarchy*. Blacksburg: Center for the Study of Public Choice, Virginia Polytechnic Institute and State University.

Gupta, Udayan. 1990. "Enterprise." *Wall Street Journal*, Jan. 24, p. B1.

Haddock, David D. 1994. "Foreseeing Confiscation by the Sovereign: Lessons from the American West." In Terry L. Anderson and Peter J. Hill, eds., *The Political Economy of the American West*. Lanham, Md.: Rowman & Littlefield.

Hanlon, Sally. 1986. "PACs Pad Taxwriters' Campaign Accounts." *Tax Notes*, 33: 529.

Louis Harris & Associates, Inc. 1983. *Consumerism in the Eighties*. Los Angeles: Atlantic Richfield.

Henderson, David R. 1985. "The Economics of Fuel Economy Standards." *Regulation*, January/February, p. 45.

Hettrick, Walter, and Stanley Winer. 1988. "Economic and Political Foundations of Tax Structure." *American Economic Review*, 78: 701.

Hirshleifer, Jack. 1976. "Comment." *Journal of Law and Economics*, 19: 241.

Hoffman, Elizabeth, and Gary D. Libecap. 1995. "The Failure of Government-Sponsored Cartels and Development of Federal Farm Policy." *Economic Inquiry*, 33: 365.

Jackson, Brooks. 1985a. "House Republicans Are Pressing PACs for Contributions." *Wall Street Journal*, June 27, p. 38.

———. 1985b. "Brewing Industry Organizes Lobbying Coalition to Head Off Any Incrase in U.S. Tax on Beer." *Wall Street Journal*, July 11, p. 52.

———. 1985c. Tax Revision Proposals Bring Big Contributions from PACs to Congressional Campaign Coffers." *Wall Street Journal*, August 9, p. 32.

———. 1985d. "Congressmen Charge All Kinds of Things to Campaign Chests." *Wall Street Journal*, Dec. 3, p. 1.

———. 1986. "Congress, Wined and Dined by Jack Valenti, Writes a Rule Giving Hollywood a Tax Break." *Wall Street Journal*, June 17, p. 64.

———. 1988. *Honest Graft: Big Money and the American Political Process*. New York: Alfred A. Knopf.

Jackson, Brooks, and Bruce Ingersoll. 1987. "Chicago Futures Industry, to Fend Off Attack, Rallies Lawmakers Who Received PAC Funds." *Wall Street Journal*, Nov. 12, p. 64.

Jackson, John D., David Saurman, and William F. Shughart II. 1994. "Instant Winners: Legal Change in Transition and the Diffusion of State Lotteries." *Public Choice*, 80: 245.

Jaroslovsky, Rich. 1989. "Industries Mobilize to Block Bush's User-Fee Plans." *Wall Street Journal*, Dec. 29, p. 1.

Jarrell, Gregg A., James A. Brickley, and Jeffrey M. Netter. 1988. "The Market for Corporate Control: The Empirical Evidence since 1980." *Journal of Economic Perspectives*, 2: 49.

Jensen, Michael, and Richard Ruback. 1983. "The Market for Corporate Control: The Empirical Evidence." *Journal of Financial Economics*, 36: 5.

Johnson, Omotunde E. G. 1975. "An Economic Analysis of Corrupt Government, with Special Application to Less Developed Countries." *Kyklos*, 28: 47.

Joskow, Paul L., and Roger G. Noll. 1981. "Regulation in Theory and Practice: An Overview." In Garry From, ed., *Studies in Public Regulation*. Cambridge, Mass.: MIT Press.

Kalt, Joseph A., and Mark Zupan. 1984. "Capture and Ideology in the Economic Theory of Politics." *American Economic Review*, 74: 279.

Kaplan, Sheila. 1990. "How Cosmetics Lobby Maintains Its Luster: Even Distant Threat of Regulation Spawns Industry Scurrying." *Legal Times*, April 30, p. 1.

Karni, Edi, and Dan Levin. 1994. "Social Attributes and Strategic Equilibrium: A Restaurant Pricing Game." *Journal of Political Economy*, 102: 822.

Kaun, David E. 1965. "Minimum Wages, Factor Substitution, and the Marginal Producer." *Quarterly Journal of Economics*, 79: 478.

Kenkel, Donald S., and David C. Ribar. 1994. "Alcohol Consumption and Young Adults' Socioeconomic Status." In *Brookings Papers on Economic Activity: Microeconomics*. Washington, D.C.: Brookings Institution.

Kiesling, Herbert J. 1990. "Economic and Political Foundations of Tax Structure: A Comment." *American Economic Review*, 80: 931.

Klein, Benjamin, Robert G. Crawford, and Armen A. Alchian. 1978. "Vertical Integration, Appropriable Rents, and the Competitive Contracting Process." *Journal of Law and Economics*, 21: 297.

Klein, Benjamin, and Keith B. Leffler. 1981. "The Role of Market Forces in Assuring Contractual Performance." *Journal of Political Economy*, 89: 615.

Klott, Gary. 1993. "House Committee OKs Another Tax Bill." *Atlanta Constitution*, Nov. 22, p. E2.

Krueger, Anne O. 1974. "The Political Economy of the Rent-Seeking Society." *American Economic Review*, 64: 291.

Kuntz, Phil. 1995. "A Day in Washington Is Just Another Day to Raise More Dollars," *Wall Street Journal*, Oct. 23, p. A1.

Kurkjian, Stephen. 1986. "Money, Pressure Seen as Keys in Gun-Bill Vote." *Boston Globe*, April 14, p. 3.

Kurtz, Michael L., and Morgan D. Peoples. 1990. *Earl K. Long: The Saga of Uncle Earl and Louisiana Politics*. Baton Rouge: Louisiana State University Press.

Laband, David. 1986. "Stoplight Sales and Sidewalk Solicitation." *Journal of Economic Organization and Behavior*, 7: 403.

Lal, Deepak. 1993. *The Repressed Economy: Causes, Consequences, Reform*. Aldershot, U.K.: Edward Elgar.

Landes, William M., and Richard A. Posner. 1975. "The Independent Judiciary in an Interest-Group Perspective." *Journal of Law and Economics*, 18: 875.

Langley, Monica, and Brooks Jackson. 1986. "Bankers Want Election Commission to Tighten Restrictions on Lending to Political Candidates." *Wall Street Journal,* Sept. 23, p. 64.

Leal, Donald. 1990. "Saving an Ecosystem: From Buffer Zone to Private Initiatives." In John A. Baden and Donald Leal, eds., *The Yellowstone Primer.* San Francisco: Pacific Research Institute for Public Policy.

Lee, Dwight R. 1985. "Rent Seeking and Its Implications for Taxation." *Southern Economic Journal,* 51: 731.

Lee, Dwight R., and Robert D. Tollison. 1988. "Optimal Taxation in a Rent-Seeking Environment." In Charles K. Rowley and Robert D. Tollison, eds., *The Political Economy of Rent Seeking.* Boston: Kluwer Academic.

Levmore, Saul X. 1990. "Just Compensation and Just Politics." *University of Connecticut Law Review,* 22: 285.

Lewis, Neil A. 1993. "Medical Industry Showers Congress with Lobby Money." *New York Times,* Dec. 13, p. A1.

———. 1994. "U.S. Drug Industry Is Battling Image for Price Gouging." *New York Times,* March 7, p. A1.

Liebowitz, S. J., and Stephen E. Margolis. 1994. "Network Externality: An Uncommon Tragedy." *Journal of Economic Perspectives,* 8: 133.

Lindgren, James. 1993. "Theory, History, and Practice of the Bribery-Extortion Distinction." *University of Pennsylvania Law Review,* 141: 1695.

Lindsay, Cotton M. 1976. "A Theory of Government Enterprise." *Journal of Political Economy,* 84: 1061.

Lott, John R., Jr. 1990. "Predation by Public Enterprises." *Journal of Public Economics,* 43: 237.

Lott, John R., and Stephen G. Bronars. 1993. "Time Series Evidence on Shirking in the U.S. House of Representatives." *Public Choice,* 76: 125.

Lott, John R., and Michael L. Davis. 1992. "A Critical Review and an Extension of the Political Shirking Literature." *Public Choice,* 74: 461.

MacAvoy, Paul W. 1970. *The Crisis of the Regulatory Commissions: An Introduction to a Current Issue of Public Policy.* New York: W. W. Norton.

Malbin, Michael J., ed. 1984. *Money and Politics in the United States.* Chatham, N.J.: Chatham House.

Maloney, Michael T., Robert E. McCormick, and Robert D. Tollison. 1984. "Economic Regulation, Competitive Governments, and Specialized Resources." *Journal of Law and Economics,* 27: 329.

Manne, Henry G., and Roger LeRoy Miller, eds. 1976. *Auto Safety Regulation: The Cure or the Problem.* Glen Ridge, N.J.: Thomas Horton and Daughters.

Maraniss, David. 1983. "PAC Heaven: Commerce Committee Members Roll Up Corporate Contributions." *Washington Post,* Aug. 21, p. A1.

McChesney, Fred S. 1986. "Government Prohibition of Volunteer Fire Fighting in Nineteenth-Century America: A Property Rights Perspective." *Journal of Legal Studies,* 15: 69.

———. 1987. "Rent Extraction and Rent Creation in the Economic Theory of Regulation." *Journal of Legal Studies,* 16: 101.

———. 1988. "The Cinderella School of Tax Reform: A Reply to Rabushka." *Contemporary Policy Issues*, 6 (October): 65.

———. 1990. "Consumer Ignorance and Consumer Protection Law: Empirical Evidence from the FTC's Funeral Rule." *Journal of Law and Politics*, 7: 1.

———. 1991. "Rent Extraction and Interest-Group Organization in a Coasean Model of Regulation." *Journal of Legal Studies*, 20: 73.

———. 1992. "Positive Economics and All That—A Review of *The Economic Structure of Corporate Law*." *George Washington Law Review*, 61: 272.

McChesney, Fred S., and William F. Shughart II. 1995. *The Causes and Consequences of Antitrust: The Public Choice Perspective*. Chicago: University of Chicago Press.

McCloskey, Donald N. 1982. *The Applied Theory of Price*. New York: Macmillan.

McCormick, Robert E. 1984. "The Strategic Use of Regulation: A Review of the Literature." In Robert A. Rogowsky and Bruce Yandle, eds., *The Political Economy of Regulation: Private Interests in the Regulatory Process*. Washington, D.C.: Federal Trade Commission.

McCormick, Robert E., William F. Shughart II, and Robert D. Tollison. 1984. "The Disinterest in Deregulation." *American Economic Review*, 74: 1075.

McCormick, Robert E., and Robert D. Tollison. 1981. *Politicians, Legislation, and the Economy: An Inquiry into the Interest-Group Theory of Government*. Boston: Martinus Nijhoff.

McGee, John S. 1960. "Ocean Freight Rate Conferences and the American Merchant Marine." *University of Chicago Law Review*, 27: 191.

McLure, Charles E., Jr., and George R. Zodrow. 1987. "Treasury I and the Tax Reform Act of 1986: The Economics and Politics of Tax Reform." *Journal of Economic Perspectives*, 1: 37.

Migué, Jean-Luc. 1977. "Controls versus Subsidies in the Economic Theory of Regulation." *Journal of Law and Economics*, 20: 213.

Mitchell, Mark L., and Michael T. Maloney. 1989. "Crisis in the Cockpit? The Role of Market Forces in Promoting Air Travel Safety." *Journal of Law and Economics*, 32: 329.

Mitchell, William C. 1988. "Virginia, Rochester, and Bloomington: Twenty-five Years of Public Choice and Political Science." *Public Choice*, 56: 101.

Mixon, Franklin G., Jr., David N. Laband, and Robert B. Ekelund, Jr. 1994. "Rent Seeking and Hidden In-Kind Resource Distortion: Some Empirical Evidence." *Public Choice*, 78: 171.

Mueller, Dennis C. 1985. *The "Virginia School" and Public Choice*. Fairfax, Va.: Center for Study of Public Choice.

Murphy, Cait. 1993. "The Indian Way of Capitalism." *Wall Street Journal*, Sept. 17, p. A10.

Murray, Alan. 1986. "Lobbyists and Chums from College Leave Imprint on Tax Bill." *Wall Street Journal*, May 16, p. 1.

Musgrave, Richard A. 1987. "Short of Euphoria." *Journal of Economic Perspectives*, 1: 59.

Neely, Mark E., Jr. 1991. *The Fate of Liberty: Abraham Lincoln and Civil Liberties.* New York: Oxford University Press.

Niskanen, William A. 1971. *Bureaucracy and Representative Government.* Chicago: Aldine Press.

Noah, Timothy. 1993. "AMA Lavishly Courts Congressional Staffers Who Will Affect Outcome of Clinton's Health Plan." *Wall Street Journal,* June 30, p. A16.

Nossiter, Adam. 1989. "Lawsuit Resurrects Old Rumors of Wallace Brother's Influence." *Atlanta Journal & Constitution,* April 2, p. A2.

O'Brien, Timothy L. 1994. "Computer-Aided Legal Research Subject of Probe." *Wall Street Journal,* Oct. 3, p. B5.

Olson, Mancur. 1965. *The Logic of Collective Action.* Cambridge, Mass.: Harvard University Press.

Olson, Mary K. 1995. "Regulatory Agency Discretion among Competing Industries." *Journal of Law, Economics, and Organization,* 11: 379.

Ornstein, Norman J., Thomas E. Mann, and Michael J. Malbin. 1994. *Vital Statistics on Congress.* Washington, D.C.: Congressional Quarterly.

Palefsky, Howard D. 1990. "FDA User Fees Are Good for Business." *Wall Street Journal,* Aug. 16, p. A14.

Pashigian, B. Peter. 1975. "On the Control of Crime and Bribery." *Journal of Legal Studies,* 4: 311.

———. 1976. "Consequences and Causes of Public Ownership of Urban Transit Facilities." *Journal of Political Economy,* 84: 1239.

Pechman, Joseph A. 1987. "Tax Reform: Theory and Practice." *Journal of Economic Perspectives,* 1: 11.

Peles, Yoram. 1971. "Rates of Amortization of Advertising Expenditures." *Journal of Political Economy,* 79: 1032.

Peltzman, Sam. 1971. "Pricing in Public and Private Enterprises: Electric Utilities in the United States." *Journal of Law and Economics,* 14: 109.

———. 1976. "Toward a More General Theory of Regulation." *Journal of Law and Economics,* 19: 211.

———. 1989. "The Economic Theory of Regulation after a Decade of Deregulation." In Martin Neil Baily and Clifford Winston, eds., *Brookings Papers on Economic Activity: Microeconomics.* Washington, D.C.: Brookings Institution.

Pogue, Thomas F., and Larry G. Sgontz. 1989. "Taxing to Control Social Costs: The Case of Alcohol." *American Economic Review,* 79: 235.

Poole, Robert. 1986. "The Iron Law of Public Policy." *Wall Street Journal,* Aug. 4, p. 15.

Porter, John 1990. "Let Workers Plan Their Own Retirement Funds . . ." *Wall Street Journal,* Feb. 1, p. A8.

Posner, Richard A. 1971. "Taxation by Regulation." *Bell Journal of Economics and Management Science,* 2: 22.

———. 1974. "Theories of Economic Regulation." *Bell Journal of Economics and Management Science,* 5: 335.

————. 1975. "The Social Costs of Monopoly and Regulation." *Journal of Political Economy,* 83: 807.

————. 1993. "Blackmail, Privacy, and Freedom of Contract." *University of Pennsylvania Law Review,* 141: 1817.

Pressman, Steven. 1985. "PAC Money, Honoraria Flow to Tax Writers." *Congressional Quarterly Weekly Report,* 43: 1806.

Rabushka, Alvin. 1988. "The Tax Reform Act of 1986: Concentrated Costs, Diffuse Benefits—An Inversion of Public Choice." *Contemporary Policy Issues,* 6 (October): 50.

Ramseyer, J. Mark. 1993. "On the Political Improbability of Efficient Tax Policy: Asset-Specificity and the Returns to Politics." In Oliver Oldman and Hiroshi Kaneko, eds., *A Final Draft Report from FAIR to the World Bank on "Taxation and Economic Growth."* Tokyo: Foundation for Advanced Information and Research (FAIR).

Ramseyer, J. Mark, and Minoru Nakazato. 1989. "Tax Transitions and the Protection Racket: A Reply to Professors Graetz and Kaplan." *Virginia Law Review,* 75: 1155.

Rasmusen, Eric, and J. Mark Ramseyer. 1994. "Cheap Bribes and the Corruption Ban: A Coordination Game among Rational Legislators." *Public Choice,* 78: 305.

Rasmussen, David W., Bruce L. Benson, and Brent D. Mast. 1994. "Entrepreneurial Police and Drug Enforcement Policy." Manuscript. Florida State University.

Reese, Thomas J. 1980. *The Politics of Taxation.* Westport, Conn.: Quorum Books.

Robbins, Lionel. 1930. *The Nature and Significance of Economic Science.* 2d ed. London: Macmillan.

Roberts, Paul Craig. 1990. ". . . That's How It's Done in Other Countries." *Wall Street Journal,* Feb. 1, p. A8.

Robinson, Jeffrey. 1994. *The Laundrymen: Inside the World's Third Largest Business.* London: Simon & Schuster.

Rogers, David. 1993a. "As GM's EDS Works to Save Software Tax Break, Its Political Contributions to Capitol Hill Soar." *Wall Street Journal,* July 27, p. A20.

————. 1993b. "Carr, with Powerful House Transportation Post, Goes Full Speed Ahead on His Own Fund Raising." *Wall Street Journal,* Sept. 24, p. A12.

Rogerson, William P. 1982. "The Social Costs of Monopoly and Regulation: A Game-Theoretic Analysis." *Bell Journal of Economics,* 13: 391.

Romano, Roberta. 1993. "Public Pension Fund Activism in Corporate Governance Reconsidered." *Columbia Law Review,* 93: 795.

Rose-Ackerman, Susan. 1978. *Corruption: A Study in Political Economy.* New York: Academic Press.

Rosenbaum, David E. 1989. "The Tax Breaks America Could Not Give Up." *New York Times,* Oct. 8, p. E1.

Rowley, Charles K., and Robert D. Tollison. 1986. "Rent-Seeking and Trade Protection." *Aussenwirtschaft*, 41: 303.

Sabato, Larry J. 1984. *PAC Power: Inside the World of Political Action Committees*. New York: W. W. Norton.

Saxton, Jim. 1994. "A Raid on America's Pension Funds." *Wall Street Journal*, Sept. 29, p. A12.

Schelling, Thomas C. 1963. *The Strategy of Conflict*. New York: Oxford University Press.

Schwartz, Alan. 1988. "The Fairness of Tender Offer Prices in Utilitarian Theory." *Journal of Legal Studies*, 17: 165.

Schwert, G. William. 1981. "Using Financial Data to Measure the Effects of Regulation." *Journal of Law and Economics*, 24: 121.

Scully, Gerald W. 1995. "The 'Growth Tax' in the United States." *Public Choice*, 85: 71.

Seabrook, Charles. 1994a. "Lawmakers Wined, Dined and Lodged." *Atlanta Journal & Constitution*, Feb. 6, p. D1.

———. 1994b. "Bank Lobbyists List $14,000 in Gifts." *Atlanta Journal & Constitution*, Feb. 19, p. C4.

Seelye, Katherine Q. 1994. "Tobacco Politics Falters Even in Congress." *New York Times*, April 2, p. 1.

Sele, Michael. 1995. "Costs of Complying with Federal Rules Weigh More Heavily on Small Firms." *Wall Street Journal*, Nov. 1, p. B2.

Shavell, Steven. 1993. "An Economic Analysis of Threats and Their Illegality: Blackmail, Extortion, and Robbery." *University of Pennsylvania Law Review*, 141: 1877.

Shelanski, Howard A., and Peter G. Klein. 1995. "Empirical Research in Transaction Cost Economics: A Review and Assessment." *Journal of Law, Economics, and Organization*, 11: 335.

Sherman, Mark. 1993. "Politicians Cash in on Campaign Leftovers: Funds Used to Buy a Car, Throw a Party." *Atlanta Journal & Constitution*, Aug. 5, p. D1.

Shleifer, Andrei, and Robert W. Vishny. 1993. "Corruption." *Quarterly Journal of Economics*, 58: 599.

Shughart, William F., II. 1987. "Durable Tax Reform." *Cato Journal*, 7: 273.

———, ed. 1997. *Taxing Choice: The Predatory Politics of Fiscal Discrimination*. New Brunswick, N.J.: Transaction.

Shughart, William F., II, Robert D. Tollison, and Richard S. Higgins. 1987. "Rational Self-Taxation: Complementary Inputs and Excise Taxation." *Canadian Journal of Economics*, 20: 527.

Simpson, Glenn R. 1995. "Oregon Firm's Success under Sen. Packwood Underscores the Benefits of a Political Patron." *Wall Street Journal*, Sept. 26, p. A20.

Smith, Adam. 1776. *The Wealth of Nations* (Cannan ed., 1937). New York: Modern Library.

Sowell, Thomas. 1980. *Knowledge and Decisions*. New York: Basic Books.

Spicer, Michael W. 1990. "On the Desirability of Tax Evasion: Conventional versus Constitutional Economic Perspectives." *Public Finance/Finances Publiques*, 45: 118.

Stigler, George J. 1971. "The Theory of Economic Regulation." *Bell Journal of Economics and Management Science*, 2: 3.

———. 1974. "Free Riders and Collective Action: An Appendix to Theories of Economic Regulation." *Bell Journal of Economics and Management Science*, 5: 359.

Stigler, George J., and Gary S. Becker. 1977. "De Gustibus Non Est Disputandum." *American Economic Review*, 67: 76.

Stigler, George J., and Claire Friedland. 1962. "What Can Regulators Regulate? The Case of Electricity," *Journal of Law and Economics*, 5: 1.

Stone, Brewer S. 1993. "Beating China's Rapacious Profiteers." *Wall Street Journal*, Oct. 4, p. A14.

Stubblebine, W. Craig. 1985. "On the Political Economy of Tax Reform." Paper presented at the annual meeting of the Western Economic Association.

Telser, Lester. 1980. "A Theory of Self-Enforcing Agreements." *Journal of Business*, 22: 337.

Thomas, Paulette. 1993. "Accused Lawmakers Get Aid From Favor Seekers as Fat Cats Raise Big Kitties in Their Defense." *Wall Street Journal*, Nov. 23, p. A18.

Tolchin, Martin. 1993. "Road Official Urges Privatizing Portions of Interstate System." *New York Times*, Oct. 1, p. A1.

Tollison, Robert D. 1982. "Rent Seeking: A Survey." *Kyklos*, 35: 575.

Tollison, Robert D., and W. Mark Crain. 1979. "Consitutional Change in an Interest-Group Perspective." *Journal of Legal Studies*, 8: 165.

Tullock, Gordon. 1967. "The Welfare Costs of Tariffs, Monopoly, and Theft." *Western Economic Journal*, 5: 224.

———, ed. 1972. *Explorations in the Theory of Anarchy*. Blacksburg: Center for the Study of Public Choice, Virginia Polytechnic Institute and State University.

———. 1974a. *The Social Dilemma: The Economics of War and Revolution*. Blacksburg, Va.: University Publications.

———, ed. 1974b. *Further Explorations in the Theory of Anarchy*. Blacksburg, Va.: University Publications.

———. 1989. *The Economics of Special Privilege and Rent Seeking*. Boston: Kluwer Academic.

———. 1993. *Rent Seeking*. Aldershot, U.K.: Edward Elgar.

Wagner, Richard E. 1997. "The Taxation of Alcohol and the Control of Social Costs." In William F. Shughart II, ed., *Taxing Choice: The Predatory Politics of Fiscal Discrimination*. New Brunswick, N.J.: Transaction.

Wang, Yongley. 1994. "The Effects of Tax and Political Uncertainty on Foreign Direct Investment in China." Paper delivered at Emory University, April 10.

Wartzman, Rick. 1993a. "Whether or Not They Benefit, Companies Decry Instability in Tax Law as a Barrier to Planning." *Wall Street Journal*, Aug. 10, p. A16.

———. 1993b. "In Health Reform Battle, Insurers Are Resisting White House Efforts to Fit Them with a Black Hat." *Wall Street Journal,* Sept. 20, p. A16.

———. 1994a. "Defending Football and Fancy Cars, Politicians Decry Effort to Limit Use of Campaign Money." *Wall Street Journal,* Jan. 12, p. A12.

———. 1994b. "Drug Firms' Lobbying to Defuse Criticism by Clintons Pays Off." *Wall Street Journal,* Aug. 16, p. A1.

Wartzman, Rick, and John Harwood. 1994. "For the Baby Bells, Government Lobbying Is Hardly Child's Play." *Wall Street Journal,* March 15, p. A1.

Wartzman, Rick, and Pauline Yoshihashi. 1994a. "As Gambling Grows across the U.S., the Industry Seeks to Hit Jackpot on National Political Scene." *Wall Street Journal,* Feb. 1, p. A16.

———. 1994b. "Gambling Industry Says Tax Means Snake Eyes, but from Washington It Looks like a Natural." *Wall Street Journal,* March 31, p. A16.

Weingast, Barry R., and Mark J. Moran. 1983. "Bureaucratic Discretion or Congressional Control? Regulatory Policymaking by the Federal Trade Commission." *Journal of Political Economy,* 91: 765.

Welch, William P. 1974. "The Economics of Campaign Funds." *Public Choice,* 17: 83.

Wenders. John T. 1986a. "A Note on Welfare Costs." Manuscript. University of Idaho.

———. 1986b. "Economic Efficiency and Income Distribution in the Electric Utility Industry." *Southern Economic Journal,* 52: 1056.

———. 1987. "On Perfect Rent Dissipation." *American Economic Review,* 77: 456.

Wessell, David, and Laurie McGinley. 1990. "Federal Tax on Air Fares May Climb." *Wall Street Journal,* Jan. 8, p. B1.

West, E. G. 1967. "The Political Economy of American Public School Legislation." *Journal of Law and Economics,* 10: 101.

White, James A. 1989. "Pension Funds to Politicians: Hands Off." *Wall Street Journal,* Dec. 5, p. C1.

———. 1991. "Back-Yard Investing Yields Big Losses, Roils Kansas Pension System." *Wall Street Journal,* Aug. 21, p. A1.

Williamson, Oliver E. 1968. "Wages Rates as a Barrier to Entry: The Pennington Case in Perspective." *Quarterly Journal of Economics,* 82: 85.

Wirl, Franz. 1994. "The Dynamics of Lobbying—A Differential Game." *Public Choice,* 80: 307.

Witte, John. 1985. *The Politics and Development of the Federal Income Tax.* Madison: University of Wisconsin Press.

Yandle, Bruce. 1983. "Bootleggers and Baptists: The Education of a Regulatory Economist." *Regulation,* May/June, p. 12.

———. 1989. "Taxation, Political Action, and Superfund." *Cato Journal,* 8: 751.

Yang, John E. 1989. "Honoraria, Bounty of Special Interest Groups, Trickle Down to Some Congressional Staffers." *Wall Street Journal,* May 26, p. A12.

Yelvington, Brenda. 1997. "Excise Taxes in Historical Perspective." In William F. Shughart II, ed., *Taxing Choice: The Predatory Politics of Fiscal Discrimination.* New Brunswick, N.J.: Transaction.

Index

Abramson, Jill, 30, 52, 162
Akerlof, George, 56
Alchian, Armen A., 10
Alm, James, 33
Anderson, Terry L., 7, 40
Aranson, Peter H., 2, 14, 30, 54
Archer, Bill, 109
Atkinson, A. B., 116
Axelrod, Robert, 21

Bacon, Kenneth H., 59
Barbash, Fred, 54
Bargaining: last-period problems, 100; players in tax legislation contracting, 103–106, 108–109; rent extraction game, 98–99
Beck, Roger, 73, 78, 79
Becker, Gary S., 21, 135, 153, 169, 170
Bell, Jeffrey, 126
Benefits: beneficiaries of tax carve-outs, 63–64; to consumers of organization, 137–141; created by regulation, 9–10; under economic model of regulation, 9, 13–14, 16; to producers of organization, 138. *See also* Rents
Bennett, James, 145
Benson, Bruce L., 154, 166
Berke, Richard L., 57
Berkman, Harvey, 54
Birnbaum, Jeffrey, 64, 65, 100, 128
Bribery, rent creation as, 31
Brickley, James A., 163
Brooke, James, 68
Buchanan, James M., 116, 137
Buckley v. Valeo (1976), 106

Califano, Joseph, 52
Campaign contributions: for favorable tax treatment, 63–64; soft money, 64; targeting of, 46–47; vague limits to and uses of, 48–50. *See also* Payments to politicians; Political action committees (PACs)
Carnevale, Mary Lu, 58
Carr, Bob, 47
Clinton administration: carve-outs of 1993 tax increase, 63–64; proposed highway privatization, 119; response to health-care proposal, 57–58, 77–78
Coase, Ronald H., 8, 143
Coelho, Tony, 164
Collor de Mello, Fernando, 68
Competition: for transfer payments, 32; among transfer seekers, 125
Congress: committee-subcommittee system, 103–106
Congressional Quarterly, 105
Connolly, Martin, 73, 78, 79
Consumer organizations: extractable surplus in, 147–148; politicians' subsidies to, 145; producer subsidies of, 152; role of, 140
Consumers: costs and benefits of organizing, 137–141; as counterbidders to producers, 140; under economic theory of regulation, 12–14, 16, 18–19; free riding on producers, 152; gain from government underpricing, 123–124; gains from suboptimal pricing, 122–123; in Olson-Stigler model of regulation, 134, 136, 140; in Peltzman-Becker

214 | Index

Politicians: choice between rent creation or extraction, 160–161; combined strategy of rent creation and extraction, 34–37; contractual opportunism of, 40–41, 89–90, 97; under economic theory of regulation, 12–13, 16–19, 157; extraction of private rents, 23–26; gains from rent extraction, 26–34; incentives for low user fees, 123–124; opportunities from consumer organization, 147–148; payments to, 1–2; in Peltzman-Becker model, 141; power of taxation, 114; raising money, 47–50; regulation choices, 146; in rent-extraction model, 19, 157; rent-extraction strategy, 38–41, 71–73, 162–165; rent extraction through earmarked funds, 130–131; in Stigler-Peltzman model of regulation, 134; threat-bribe strategy, 22–23; threats to expropriate, 97; threats to transfer surplus, 142–145; transaction costs, 144; turnover rates and tenure, 101–108. *See also* Payments to politicians

Poole, Robert, 156

Porter, John, 126

Posner, Richard, 8, 14, 42, 133

Pressman, Steven, 65, 66

Price controls: in proposed Clinton health-care bill, 56–57, 77; threats of, 26–27, 56–58

Prices: government user charges as, 116–120; legislation as method to lower, 26–29; threats to lower, 55–61

Producer organizations, costs and benefits of, 138–141

Producers: consumers free riding on, 152; under economic theory of regulation, 12–14; enlisting consumer support, 152–153; government as, 116–122; profit maximization incentive, 120; raising-rivals'-costs model of regulation, 14–15. *See also* Surplus, producer

Rabushka, Alvin, 94

Raising-rivals'-costs model of regulation, 14–17, 24

Ramseyer, J. Mark, 114, 163

Rasmusen, Eric, 163

Rasmussen, David W., 166

Reese, Thomas J., 102

Regulation: gains with durability of, 23; raising-rivals'-costs model of regulation, 14–16; rent-creating functions, 11–12, 133–134; Stigler-Peltzman model of, 133–134; Stigler's model, 8–13; welfare model of, 7–8

Regulatory auction: allocation of surplus in, 141; consumers and producers in, 135–140; extraction of consumer surplus in, 145–147; information for politicians in, 36–37; limitations in static models of, 145–146; payment by winners and losers, 161–162; under Stigler-Peltzman theory of regulation, 16–17, 20

Rent creation: conditions for tax-based, 99–100; disincentives for, 89–90; in economic theory of regulation, 10–14, 16, 19–20, 31; extension of economic model of regulation, 14; outside the United States, 66; political, 35, 158; reasons for politicians' choice of, 160–161

Rent extraction: conditions for, 75; economists' lack of interest in, 158; experience of Canadian firms, 73–77, 79–82; game strategy, 38–41; incentives for, 90; methods, 26–34; mud farming as, 3; notion of, 2–3; outside the United States, 66–68; payments to politicians as, 2–3; politicians' returns from, 162–165; of privately created rents, 23–34; problems of, 97; reason for politicians' choice of, 160–161; related to proposed Clinton health-care bill, 77, 83–85; with restricted output, 35; by threatening price controls, 26–27; by threats of taxation, 62–66. *See also* Contracts, rent-extraction

Rent-extraction model: analyses to corroborate, 73–85; application to regulation, 3; focus of, 157; function of, 70; politician in, 19; predictions of, 72–73; statement of, 23–34, 45; as supplement to rent-creating model, 41; transaction costs of politicians, 144

Rents: benefits from regulation as, 10; defined, 10; in economic theory of regulation, 10; political, 34–37, 45–55;